Economic Liberalization and Labor Markets

Recent Titles in
Contributions in Labor Studies

Farewell to the Self-Employed: Deconstructing a Socioeconomic and Legal Solipsism
Marc Linder

Trade Unionism and Industrial Relations in the Commonwealth Caribbean: History, Contemporary Practice and Prospect
Lawrence A. Nurse

Eastern's Armageddon
Martha Dunagin Saunders

A State Within a State: Industrial Relations in Israel, 1965–1987
Ran Chermesh

Culture, Gender, Race, and U.S. Labor History
Ronald C. Kent, Sara Markham, David R. Roediger, and Herbert Shapiro, editors

Infighting in the UAW: The 1946 Election and the Ascendancy of Walter Reuther
Bill Goode

American Labor in the Era of World War II
Sally M. Miller

The American Labor Movement, 1955–1995
Walter Galenson

The American Fund for Public Service: Charles Garland and Radical Philanthropy, 1922–1941
Gloria Garrett Samson

Black Unemployment: Part of Unskilled Unemployment
David Schwartzman

The Quest for a Living Wage: The History of the Federal Minimum Wage Program
Willis J. Nordlund

Irish Voice and Organized Labor in America: A Biographical Study
L. A. O'Donnell

Economic Liberalization and Labor Markets

Edited by
Parviz Dabir-Alai
and Mehmet Odekon
Foreword by Hans W. Singer

Contributions in Labor Studies, Number 51

Greenwood Press
Westport, Connecticut • London

Library of Congress Cataloging-in-Publication Data

Economic liberalization and labor markets / edited by Parviz Dabir-
   Alai and Mehmet Odekon ; foreword by Hans W. Singer.
      p.   cm.—(Contributions in labor studies, ISSN 0886–8239 ;
   no. 51)
      Includes bibliographical references and index.
      ISBN 0–313–30358–4 (alk. paper)
      1. Foreign trade and employment.   2. Free trade.   3. Labor market.
   I. Dabir-Alai, Parviz, 1955– II. Odekon, Mehmet.   III. Series.
   HD5710.7.E25   1998
   331.12—DC21   97–37971

British Library Cataloguing in Publication Data is available.

Library of Congress Catalog Card Number: 97–37971
ISBN: 0–313–30358–4
ISSN: 0886–8239

First published in 1998

Greenwood Press, 88 Post Road West, Westport, CT 06881
An imprint of Greenwood Publishing Group, Inc.

Printed in the United States of America

The paper used in this book complies with the
Permanent Paper Standard issued by the National
Information Standards Organization (Z39.48–1984).

10 9 8 7 6 5 4 3 2 1

Contents

Illustrations

FIGURES

Foreword

Hans W. Singer

Employment in a productive job under decent conditions is an essential (although not sufficient) part of the attack on poverty which, by general agreement, has moved into the center of the development debate. Notwithstanding this, the process referred to as economic liberalization has also spread to many parts of the world. Hence a publication examining the relation between the two appears at a most opportune moment. There is still current debate on the impact of trade liberalization (accompanied by other features of globalization) on labor markets in all different types of economies—developed, transition, middle income, low income—especially on skilled versus unskilled labor and, related to this, on the divergence and convergence of wages both within and between different kinds of countries and different labor market regimes.

We are still at the stage where more empirical evidence and the trying out of new approaches are needed before confident conclusions and confident recommendations on the organization of labor markets can be made. This book should make a significant impact on the process of evidence collection and thus contribute to enhancing debate in this area. The country-specific, as well as regional focus of the chapters is particularly useful in bringing home to the reader the diversity of conditions, issues, and policies. This, and other aspects of the book, will help us better understand the differences observed in the employment intensity of growth experiences. In short, the discussion ought to confirm that the pattern of growth is as important as the rate of growth and should thus help the development debate in this direction.

Acknowledgments

We thank Gina Ponessa Swift (Skidmore College) for her excellent typing, and Carol Lloyd, David Maswick, Amanda Corradino, Ben Running (Skidmore College) and Adebayo Akanji, Mourad Khediri, and Mark Toole (Richmond, the American International University in London) for their computer assistance.

The project was partially supported by the Office of the Dean of Faculty at Skidmore College and the Faculty Development Committee at Richmond, the American International University in London. Additionally, Parviz Dabir-Alai acknowledges the congenial research environment offered by the University of the West Indies in Trinidad and Tobago and Suntory and Toyota International Centres for Economics and Related Disciplines (STICERD) at the London School of Economics in London, England.

We owe a great debt to our contributors, who responded to our many and varied requests promptly and with care.

Closer to home, we extend our gratitude to our respective families for the vast hours of absence they tolerated from us.

Introduction

Even a casual reflection on the enormous strides made in recent years within the fields of arts and sciences leaves one wondering why these successes have not been replicated within the domain of socioeconomic development of nations. Problems such as low productivity at work, widespread imbalances in asset ownership and income poverty, and premature mortality for millions of hapless individuals each year are nothing more than the tip of a very large *underdevelopment* iceberg which has plagued the world for many years. That these and other difficulties have become so endurable is a sad indictment of the way in which national and international institutions have been molded into shape by the passage of history. That history is rich in fortune as well as misfortune: the microchip and space travel, but also wars and famines—all happily existing side by side. Our propensity for such a diverse set of experiences has encouraged the acceptance of institutional arrangements under whose aegis untold deprivation and stratospheric opulence are increasingly commonplace.

It is inconceivable to imagine that any single collection of readings can adequately deal with the often grotesque nature of the root causes of the kind of problems alluded to above or explain the reasons for the successes seen. This is simply not possible and its achievement has not been our goal. In conceptualizing this collection of chapters our intention has been to be creative and helpful in a much more limited way. Our fundamental premise has been that the process of economic liberalization, in its many forms, has had and will continue to have significant implications for workers everywhere. With this broadly defined relationship in mind, and aware that not much work exists in this area, each one of the thirteen authors presents a particular view drawing on his or her own research and reflection.

The first chapter, by Parviz Dabir-Alai, describes some of the broader parameters of the issues involving economic liberalization and how this impacts on labor's absorption within the economic process. The chapter places considerable emphasis on describing the relevance of an analytical framework looking to classical political economy for much of its inspiration. A brief reflection on the experience of planning provides the chapter with its motivation to consider the merits of a liberalized economy. In assessing the chances of success at economic liberalization, the chapter looks at a number of records from developing and transition economies in the key areas of fiscal policy, achievement of resource balance (exchange rate position), and monetary policy, all in the light of recent information published by the World Bank. The emerging picture, unsurprisingly, is somewhat mixed. However, it is noticeable that relative success at the experience of economic liberalization belongs to those economies managing to achieve internal, resource, and external balance. This then confirms the chapter's general contention that sustainable growth and development, being linked to sensible domestic financial housekeeping, remains incontrovertible.

The chapter's general description of the relationship between liberalization and the labor market is enhanced through consideration of employment elasticity and other labor-related data for a number of countries as made available through a recently published report by the International Labor Office. Here we see that the employment content of value-added has had a tendency to fluctuate much in recent years. The chapter's observation that employment growth has generally failed to keep pace with labor force growth adds extra impetus to the analysis presented elsewhere within the volume.

The chapter ends with a brief discussion of how the problem of factor price distortions has contributed to the sluggish absorption of labor resources as compared with capital resources. It is suggested that removal of these distortions cannot but help labor's absorption within developing and transition economies.

The remaining chapters are intentionally more focused. Kwan S. Kim's chapter is distinctly comparative. His research focuses on the impact of globalization—which he defines as "movement toward freer international trade and capital investments"—on economies within the North and the South. With respect to his discussion of the impact of globalization on the North, Kim observes that production outsourcing has had the expected result of weakening domestic labor's position. In turn, this process has contributed to rising corporate profit income relative to labor's wage earnings. Neoclassical trade theory predicts faster growth rates for developing countries that engage in a dismantling of their protective shield. Kim concedes this point but argues that the benefits of any opening up have been "very uneven" across countries in the South. This, he maintains, is due to the kind of problems arising from the need to adjust to changed world circumstances. Specifically, the transition from inward-oriented development to an outward-oriented regime is more costly than is often recognized. These rigidities dilute many of the benefits normally expected from a more liberalized environment.

Kim recognizes that the impact of any liberalization will be felt differently by the members of a segmented labor market. The segmentation is largely due to skill-intensity differentials which manifest themselves in terms of uneven employment and wage opportunities. Kim's chapter confirms the findings of others that within the industrialized North employment of less intensively skilled labor has declined in a structural sense. He further notes that the problems of unemployment, and the general stagnation in wages, have been accompanied by sharply diminished roles for labor organizations.

As for the South, Kim highlights the fact that already exporting East Asians continued to enjoy fast economic growth throughout the early 1990s. During this period, economic growth remained somewhat elusive in most of the remaining transition economies in Africa, Eastern Europe, and Latin America. Of equal concern for this latter grouping has been the phenomenon of rising income inequality, which acts as a reasonably accurate measure of overall deprivation. The consequences for labor as a whole of the differential skill intensities mentioned earlier apply to the South as well. Kim notes that, within Latin America, the middle-income countries have seen a more sizable impact on their labor markets—following liberalization—than have others. In this group, investment flows have raised the demand for skilled labor relative to those with less skill.

The chapter by Fabrizio Coricelli focuses on the problem of unemployment dynamics within the previously centrally planned economies (PCPEs) and the former Soviet Union (FSU). The chapter takes a largely theoretical perspective and introduces several interesting insights into the experience of unemployment dynamics within the group of countries looked at. For example, Coricelli notes that unemployment during transition is as much a function of the extent of restructuring and reallocation of resources, and of the policy framework and institutional arrangements, as it is related to fluctuations in the economy's level of output.

Within transition economies much of the experience of unemployment has befallen the old state sector. At the same time, Coricelli notes, the newer firms, operating within the private sectors, have developed quickly and absorbed large numbers of workers. As such, a critical aspect of Coricelli's analysis later on in his chapter is the recognition of the asymmetrical behavior of different firms and sectors. For those economies choosing to engage in fast reforms, Coricelli's chapter finds that large falls in employment within the state sector and a buoyant private sector are, with the exception of the findings for the Czech Republic, correlated with a rapid increase in unemployment.

Before presenting its empirical findings, the chapter explores the usefulness of several theoretical models for the task of explaining transition-economy unemployment. Even though their emphasis on the role of changing labor market institutions is welcome, the early versions of these search models are said to be quite limited in their scope. This arises from their inability to address the whole issue of transitional unemployment and, from their focus instead on factors influencing long-run unemployment. These models' least attractive feature is that they are essentially steady-state and thus nondynamic in nature. Other problems include their inability to reflect, and take into account, labor force heterogeneity.

Extensions of the basic models are also presented by Coricelli. These extensions place considerable emphasis on the role played by private-sector firms, whose behavior is dependent on whether they are myopic, that is, looking to current profitability, or forward looking, that is, looking to current as well as future profitability levels. From a theoretical perspective of the behavior of such firms, Coricelli notes an important role for labor market institutions. These institutions are seen to be as varied as unemployment benefit levels, the efficiency of job-search mechanisms, and the existence of income policies.

Further extensions developed by Coricelli explicitly model investment within the private sector; assume adjustment costs to be higher in capital than in labor markets; and regard restructuring as an endogenous process determined by the choices of workers within state firms. Coricelli's theoretical discussion of the extensions to the basic search models results in a set of four findings. First, unemployment and output are related by a highly nonlinear function. Second, the growth of the private sector is associated with higher unemployment. Third, private-sector growth affects output negatively only in the short run. Fourth, in the long run private-sector growth affects output positively. The chapter ends with a brief discussion of income distribution issues and how these relate to labor market characteristics.

Fidel Ezeala-Harrison's chapter focuses on the employment effects of structural reform within Africa. This chapter raises a number of core issues that are central to the understanding of the relationship between reform and employment, not just within its African context, but more generally. For example, the chapter notes that even a genuinely strong political commitment to reform need not imply adherence to the basic tenets of economic liberalization. Ezeala-Harrison's reflection on this brings out the all-important (but mostly neglected) question: What exactly needs reforming in African countries? The rest of his chapter addresses this and various other critical issues.

For Ezeala-Harrison social and political liberalization is a necessary complement to the whole process of economic reform. These reforms will have to extend and embrace the difficult area of property rights, particularly as they relate to the distribution and ownership rights over land. The chapter insists on a proactive role for the providers of social overhead capital, as well as improvements in the area of political leadership and accountability.

The chapter's central theoretical core presents some useful reflections on how reform-related economic growth may be decomposed into various constituent elements including labor. This discussion then moves to a more policy-oriented view of the nature of the problems faced by African countries from the specific perspective of the role of trade. For example, Ezeala-Harrison notes that only about 5 percent of intraregional trade occurs among all African economies. Greater economic security for the region must be closely associated with raising the level of this trade, and the chapter calls for this in unequivocal terms. It is also clear that greater intraregional trade will ultimately assist African economies' efforts at meeting their external debt obligations. In this regard, the chapter reminds us of how important it is for the grouping of Organization for Economic Co-operation and Development (OECD) countries as well as the multilaterals to become more sensitive to the whole issue of debt repayment. It is argued that the debt positions we see are largely the result of harsh economic reforms. The position of labor within all of this cannot be healthy. Labor, as do other factors, performs well and receives good rewards when the rest of the economy is in a position to prosper. It is rare for one to occur sustainably without the other. Ezeala-Harrison's chapter reminds us of the need to continue the effort in asking difficult and uncomfortable questions.

The fifth chapter is by Alexander Sarris. This is the first of five chapters with a predominantly single-country focus (the others being Riveros on Chile, Vacs and Renwick on Argentina, Rambarran on Trinidad and Tobago, and Nas and Odekon on Turkey). Sarris's contribution focuses on the trade and employment effects of the economic integration of Greece with the European Union (EU). This focus is entirely appropriate as Sarris chooses to interpret Greece's accession to the European Union as a firm indication of Greece's decision to embark upon the path of trade and economic liberalization. The chapter charts the developing structure of Greek trade over a wide period starting with the early 1960s. This is an extensive exercise and helps in placing the subsequent discussion of labor market issues within its appropriate context.

The Greek labor market is described as being burdened with extensive duality and serious structural rigidities. These difficulties are described as having become more accentuated through the impact of a number of exogenous macroeconomic shocks. Chief among these have been the second oil shock, the fall of communism within Eastern Europe, accession to the European Union, and the government's growing appetite for intervention within the labor market. Partly in response to these shocks, the structure of the Greek labor market has undergone some significant change in recent years. For example, the previously dominant agricultural sector has seen its share within Gross Domestic Product (GDP) decline vis-à-vis the services sector. This factor dominates the productivity slow-down seen within the Greek economy. Another sign of the rigidities mentioned is the lack of significant responsiveness of wages to productivity differences and demand fluctuations.

Sarris's chapter presents a detailed account of the data preparation exercise carried out in anticipation of the empirical work that followed. The impact of the opening up of trade, as reflected by Greece's accession to the EU, on the labor market is measured through the introduction of an accounting decomposition for a large number of manufacturing industries. So as to be able to draw some inference on the direction of any causality between employment and trade performance, Sarris relies on the use of cross-section regression analysis. In this way Sarris correlates changes in employment to a variety of trade variables and finds that, overall, the relationships are all fairly robust.

Luis A. Riveros's contribution is another one of the country-specific chapters, this one dealing with labor market developments within Chile. Within the whole of Latin America, the Chilean experience of reform has been quite impressive. Riveros's chapter draws out the main aspects of this experience in its discussion of several distinct phases of economic policy making, starting with the Socialist experiment of the early 1970s under President Allende. Riveros notes that the post-1973 military government was intent on improving on the economy's record on efficiency within the context of an increasingly open economy. This was achieved through a wide-ranging program of reform measures in the areas of fiscal and monetary policy (basically amounting to further tightening); trade liberalization (fewer controls and more incentives for inward investment); speeding up the privatization program and public-sector reform; and, finally, wide-scale price deregulation in both goods and factor markets. The pace of rapid reform continued and touched the key areas of education and health, social security, and labor market legislation. Riveros attributes the slowdown in economic activity in the late 1980s to the financial crisis of 1982–85, which was brought on through the introduction of a series of unsustainable macroeconomic policy measures in the 1970s. The period spanning 1985 to 1990 was one of adjustment. The main ingredients were the maintenance of a high real exchange rate, more incentives for export sectors, further privatization, and better targeted social spending for the poor. Riveros notes that the postmilitary regime, contrary to some expectations, engaged in the consolidation of the economic liberalization policies started earlier. These, together with some major changes on the fiscal side, have contributed to a substantial decline in household poverty within Chile.

Beyond his comprehensive treatment of the background to Chilean reforms, Riveros considers the role and contribution of labor and the labor market. Historically speaking, and particularly during the prere-form period, labor markets within Chile have been characterized by high and persistent levels of unemployment and low real wages. The labor market, like its counterparts in the rest of Latin America, has featured a significant amount of regulation. Riveros's analysis implies that the motivation for tolerating an overregulated labor market, in the pre-1973 period, lay in the state's traditional distrust of the market. With the onset of economic liberalization policies, some deregulation of the labor market followed. Riveros's research points to a welcome structural increase within the employment-output elasticity after the labor market reforms of the early 1980s. The improvements noted are explained in terms of a more relaxed (that is, control-free) labor market and improved macroeconomic performance.

The chapter by Aldo C. Vacs and Trudi J. Renwick addresses political economy issues relating to what is described as "neoliberal restructur-ing" and labor market issues for Argentina. The chapter argues that prior to the 1960s, labor markets in Argentina were generally charac-terized by low unemployment, high real wages, and strong labor organi-zations. It is since then that the deterioration has set in. The decline is attributed to falling productivity, high and persistent inflation levels, population growth, and general political instability which, inevitably, has contributed to falling investment inflows. One of the major causes of the period of economic decline is described as arising from Argentina's failure to maintain a viable import-substituting industrialization (ISI) strategy. Eventual exhaustion of economic opportunities is of course a feature of most ISI regimes, so the difficulties encountered by Argentina are not really that surprising. What is a little puzzling, and Vacs and Renwick do refer to this, is Argentina's efforts at implementing a program of reform while simultaneously trying to uphold many of the key aspects of its dated ISI strategies. The results of pursuing such inherently contradictory policies were not encouraging for the economy. Further, the overtly political motives underlying the economic program of the military regime did little to win the requisite level of credibility.

Real progress on the economy did not come until the reestablishment of democratic rule in 1983. However, as described by Vacs and Renwick, there were several policy reversals during the 1983–89 period which created further vulnerability for the economy in its attempts to control both the levels of inflation and the fiscal deficit. With the policy reversals behind them, the Menem administration started the task of implement-ing the so-called neoliberal restructuring of the economy. The key elements of this program included elimination of state subsidies, devaluation of the currency, tax reform, and a freezing of wages and salaries. Menem's plans were met with some political opposition which, despite its intensity, did not deflect the government from its central goal of implementing the reforms.

A critical aspect of the reform measures was an accelerated privatization program. These measures assumed an even greater importance under the economic leadership of Domingo Cavallo and his Convertibility Plan. Despite Cavallo's evident successes, the problem of unemployment remained and, in fact, deteriorated somewhat. The main reason for this may be attributed to a combination of overzealous privatization and the continuing impact of factor price distortions, along the lines described in the first chapter, on labor's absorption. A natural consequence of high and persistent unemployment has been major labor unrest. Most of the discontented workers belonged to many of the affected public-sector firms. Despite this, however, support for the reform program remained high among the population as a whole.

Vacs and Renwick argue that the mid-1990s picture on unemployment continues to be a source of serious concern. This problem shows little sign of abatement in spite of Argentina's impressive achievements in the area of economic reform.

Tim Koechlin's chapter analyzes the effects of economic liberalization on Mexican labor markets. Koechlin begins his chapter with a critical review of the assumptions of the classical trade theory. He argues that the optimistic projections of mainstream studies of the North American Free Trade Agreement (NAFTA) have more to do with their assumptions of full employment and immobile capital than with the reality of North American integration. Koechlin goes on to show that, contrary to the predictions of classical trade theory and mainstream studies of NAFTA, the liberalization of the labor-abundant Mexican economy has been associated with reductions in labor demand and stagnant real wages. He concludes by arguing that trade agreements ought to include provisions designed to ensure that the gains from trade are distributed equitably.

Anston Rambarran's chapter presents a persuasive account of the relevance of the labor market to the success of economic reform programs. The context of his chapter is that of a small open economy still dominated by the oil sector, such as that represented by the Republic of Trinidad and Tobago. The chapter describes a number of adjustment measures in place during the 1983–95 period. These span several items, including salary reductions for public servants, suspension of the cost of living allowance (COLA), and the introduction of a value-added tax system. Allied with all this has been the introduction of several measures on the monetary side. The most visible of these include the setting of monetary targets (so as to limit commercial bank lending) and some

Central Bank participation in the management of the levels of liquidity preference within the economy. The impact of these and several other measures on the labor markets of Trinidad and Tobago are highlighted within the chapter. The chapter notes that the economy's reliance on the capital-intensive energy sector has resulted in a relatively high level of open unemployment. The burden of this problem seems to have fallen disproportionately on the young and the unskilled. The female workers are also disadvantaged by this. The kind of marginalization alluded to here was accentuated through high levels of underemployment and a significant shift to less informal types of labor market participation.

The problems experienced by the economy were in many ways typical of what one might expect from a small economy with a single booming sector. The famed Dutch Disease effect came into play in that, on the back of a rising value for the exchange rate, employment activity within the nontradable sectors became ever more dominant. This position was not sustained by the turn of events, as the economy was hit by quite a severe and long-lasting recession around 1983–84.

Rambarran argues that despite the existence of strong labor institutions, the labor market as a whole retained a reasonable level of flexibility as reflected in downward movements in real wages. The chapter provides a stark reminder that wage flexibility is not a sufficient guarantor of success at reform. The experience of the research presented in this chapter provides a convincing case against much of what many have taken for granted. Sadly, for Trinidad and Tobago, the sectoral shifts within the labor market have not provided enough relief away from the endemic problems of poverty and marginalization for many of its peoples. In short, the future economic path must benefit from greater diversification, deliver more versatile workers, create greater partnership opportunities between the state and labor organizations, and make concrete proposals on how the existing groups of have-nots can be productively integrated. Rambarran's analysis fruitfully considers many of these issues in some detail.

The chapter by Dhanayshar Mahabir presents a valuable contribution to the volume. While the inevitability of some unemployment following the experience of structural adjustment is acknowledged, the chapter's main contribution lies in its advocacy of unemployment insurance as a means toward mitigating the damaging effects of the process of adjustment. The chapter's declared focus is the Caribbean region; however, the analysis has applicability to other parts of the world in which the small open economy (SOE) model is dominant.

Mahabir discusses some of the hazards facing the SOE when it embarks on a process of adjustment. These hazards may involve major short-term shocks in the areas of trade and international liquidity management. The chapter addresses some of the specifics of these problems within the broad context of the Caribbean and suggests some measures for dealing with them. Within the context of labor markets, Mahabir proposes, given the problem of unemployment hysteresis traceable to various adjustment programs, special measures to alleviate labor market imbalance. A useful approach considered is the introduction of unemployment insurance (UI) to the fragile economies of the Caribbean. Mahabir's chapter is cognizant of the usual problems of moral hazard associated with most forms of insurance schemes. He argues that because of these and other difficulties such as small size, the role of government agencies is paramount. The chapter presents a balance sheet of possible costs and benefits associated with any introduction of a UI scheme.

The latter part of the chapter deals with the actual design aspects of UI schemes. It proposes specific guidelines on, for example, the use of a sliding-scale arrangement, to wean the unemployed off benefits. The very last section of the chapter presents some additional measures directed at the unemployed within the Caribbean region as a whole.

According to the advocates of economic liberalization, the more efficient allocation of resources and opening up of the economy to trade would, after a short-run adjustment period, lead to an increase in employment. The temporary rise in unemployment would be more than offset by the creation of employment in newly expanding industries. The final chapter by Tevfik F. Nas and Mehmet Odekon looks at this issue within the context of Turkey. Nas and Odekon argue that employment creation in Turkey in the post-1980 era has been limited, in spite of the fact that real wages in manufacturing have plummeted. A discussion for the reasons of high and persistent unemployment is followed by an attempt to quantify the effects of the Turkish economic liberalization program on firms' labor demand. The authors conclude that economic liberalization alone will not be enough to solve the problems facing the labor market in Turkey.

1

Political Economy, Liberalization, and Labor's Absorption: A Generalized View of Recent Experiences

Parviz Dabir-Alai

INTRODUCTION

The objective of this chapter is to make a general assessment of the impact of economic liberalization policies on the labor markets of a number of economies in which such policy initiatives have been implemented. The material used relies on several key sources of information among which the World Bank (1996) and International Labor Organization (ILO, 1996) are prominent.[1] The chapter has four main sections. We begin by setting the scene quite generally. Here, we present a discussion of some broad political economy issues, including the relevance of Keynesian economics to the popularity of the planned economies favored in the immediate decades after the ending of the Second World War. Following that, there is a brief discussion of why planning, as an economic methodology, underwent its decline. Here some of the reasons for the success of the relatively unplanned economies of the Far East are also presented. That discussion provides the necessary springboard with which to analyze the liberalization phenomenon which has been sweeping across much of the globe in recent years. We essentially present and discuss the findings of a few recent studies inspired by the work of multilaterals such as the World Bank. Here a few brief country-specific experiences, with respect to the attainment of key liberalization-success indicators, are presented. We then present a discussion of some labor market issues and attempt to link these with the aforementioned process of economic liberalization. Again the exploration is carried out fairly generally. While the chapter as a whole does not have a specific geographical focus, there is a tendency to rely more on developing and transition-country information.

POLITICAL ECONOMY ISSUES

Certainly from the perspective of a West European and/or North American liberal democratic framework, Adam Smith is the acknowledged founding father of classical political economy.[2] It was basically Smith's exposition of the virtues of classical political economy that paved the way for a tradition of thinking referred to by Will Hutton as the "liberal heritage."[3] The essential elements of this liberal heritage may be regarded quite simply as lying within a set of doctrines promoting the virtues commonly associated with, and expected of, a harmonious society. It is frequently claimed that progress, be it economic, societal, or political, rests on each community's sense of respect for these doctrines. After all, without the development of this particular type of collaborative and collegial approach, the necessary institutions on whose healthy operation sustained progress must depend would not come into being in the first place. In this sense, the economic development of nations throughout most of the eighteenth, nineteenth, and twentieth centuries may, at least partly, be seen in terms of how well a particular society has managed its affairs vis-à-vis its pursuit of the so-called liberal heritage.

Clearly, this view will not settle well with those subscribing to a more radical view of how we have arrived at the current state of the world economy. Perhaps the common element of the myriad of radical views one finds describes development, or more appropriately underdevelopment, as being indistinguishable from the process of exploitation. These views typically consider core-periphery relationships as lying at the heart of any explanation of why we have the present unbalanced clustering of the haves and the have-nots of nation-states and within nation-states, of individuals.

Taking a nonradical and more libertarian approach to the history of economic development of nation-states leads to an unassailable view. This view ascribes the majority of modern economic development experiences to such factors as the existence of strong, democratically driven institutions accountable to a wide constituency of reasonably well informed individuals.

Good governance, in the sense just described, has certainly played a major part in the developmental experience of nation-states. But there is more to success on the economic front than the mere presence of good governance.[4] Good economics has also contributed to the onset of an enabling environment for modern economic development.

However, unlike many familiar and traditional views on good governance, what has been considered good economics has had a tendency to vary over time. Take Keynesian economic doctrine as an example. Few mainstream and doctrinal approaches to economic analysis have been regarded with as much disdain and, at the same time, as much admiration by different groups, both concurrently and over time.

An important principle on which Keynesian analysis rests is the notion that government intervention may be not only desirable, but critical to ensuring the avoidance of long periods of unemployment and stagnation. Followers of some other (rival) lines of thinking note that reasonably healthy economic activity may coexist with severe bouts of unemployment. The description of an otherwise robust economic environment, with good intersectoral linkages, tolerating large-scale, long-term structural unemployment will be familiar to neoclassical purists and the like.

It is within the context of its advocating government intervention, with the purpose of ridding the economy of the evil of unemployment, that Keynesian economics promotes use of demand management policies. Such policies pursued through the introduction of mostly fiscal measures are frequently cited as contributing to the success of economies in Europe and the United States during much of the 1940s, 1950s, and 1960s. For most of this period, it would seem that Keynesian macroeconomic analysis could, quite simply, do no wrong.

It was not just the Western economies that were sold on the seductive messages underlying the Keynesian viewpoint. Among many of the world's community of developing countries the Keynesian message was taking firm hold as well. However, it is important to note that Keynesian economics was played out somewhat differently here than in the West. In its Western context, Keynesianism was embraced within the framework of economies that were predominantly market driven. After decades of colonial history, many of the then-emerging nations were understandably anxious to avoid tying their economic fortunes with those of their recent masters. Largely unaware of the full extent of their development path options and, at the same time, fearful of the abandonment of their newly acquired principles of political nonalignment, many of these nations were led toward the economic middle path. For several of these nations, steering through this so-called economic middle path has meant reliance on some form of planning and extensive use of regulation. Countries as diverse as Egypt, India, Mozambique, South Korea, Sri Lanka, and Tanzania, for example, all benefited from some form of a regulated approach to the organization of both their micro- and macroeconomic decision-making structures. While these experiences have all been quite different from each other, what is patently true is that much of their underlying philosophical traits have been grounded in the Keynesian tradition of demand management.[5]

Another important distinguishing aspect of the planning process, shared by many of its adherents, has been its almost total commitment to the ideal of self-reliance. It is in this sense that the experience of planning and the pursuit of autarky have come to be closely associated.

PLANNING AND ITS DEMISE

Depending on one's perspective, one would regard the era of planning, and the demand management that went along with that, as having been either wholly necessary or an example of the type of historical legacy one would wish to dispel very quickly. Bagchi, for example, sums up one side of this view well when he outlines: "In the general atmosphere of crisis in the world economy, there is sometimes an agreement between proponents at both extremes of the political spectrum that development planning is impossible in Third World countries."[6]

Bagchi maintains that the implementation of (development) plans will always be problematic and fraught with contradictions. Bagchi's insight is correct in the sense that one tends to encounter more examples of extremes among Third World countries. These imbalances manifest themselves in terms of regional differences in skill endowments, work habits, extent of economic well-being, investment flows from the center and from abroad, prevailing political and ethnic tensions, and so on. As against the type of inherent contradictions highlighted by Bagchi, one can also think of ways in which the experience of planning has been helpful to the overall development effort of Third World, and other, countries. For example, the virtual eradication of famines in India is frequently credited to Indian governmental and quasi-governmental agencies that, with the assistance of various public action programs, have managed to deal with what used to be a fairly recurring and nightmarish experience for large numbers of the country's inhabitants.[7] In this context, and as noted by Drèze, the central management of food stocks may extend beyond food aid and include commercial food imports by governments.[8]

Indian success at engaging in planning is not limited to a record on famine prevention. At least in the early days, after independence in 1947, India was remarkably successful in finding a role for the state in promoting its various developmental initiatives. Major parliamentary initiatives, such as the Industrial Policy Resolution of 1948, as well as the advent of the first and second five-year plans, provided the necessary framework for the launch of a variety of different types of industrial activities.

Part of the success of the early Indian attempts at planning resulted from the planners' willingness to look to other experiences and their propensity to learn from them. The work of Hanson, for example, testifies to this. He maintains: "throughout the remainder of his life, Nehru (the Guru of the Planning Commission) dreamed of combining economic mobilization with political conciliation, a 'Soviet economy with a Western polity.' "[9] Or, as re-phrased by Dabir-Alai, and in keeping with a more modern parlance: "achieving Glasnost without having to endure Perestroika."[10]

Within the context of the economic experiences of the Soviet Union, especially during the 1930s to the 1970s, one can discern a distinct role for the planning process as well. It was the Soviet Union's reliance on planning as an economic strategy that enabled it to engage in large-scale industrialization. As long as the pursuit of industrialization is considered an appropriate means of achieving a reasonably viable (economic) future, then the Soviet experiment must receive its share of credit for its contribution to this process.[11]

Overall, and despite all the examples of success, planning as an economic approach has been on the decline for at least the past ten to twenty years. A number of fairly obvious factors provide us with the clues for this.

First, the relative tranquillity of the world economy during the 1950s and 1960s came to a thundering crash in the 1970s. The oil price crisis, and the untold shocks associated with it, best illustrate the impossibility of running an economy on the basis of something as restrictive as a fixed-period plan whose full implementation must depend on *predictable* assumptions about the future. That period of crisis revealed quite clearly the need for economic flexibility and the difficulties associated with not maintaining one's versatility in the management of economic resources. Both of these requirements illustrate rather starkly the need to be able to adjust to new and changing circumstances fairly speedily. Few if any of these traits have been associated with economies in which the planning experience has been at the fore. Because of these as well as other reasons, there was a creeping realization that traditional forms of planning could not respond to the economic challenges of the modern age.[12]

Second, throughout the 1960s and the 1970s, a new breed of economic superpower was being shaped. Some of these countries, subsequently labeled as newly industrializing (NICs) and later as "Tigers," engaged in a series of successful transitions over a relatively short period of time. The most thriving examples of these, Hong Kong, South Korea, Taiwan, and Singapore, relied on a system of selective promotion of their core areas of economic and industrial expertise. Coupled with sound management of both their fiscal and monetary affairs, the so-called Tigers achieved enormous economic success.

The Tigers' success was rooted in their early ability to see the pitfalls associated with too much, and undiscriminating, control. They recognized that while market intervention would encourage some industrial activity initially, the long-term prospects of indiscriminate control could only mean stagnation. Measures such as price intervention usually end up with unpredictable and normally negative consequences. Economic initiatives such as interest rate ceilings prevent productive investment as they tend to depress savings. Caps on food and other agricultural-sector prices discourage investment in those areas. The issuing of industrial licenses creates and promotes rent-seeking behavior among those entitled to them.[13]

The Tigers' decision to avoid many of the different types of control mechanisms just described is, of course, part foresight and part luck. The element of luck is not to be overlooked as, at the time when their economic experiments were being initiated, there was very little precedent for the successful implementation of export-oriented development strategies among economies, other than perhaps a few belonging to the so-called developed world.

The successful experience of the Tigers, more than any other single fact, has prompted the view that an export-led approach to development can bring on desirable economic outcomes for the economy in question.[14]

However, this export-led strategy has not always been in the ascendancy. For example, as far back as 1950, both Singer and Prebisch were influential in putting across the view that growth in world demand may not be high enough for it to accommodate the fast rate of increase in commodity exports on which less developed countries (LDCs) in general were dependent.[15] The essential assumptions of Singer and Prebisch have had a certain timelessness that is rare in applied economic thinking.

More recent research has highlighted the relevance of other complementary elements. For example, the work of Sachs and Warner (1995) has established clear links between the principles of market orientation with the phenomenon of economic growth.[16] Their approach concentrates on assessing two sets of market-based economic criteria: the security of property rights and economic openness. By security of property rights, they are referring to a situation in which socialist economic structures and other socioeconomic "destabilizing" influences, such as war and human rights violations, are absent. By economic openness, the authors imply conditions in which only a small amount of imports are covered by quantitative restrictions (QRs) and a free-market exchange rate that is within 20 percent of any official rate. For a twenty-year period ending in 1989, Sachs and Warner identify only thirteen countries (out of seventy-five) for which all the conditions are met.[17]

Studies such as those just mentioned clearly support the positive role that is possible for markets within the overall development process. More significant perhaps, these studies, as well as several others, strongly suggest that economic openness promotes competition and, by extension, productivity.[18] It is the link between openness and the prospect of more productive resources, especially that relating to labor resources, that justifies our focus for the remaining sections of this chapter.

LIBERALIZATION AND ITS AFTERMATH

A significant initiative sweeping across many parts of both the developed and developing world in recent years has been the process commonly referred to as economic liberalization. Perhaps the single most powerful motivating influence behind this drive has been the desire to avoid a severe macroeconomic imbalance or correct an existing one. The remaining parts of this chapter will focus on making a general assessment of the impact of economic liberalization policies on the labor markets of a number of economies in which such policy initiatives have been implemented.[19] Our discussion of liberalization policies and their link with the labor market is in recognition of the expected (and proven) impact of openness on productivity mentioned above.

Given our remaining objective in this chapter, the first task must be to outline a basic understanding of what is commonly understood by the use of the term *economic liberalization* beyond what has been implied by our discussions so far.

The most widely used context is one that sees liberalization as a process whereby the role of government and government-sponsored agencies is reduced within the entire microeconomic decision-making structures of the economy. This view sees an increasing reliance on the price mechanism, rather than controls and regulation, and calls for an increasing level of integration of the national economies into the world economy.[20]

Economic liberalization policies have been introduced through several different means. Perhaps the most widely used mechanisms have relied on varying doses of structural adjustment (SAPs) and stabilization programs (SPs). SAPs and SPs are, of course, not the same. Essentially, they constitute two of the main complementary elements among several initiatives pursued around the world in recent years.[21]

For many of the more successful experiments, one finds that macroeconomic stabilization has presupposed budgetary discipline. As already implied, this is seen as providing any liberalization experiment with one of its fundamental cornerstones. The other key requirement is a firm commitment to combating inflationary pressure within the economy, at least that part which is domestically fueled and, therefore, subject to some control. Structural adjustment, on the other hand, is the longer-term attempt to provide the economy with its steady long-term growth.

It is important to note that the relatively more successful experiments have all had a tendency to see the whole process of liberalization and adjustment as being conducted along a continuum. The viability of this continuum is supported by a number of elements including, but not limited to, the presence of a clear sense of commitment—on the part of public and private economic agents—to the principal objectives of the reforms, the political will to carry these through, and the necessary propensity to withstand any of the adverse short-term costs that may result. Largely in acknowledgment of these points, we see that many of the more sober pronouncements of the 1990s have called for better harmonization of SAPs and SPs. This is also in recognition of the deleterious consequences of creating policy in a vacuum. This call for greater harmonization of such policy initiatives may also be seen as a call for better coordination among their chief sponsoring agencies, namely, the World Bank and the International Monetary Fund (IMF), respectively.[22] Another important point is that while the so-called Washington consensus has played an important role in determining the priorities within most SAPs and SPs, several alternative and complementary approaches to these have been proposed as well. In this regard, reference to the work of Singer (1993) is particularly important.[23]

Arguments linking the effects of SAPs and SPs on the labor market are often presented through the lubricating mechanisms of accelerating growth, provision of adequate public spending, and the introduction and funding of a viable social safety net system. Briefly, economic growth, among other things, provides an opportunity for the expansion of productive employment. Adequate public spending, when present, enhances the possibility that those goods and services not normally provided by the market will become more readily available. Public spending on public goods, such as education, training, and other social infrastructure items, can only have positive implications for both the enhancement of labor resources and their utilization. When the market is failing its various constituents, a reasonable backup system, in the form of a financially viable social safety net, may be called upon to cushion the plight of the most vulnerable segments.

Any complete assessment of the effects of SPs and SAPs on the labor market will benefit from a consideration of the issues just raised. However, the kind of complete assessment called for, particularly if interpreted as requiring a formal treatment, implies the use of a far more sophisticated approach. In this context, one could rely on the use of computable general equilibrium (CGE) models. However, it is not our intention to employ such a technique here in this chapter, as interpreting the results of CGE models adds a level of intricacy to the analysis which, unfortunately, is not supported by available data. Instead, and in keeping with this first chapter's objective of providing a general overview, we report on one or two key pieces of research and provide some analysis of their major findings. The authoritative study by Choksi, Michaely, and Papageorgiou (1991) is one that we shall briefly discuss.[24]

Choksi et al. outline a systematic approach to the analysis of success and failure of the experience of trade and economic liberalization for nineteen economies over a thirty-to-thirty-five-year period. The route taken by them benefits from a clear and accessible synthesis which is not available to more formal approaches based on the likes of those dependent on the CGE-type models. Their comprehensive study includes looking at the experience of economies based within Asia, Latin America, the Mediterranean, and the Pacific Rim regions. By reviewing the set of liberalization experiments at several distinct points in time, the authors effectively draw on the experiences of thirty-six separate liberalization attempts. Their approach to analyzing their sample looks at trade and other issues. Within the area of trade, for example, Choksi et al. consider each economy's record with respect to its relaxation of quantitative restrictions (QRs) and any reduction of tariff rates achieved. They also consider what the World Bank has referred to as "resource balance" issues, namely, each economy's track record in moving toward a realistic valuation for its exchange rate.[25] While several other issues are also considered (such as each economy's record on income distribution, and on meeting employment/unemployment targets and their balance of payments targets), the remaining major focus of the study has been on adopted fiscal and monetary regimes. A further significant contribution of the Choksi et al. study has been its recognition of the role of time in judging success and failure.[26] Relatedly, another key feature of the Choksi et al. study is its consideration of the intensity of the introduced reform packages. The relevant distinctions here are between reform packages that are either strong or weak. The yardstick used by the study to define a reform package as strong amounts to finding evidence of a radical shake-up of the system of QRs. Weak packages are so identified because of their lack of commitment to the shake-up of QRs.

A more recent attempt at judging the success of introduced reforms, among a wide grouping of countries, is represented by the World Bank (1996).[27] That particular study's approach to judging the success (or failure) of introduced reforms relies on assessing the overall strength of the ensuing macroeconomic framework. In what follows, the salient features of that particular perspective are briefly discussed.

The World Bank study looked at the experience of adjustment in fifty-three countries, spanning the early 1980s to the early 1990s. Assessment of the success of reform for the fifty-three countries studied by the World Bank, including the selected group of twenty-nine, was judged on a set of criteria impinging on the conditions associated with the overall macroeconomic stability. Essentially, three principal criteria were used: first, each country's record in the area of fiscal policy and internal balance; second, the countries' respective resource balance and the exchange rate positions; and, third, each economy's particular monetary regime and the external balance achieved. These will be looked at in turn below and the more notable individual country experiences highlighted. It will be remembered that the forthcoming discussion on each economy's success or failure in meeting the above three principles assumes at least an implicit impact on labor's absorption.

Fiscal Policy and the Internal Balance

Overall, engaging in a program of fiscal contraction remained a key component of the adjustment program for most of the economies reviewed. The principal motivation was to try and restore internal balance, as indicated by the strength or otherwise of domestic inflationary pressure. According to the World Bank study, twenty-seven of the fifty-one countries for which fiscal and inflation data were available reduced both their fiscal deficits and inflation rates.[28] These twenty-seven economies are loosely described as having been successful. Against these twenty-seven successful episodes one finds a large number of unsuccessful attempts at fiscal and internal balance reform. For example, the study reveals that sixteen countries failed to engage in any fiscal tightening. Of these sixteen, nine experienced increases in their inflation rates during the adjustment period. This kind of relative failure is often caused by a lack of internal discipline or some supply shock or both. For example, in the case of both Colombia and Nigeria, the supply shock came in the form of sharp increases in food prices.[29] These two economies plus Bolivia, Sudan, and Turkey engaged in a high degree of monetization of their rising fiscal deficits. However, their efforts at controlling the situation were largely stifled by political and social unrest during their respective adjustment periods.

According to the above-mentioned World Bank study, seven of the countries that did not tighten fiscally managed to control their inflation. The mechanism used to achieve this was price control. These economies also used a combination of trade liberalization and the implementation of some industrial reorganization measures, such as the abolishing of certain of their monopolies. In summary, then, the seven countries, which include Burundi, Côte d'Ivoire, Niger, and Pakistan, started with relatively low inflation rates, relaxed their fiscal position, and managed to successfully postpone their adverse inflationary consequences. All of this, at least potentially, bodes well for improved factor productivity in general and, hence, labor's employability in the long term.

For eight of the countries studied, reductions in their fiscal deficits were accompanied by inflationary pressure. The price increases were all because of a number of internal and external supply shocks. Of these eight, Costa Rica experienced the smallest increase (10 percent to reach 23) and Zaire the largest (by more than 600 percent to reach 700!).[30] Several other countries relied on a system of monetizing their foreign exchange reserves (e.g., Ecuador and Tanzania) in order to lend support to their domestic spending.

The experiences summarized above pose uncomfortable questions and confront policymakers with a set of difficult choices in the area of fiscal policy and the achievement of internal balance. Success in one area has been tempered with some setbacks in others, while certain failures have occurred in the face of apparently correct decisions. It is this reality that focuses the mind on the challenges that lie ahead. Such challenges have been met before. What is a matter for concern, however, is the case of a few countries, identified by the World Bank study and numbering about eight, for which the political will with which to attempt stabilization and fiscal prudence seems to have been lacking.[31]

Resource Balance and Exchange Rate Positions

Large current account deficits, particularly those unsustainable over a period of time, may call for a real devaluation of the currency. However, such a policy may be both inflationary and lead to some instability within the capital account (through, say, capital flight). To avert such an outcome after a devaluation, it may be necessary to engage in short- to medium-term fiscal and monetary tightening.

As compared with experience in achieving internal balance, a relatively larger number of the fifty-three countries already referred to managed to achieve real devaluations of their currencies during their respective periods of adjustment. Furthermore, the thirty-nine economies managing a successful devaluation also managed to increase their resource balance, that is, reduce their deficit. Of the rest, Sudan experienced both a real appreciation of its currency and a decrease in its resource balance. Four others, comprising Bolivia, Brazil, Côte d'Ivoire, and the Gambia, had improvements in their resource balances while experiencing an appreciation. Despite engaging in real devaluations, Ghana, Togo, and Zambia saw a worsening in their resource balance positions.

Of the last set of countries mentioned, Ghana probably represents the most interesting case. Ghana has experienced increases in both its exports and imports. However, overall, its terms of trade worsened, contributing to a deterioration in its ability to service its external debts. Within the context of the Ghanaian economy, the experience of growing imports and an increase in the inflow of public capital coincided. A significant part of this capital inflow may be ascribed to the World Bank's adjustment lending in order to support Ghana's imports. The bank acknowledges that such a policy is of long-term value, as far as the labor and other markets are concerned, only if it contributes meaningfully to the overall growth and development effort.[32] The World Bank study (1996) summarizes some of the discussion presented above and that contained within the next sub-section.

Monetary Policy and the External Balance

One of the problems faced by many of the economies reviewed by the aforementioned World Bank study was that they had grown accustomed to enduring real (that is, inflation-adjusted) interest rates that were below international levels. Their chosen method of combating the resultant capital outflows was mainly through capital controls. Insofar as the employment of labor is concerned, such capital controls are generally unwelcome as they act as a disincentive to inward flows of investment by corporate interests. Additionally, we would expect such controls to have a discouraging effect on both expatriate and nonresident nationals' flows.

It is not surprising, therefore, to see that a major plank of the World Bank's assessment of success at adjustment rests on a view of each economy's progress with its monetary policy and the maintenance, or improvement, of its external balance. Consequently, many of the adjustment processes have involved a tightening of monetary policy. This has contributed to an increase in interest rates which has helped in reducing the size of the negative interest rates prevailing earlier. It is generally recognized that a positive real interest rate differential should discourage capital outflows and thus help the economy's efforts at building up its foreign exchange reserves. Almost forty of the fifty-three countries studied managed to raise their interest rates over their respective adjustment periods. Of these, more than thirty succeeded in increasing their reserves of foreign exchange.[33]

The importance of following a tight monetary policy is perhaps best illustrated by the experience of Argentina, Bolivia, and Sudan. All three of these countries reduced their interest rates over their respective adjustment periods and lost reserves. All three were also high inflation economies that had chosen not to adjust their nominal interest rates.[34]

Other country examples highlight the importance of factors other than the pursuit of a tight monetary policy. For example, seven countries experiencing some monetary tightening also witnessed a decline in their reserves. These economies, which included Kenya, Madagascar, and Pakistan, all had fairly high debt-service ratios as well as current account deficits. In the case of the Philippines, it is suggested that the massive capital outflows may have been caused by expectations of policy reversals on monetary policy.

Not surprisingly, perhaps the overall picture is somewhat mixed. However, the key message of sustainable growth and development being linked to sensible domestic housekeeping, in both monetary and fiscal areas, remains unassailable.

INTERCONNECTIONS WITH THE LABOR MARKET

By Western standards those developing- and transition-country residents fortunate enough to be in work are not only badly paid but often feel a great deal of insecurity with respect to both their conditions and their tenure. For those not in work, the picture is yet more bleak. With net population growth rates for many developing and some transition economies exceeding the 2 percent mark, the major challenge must remain one in which large quantities of productive employment opportunities have to be found.[35] Without this, one may expect that major income distributional imbalances currently in place will not be addressed and that the gap between the rich and the poor will continue to widen at both national and international levels. There are clear moral imperatives which dictate the need for such gaps to be narrowed. Perhaps the strongest case for insisting on the upholding of these moral imperatives emanates from the need to promote distributive, or economic, justice.[36]

Even if one were to put aside the moral imperatives, one can legitimately argue that a situation in which increasing numbers of citizens found themselves losing out to the economic elites, and thus ending up with no greater role in the economic process than that of spectator, will be highly destabilizing to the very foundations of the capitalist system. If this is the case, then, apart from any moral obligation to the poor, the present predominantly market-driven and capitalist-based economies will find it in their self-interest to move toward a major redressing of the current imbalance.

Given that redistribution must continue to be a priority, the issue then becomes one in which the most appropriate mechanism for achieving this has to be found. Productive employment generation must be close to the top of any balanced list of available options. However, any realistic assessment of the rate at which productive employment opportunities have to be found is enough to dampen the enthusiasm of the most determined of policymakers. This growth rate has a more or less linear relationship with the fast population growth rates mentioned and, in addition, will most certainly have to take note of existing levels of labor underutilization. In connection with this, the only other significant point to note is that the relationship is necessarily delayed as, obviously, every generation of newborns needs to age fifteen to twenty years before it has the opportunity to play an active, and hopefully productive, role within the economic process and society.

Stabilization and adjustment programs contribute to the creation of environments in which long-term, and sustainable, economic expansion becomes more likely. As we have seen already, stabilization aims to secure reductions in the rate of inflation and lend sustainability to any outstanding current account deficits in the medium to long term. The short-term consequences of SPs, however, is to reduce demand and retard economic growth.[37]

Further, structural adjustment measures have the immediate effect of adding to any prevailing climate of uncertainty. Apart from having to be workable, the effectiveness of policy initiatives depends on the extent to which they are credible. Generally, economic agents require time in order to assess the sustainability of any new initiative. This kind of continued uncertainty is typical of the type of environment in which low investment levels eventually lead to a protracted recessionary period and severely dampen the economy's prospects for growth in the medium term. As such, and as said already, while SPs and SAPs should bring long-term benefits, their short- and medium-term economic effects are not always positive. Nowhere are these negative consequences felt more than in the area of labor's absorption within the overall economic process. Recent developing- and transition-economy experience everywhere testifies to the short-term negative consequences of SPs and SAPs on the labor market. One important manifestation of this is the significant swelling of the numbers of disenchanted former formal-sector workers who find solace by redeploying themselves within the informal sectors, particularly of developing countries.[38]

Recognition of the fact that labor continues to remain heavily underutilized, through either unemployment and/or underemployment, leads to the long-suspected and rather gloomy observation that the combined might of existing policy-making frameworks may be totally insufficient in meeting the challenges faced by the labor markets of developing and transition countries for some time to come.

Before delving into any policy issues, it may be appropriate to present some recently published labor market statistics for a few developing economies around the world. Table 1.1 provides such statistics, from a study by ILO.

Table 1.1 points to a number of interesting observations. First, during the 1975 to 1980 period, the increase in the various country-specific labor forces was more than matched by increases in employment growth. This should suggest falling levels of unemployment for the economies concerned. However, during the period coinciding with the debt crisis of 1981 to 1985, we see that, with few exceptions, employment growth lagged behind labor force growth.[39] A more or less similar observation can be made for the 1986 to 1993 period. This relatively long time span coincides with a period of debt-position consolidation for many of the countries and with the early 1990s recessionary trends experienced worldwide.

Another useful measure of the consequence of the overall liberalization experience on labor markets may be found in a discussion of the

Table 1.1
Labor Force Data: Selected Developing Countries, 1975–93
(percentage, annual averages)

	Labor Force Growth			Total Employment Growth		
	1975–1980	*1981–1985*	*1986–1993*	*1975–1980*	*1981–1985*	*1986–1993*
Bolivia	2.13	2.70	2.71	2.68	–0.38	1.97
Brazil	3.37	2.33	2.12	3.94	4.30	2.93
Costa Rica	4.03	3.07	2.47	4.01	2.74	3.62
Pakistan	2.97	3.24	2.66	3.32	2.07	1.93
Philippines	2.09	2.54	2.50	1.11	3.47	2.34
Côte d'Ivoire	2.38	2.70	2.54	6.68	–2.89	–1.04
Ghana	2.69	2.66	2.85	1.48	11.04	–13.29
Kenya	3.73	3.47	3.63	4.21	3.16	3.48
Zimbabwe	2.96	2.74	2.90	–0.76	0.89	1.92
Turkey	1.59	2.30	2.05	—	—	8.03

Source: Selected information from International Labor Organization (1996).

employment elasticity. This is basically an indicator of the employment content of an economy's output and measures the extent of its intensity.[40] As its numerical value is inversely related to labor productivity, a decline in its value does not necessarily carry negative connotations. Any corrective policy action on the unemployment issue must therefore depend on an assessment of trend changes, as well as the direction of these changes. According to the aforementioned ILO study, an initial value of greater than 1.0 would usually indicate that employment growth is linked with falling labor productivity. From a policy perspective, it might be desirable to seek to reverse this trend. The data in Table 1.2 provide an opportunity for further discussion in this area.

We notice several examples of declining values for the employment elasticity in Table 1.2. For Brazil, Colombia, Kenya, Zimbabwe, India, Pakistan, Korea, Thailand, Philippines, and Turkey, the elasticity measure falls during the 1975 to 1985 period. For some of these, the decline extends to the whole period. Falling values for the elasticity of output measure have to be seen within the context of developments elsewhere within the respective economies. For example, as in the case of Kenya, Korea, and Thailand, employment growth remained strong. The more worrisome cases involve countries such as India, in which low employ-

Table 1.2
Employment Elasticity, Employment Growth, and Output Growth:
Selected Developing Countries, 1975–92

Country	Variable	1975–80	1981–85	1986–92
Brazil	Value-added growth	12.06	4.22	–5.08
	Employment growth	10.58	0.06	–0.93
	Elasticity of employment	0.88	0.01	—
Colombia	Value-added growth	6.63	0.95	4.64
	Employment growth	2.46	–2.84	1.67
	Elasticity of employment	—	—	0.36
Jamaica	Value-added growth	–8.30	4.79	5.55
	Employment growth	–3.53	1.03	5.09
	Elasticity of employment	—	0.22	0.92
Kenya	Value-added growth	2.50	1.37	2.53
	Employment growth	6.71	2.64	2.83
	Elasticity of employment	2.68	1.93	1.12
Zimbabwe	Value-added growth	3.02	1.74	7.16
	Employment growth	1.27	0.43	1.90
	Elasticity of employment	0.42	0.24	0.26
India	Value-added growth	6.26	3.66	7.18
	Employment growth	4.26	–1.18	1.41
	Elasticity of employment	0.68	—	0.20
Pakistan	Value-added growth	10.96	8.40	7.67
	Employment growth	0.08	1.78	1.54
	Elasticity of employment	0.01	0.21	0.20
Republic of	Value-added growth	15.05	9.97	12.42
Korea	Employment growth	7.96	3.55	3.70
	Elasticity of employment	0.53	0.36	0.30
Thailand	Value-added growth	6.56	4.82	9.84
	Employment growth	4.01	3.29	3.76
	Elasticity of employment	0.61	0.68	0.38
Philippines	Value-added growth	3.86	–3.38	16.76
	Employment growth	14.14	–7.49	6.47
	Elasticity of employment	3.66	—	0.39
Turkey	Value-added growth	4.33	5.92	7.28
	Employment growth	2.42	1.45	2.15
	Elasticity of employment	0.56	0.24	0.29

Source: Selected information from International Labor Organization (1996).

ment elasticity has been accompanied by insignificant, or negative, changes to employment growth. A number of reasons account for this. The common thread among the myriad of available explanations describes a series of market conditions that ultimately provide the economy in general and the labor markets in particular with the wrong signals. Essentially, the problem seems to be one of distorted factor prices. We shall return to this theme below.

Clearly, for any particular work force to make a significant contribution to the prosperity of the nation it belongs to, it has to be appropriately skilled, supported with complementary inputs, and well motivated and rewarded. Further, it is essential that the policy environment is one that is broadly consistent with the need to absorb and use labor resources effectively. It is virtually inconceivable, with meaningful development in mind, for these basic elements to go unmet for long periods of time. Looking at the developmental experiences of many of the world's poorer nations suggests, at best, only a partial fulfillment of these requirements. Often the reason for this has little to do with lack of goodwill or fine intent on the part of those in charge. Most commonly, labor's contribution to the development process is reduced through there not being in position a varied and sufficiently viable set of complementary activities that can assist with its absorption. For example, and despite Lewis's (1955) famed contribution, it is now well known that the expansion of economic activity via the industrial sectors does not necessarily result in a significant expansion in labor's integration within the economy.[41] As far as the manufacturing sector is concerned, the most intensively used resources tend to be capital or capital-based items. This suggests only marginal improvements for labor's ability to play its part fully. The main causes of this lie in what is normally referred to as the problem of factor price distortions, or FPDs. In what appears below, we provide a few brief comments on how FPDs may arise and, within the context of our earlier discussion, how they may be eliminated.

FPDs occur due to a variety of institutionally determined reasons. The first is capital market imperfections. Within developing countries, such imperfections often manifest themselves in the form of interest-rate ceilings. Such capped rates can only result in the price of traded inputs (such as capital equipment) being *artificially* held below those of other inputs (such as labor resources). Capital market imperfections are also responsible for the structure of credit provision within developing countries. Recent significant strides in alerting governments and government-sponsored agencies to the benefits of nontraditional forms of credit do not seem to have had much impact in enabling poorer and less collateral-rich entrepreneurs to increase their participation in economic activity in many developing regions.[42]

The second deals with labor-wage legislation. It is sometimes claimed that policy initiatives such as minimum-wage legislation raise the cost of employing labor within formal labor markets.[43] The natural consequence of this, if proven to be widespread, will be to discourage labor's absorption within the manufacturing and other economic processes of developing, transition and developed countries. In connection with this, it is interesting to note that the ratio of the minimum wage to the average wage has usually been allowed to fall during periods of economic reform. If this ratio is seen as a kind of barometer of the labor market's flexibility, then its reduction must be interpreted as reflecting the authorities view that a more elastic, and less tightly regulated market will be good for the purposes of achieving reform.[44]

Finally, within the specific context of developing and transition economies, it is frequently claimed that multinational enterprises, because they are responsible for the permeation of the bulk of foreign direct investments and because they seek the highest returns on investment, employ predominantly capital-intensive processes.[45]

Clearly, any set of policies intent on raising labor's utilization within the overall economic process must take into account issues such as those arising from FPDs. For not doing so will force certain types of labor, particularly the low skilled, but others also, to continue their current marginalized status.

It is recognized that the elimination of FPDs will not eradicate the problem of unemployment and underemployment of labor. However, such action will contribute to the trends being at least halted and given the presence of other complementary elements, possibly reversed over the long term. The next section reflects on some of the opportunities for labor if and when FPDs are removed. The section also provides a brief summary and concludes the chapter.

CONCLUSIONS

By common consent, one of the major challenges facing the world economy today must be the problem of efficiently maximizing the availability of productive employment opportunities. The meeting of this challenge has been complicated by a number of major world events which have contributed to the accentuation of an already wide opportunity gap among the richer and poorer nations—events such as the unprecedented number of countries gaining independence in the 1960s, the 1970s oil price crisis, the 1980s period of debt, and the recessionary conditions of the early 1990s. The widening gap referred to, as well as improvements in our understanding of some of those enabling factors necessary for sustained economic growth and development, has prompted a more or less wholesale adoption of micro- and macroeconomic policies inspired by the workings of the market. The key tenets underlying such policies have increasingly found favor with influential multilateral banking and finance institutions.

The liberalization episodes experienced by developing, transition, and developed countries alike have taken an early and sustained heavy toll on their labor markets. This chapter focused on the relative success of a number of economies, in the area of progress toward reform, from the perspective of their achievement of certain macroeconomic objectives. Some were found to be clearly deficient in this respect. One would expect that failure to achieve macroeconomic balance would adversely affect opportunities within the labor market. On the other hand, a good level of performance in the area of macroeconomic balance must augur well for those in work or seeking work. The common sense here is that healthy economies that are growing in a sustainable manner also employ factors that are more gainfully employed and, hence, more productive. Like virtuous circles everywhere, the direction of causality is several.

Removal of some of the distortions, such as some of the examples of FPDs mentioned above, should facilitate labor's absorption within the overall economic process in the longer term. While some distortions will have to be eliminated, others may have to be actively encouraged, at least in the short term. For example, we know that the rapid pace of technological change within the workplace has added to growing levels of job insecurity in many parts of the world. In an increasingly global economic environment, the nature of competitive pressures in place will most likely continue this type of capital deepening. In such circumstances, it may be necessary to consider a role for a supranational agency responsible for the provision of transitional relief to the most affected groups of workers, their sectors, or their governments. While displaced workers will remain the ultimate beneficiaries of any system of relief introduced, the supranational agency may be charged with the responsibility of prioritizing the level of involvement of any intermediary. For example, it may be judged that any allocation of funds can best benefit workers if it were earmarked for a particular form of re-training program. Alternatively, any allocation may serve to alleviate only short-term consumption needs of displaced workers. In the short term, such an agency could look to national governments for financial and logistical support. In the longer term, it may be desirable to oblige the best financially endowed multinational corporations, those responsible for capital deepening, to contribute to the agency's funding requirements.

Other less bureaucratically driven initiatives for enhancing the opportunities for labor are also connected with creating an enabling environment in a number of different but interrelated areas.

First is a commitment to the pursuit of open and fair trade and economic practices. This is essential if we are to avoid the coming into being of a comparative advantage that is distorted yet effective for the perpetrators. If permitted to arise, such distortions will discourage sustainable development among the very nations and sectors where it is most needed. Second, extra help, beyond that currently pledged, must be given to the poorest countries so as to enable them to adjust to the harsh realities of following their particular experience of SPs and SAPs. Third, a mechanism must be introduced that is designed to reduce the flows of speculative short-term capital transactions. Such flows, left unchecked, may result in financial and political uncertainty, fluctuating investment levels, productivity downturns, and employment insecurity. Some of the benefits gained from the ending of speculative flows could be channeled toward the development of small- and medium-sized enterprises. Fourth, measures must be promoted which, while encouraging labor market flexibility, would not hamper cooperation among seemingly competitive elements. In this regard, it is important to encourage dialogue among employers and employees, as well as among private and public enterprises. Fifth, gender or any other form of labor market inequality must be discouraged. Women and other minority groups continue to play an active and important role in ensuring national economic success in many economies. The sooner their contribution is recognized and their rights protected, the more their long-term bestowal to the economy is likely to be. Such a contribution is particularly notable within the informal sectors of some of the poorest countries.

This listing is suggestive and, as such, by no means complete. It is an attempt at identifying what was earlier referred to as the need to practice good economics.

ACKNOWLEDGMENTS

Helpful comments from Shahin Shojai and Hans Singer are kindly acknowledged.

NOTES

1. World Bank (1996) and International Labor Organization (1996).

2. Needless to say, other socioeconomic and cultural traditions may very well acknowledge Smith's contribution somewhat differently.

3. See Hutton (1986:3).

4. See Ezeala-Harrison (1994) for a succinct account of a related issue, that of the role of bad government within the context of Sub-Saharan Africa.

5. Another motivating element driving many of the developing nations toward this planned approach was, of course, the perception of relative economic successes of the Stalinist collectivization experience of the 1930s Soviet Union.

6. See Bagchi (1989:106).

7. For an authoritative account of the experiences of India and other countries with famine prevention, see Drèze and Sen (1990).

8. See Drèze (1993).

9. See Hanson (1968).

10. See Dabir-Alai (1996).

11. Within both its Indian and Soviet contexts, planning provided the state apparatus with an opportunity to engage in economic as well as political nationalism. As will be appreciated, without a detailed case-by-case study, it is not possible to comment on the specific economic costs and benefits associated with this kind of experience.

12. Bruton (1970) is an early example of the type of research suggesting the demise of planning and import substitution as approaches to constructing a viable economic framework.

13. In this connection, see the celebrated piece by Krueger (1974).

14. It will be recalled that, in general, the various planning experiments have emphasized the need to import substitute rather than promote exports.

15. See Singer (1950) and Prebisch's work for the United Nations (1950).

16. See Sachs and Warner (1995).

17. See the text by Gillis et al. (1996) for a good summary of the Sachs and Warner paper.

18. For a recent comprehensive multicountry study of the links between macroeconomic stability and economic growth, see the work by S. Fischer (1993).

19. Unlike the material presented elsewhere in this volume, and as already mentioned, the discussion in this chapter is quite general in that it does not have a specific country or regional focus.

20. One well-known source adopting this denotation is Köves and Marer (1991; Chapter 1). They provide a comprehensive treatment of many of the relevant issues pertaining to the liberalization experience.

21. See Toye (1995), especially his Chapter 2, for a succinct assessment of SAPs and SPs.

22. The work of other multilateral lending agencies, such as the European Bank for Reconstruction and Development (EBRD) and the Inter-American Development Bank (IDB), plays an increasingly important role in this process.

23. See Singer (1993).

24. See the chapter by Choksi, Michaely and Papageorgiou in Köves and Marer (1991; Chapter 2).

25. For example, see World Bank (1996:36).

26. The terminology they use is *pace*. The pace of reforms is said to have been either fast or slow. That study defined fast as a period not exceeding six years. How was the choice of six years justified? The authors contend that, under normal circumstances, a government may be expected to change within any given six-year period. If the introduced reforms withstand a change of government, then they are likely to be sustained. While not entirely scientifically based, the six-year rule of thumb seems to have been based on reasonable assumptions.

27. World Bank (1996).

28. The total number of countries studied, as already mentioned, was fifty-three.

29. It is worth noting that the average annual urban unemployment rate in Colombia fell from 14.1 to 9.9 percent during its period of adjustment (that is, 1985 to 1989). See World Bank (1995a:8).

30. In the case of Costa Rica, the average annual urban unemployment rate was almost halved to 3.7 percent during its adjustment period (that is, 1982 to 1989). Further, compared to the 1980 levels, average real wages in Costa Rica had declined by about 15 percent. See World Bank (1995a).

31. These include Bolivia, Colombia, Guyana, Nigeria, Sudan, and Zambia.

32. See World Bank (1996:39).

33. World Bank (1996:40).

34. Even though Argentina had a generally high level of inflation throughout its adjustment period, the average real wages declined fairly steadily and eventually declined by close to 20 percent of its 1980 levels. See World Bank (1993a:8).

35. Based on detailed estimates for 209 economies, the World Bank notes the following population growth rates between 1985 and 1994: thirty-four had growth rates of more than 3.0 percent; growth rates between 2.2 and 3.0 percent were noted for fifty-six economies; and another thirty-four had population growth rates of between 1.5 and 2.1 percent. Yet another twenty-two economies recorded population growth rates of between 1.0 and 1.4 percent; for sixty-three economies the growth rate was either less than 1.0 percent or the relevant data were not available. Data are taken from the World Bank (1995b:10).

36. For a succinct discussion of some related issues, see Phelps (1991).

37. The aforementioned study by Choksi et al. provides a mixed picture for the impact of liberalization on manufacturing employment in the short run.

38. International Labor Organization (1996; Table 5.5) provides data on non-agricultural employment for thirteen Central and Latin American states for 1990 and 1994. Eleven of these (the exceptions being Honduras and Panama) record a significant increase in this indicator. The smallest increase occurs in Chile (1.1 percent) and the largest in Paraguay (7.5 percent).

39. It is interesting to note that the 1981-85 period overlapped with the various adjustment periods noted earlier in Table 1.1.

40. See International Labor Organization (1996; Chapter 5) for further elaboration.

41. See Lewis (1955).

42. The reader may wish to consult the minutes of the interministerial meetings of November 1994 in connection with the preparatory rounds of the Summit of Americas meetings held in Port-of-Spain, Trinidad. At those meetings and the subsequent summit in Miami, in December 1994, there was extensive discussion on the role and mechanisms for providing micro credit to small enterprises within the Americas.

43. This remains a controversial and much debated issue. For some international evidence contrary to the point made in the text, see International Labor Organization (1996).

44. See World Bank (1995c; Chapter 17) for a discussion of the kind of changes mentioned. There it is seen that a wide selection of developing and transition economies, including Chile, Hungary, Kenya, Mexico, and Russia, were affected in this way.

45. This raises the thorny issue of the employment, or the nonemployment, of what is often referred to as "appropriate technology."

REFERENCES

Bagchi, A. K. 1989. Development planning. In *The New Palgrave: Economic Development*, edited by J. Eatwell, M. Milgate, and P. Newman, 98–108. London: Macmillan.

Bruton, H. J. 1970. The import substitution strategy of economic development. *Pakistan Development Review* 10:123–46.

Dabir-Alai, P. 1996. Planning in India: An overview of key objectives and a few achievements—the first 20 years. In *Study of Indian History and Culture*, edited by H. D. Vinod, 466–86. Bombay: Bhishma.

Drèze, J. 1993. Dealing with famines. *Briefing Notes in Economics* 3 (March).

Drèze, J., and A. K. Sen. 1990. *The Political Economy of Hunger*. Oxford: Clarendon Press.

Eatwell, J., M. Milgate, and P. Newman, eds. 1989. *The New Palgrave: Economic Development*. London: Macmillan.

Ezeala-Harrison, F. 1994. Over-stretched economic underdevelopment in sub-Saharan Africa. *Briefing Notes in Economics* 14 (January).

Fischer, S. 1993. The role of macroeconomic factors in growth. *Journal of Monetary Economics* 32(1):485–512.

Gillis, M., D. H. Perkins, M. Roemer, and D. R. Snodgrass. 1996. *Economics of Development*. New York: Norton.

Hanson, A. H. 1968. Power shifts and regional balances. In *The Crisis of Indian Planning*, edited by P. Streeten and M. Lipton, 19–60. London: Oxford University Press.

Hutton, W. 1986. *The Revolution That Never Was: An Assessment of Keynesian Economics*. London: Longman.

International Labor Organization. 1996. *World Employment 1996/97: National Policies in a Global Context*. Geneva: International Labor Organization.

Köves, A., and P. Marer. 1991. *Foreign Economic Liberalization: Transformations in Socialist and Market Economies*. Boulder, CO: Westview Press.

Krueger, A. O. 1974. The political economy of rent-seeking. *American Economic Review* 64(3):291–323.

Lewis, W. A. 1955. Economic development with unlimited supplies of labor. *The Manchester School* 22:139–91.

Phelps, E. S. 1991. Distributive justice. In *The New Palgrave: The World of Economics*, edited by J. Eatwell, M. Milgate, and P. Newman, 164–67. London: Macmillan.

Prebisch, R., ed. 1950. *The Economic Development of Latin America and its Principal Problems*. Lake Success, NY: United Nations.

Sachs, J. D., and A. Warner. 1995. *Economic Convergence and Economic Policies*. Development Discussion Paper 502. Cambridge, MA: Harvard Institute for International Development.

Singer, H. W. 1950. The distribution of trade between investing and borrowing countries. *American Economic Review* 40(1):470–85.

———. 1993. Alternative approaches to adjustment and stabilization. *Third World Economics* 72:12–14.

Streeten, P., and M. Lipton, eds. 1968. *The Crisis of Indian Planning*. London: Oxford University Press.

Toye, J. 1995. *Structural Adjustment & Employment Policy: Issues and Experience*. Geneva: International Labor Organization.

Vinod, H. D. 1996. *Study of Indian History and Culture*. Bombay: Bhishma.

World Bank. 1995a. *Labor and Economic Reforms in Latin America and the Caribbean*. Washington, DC: World Bank.

———. 1995b. *The World Bank Atlas—1996*. Washington, DC: World Bank.

———. 1995c. *World Development Report 1995: Workers in an Integrating World*. Washington, DC: World Bank.

———. 1996. *Social Dimensions of Adjustment*. Washington, DC: World Bank.

2

Global Integration, Capital, and Labor: A North-South Comparative Perspective

Kwan S. Kim

Most nations—rich and poor—have, in the recent past, increased integration of their economies to global markets by reducing international trade and investment barriers. While global integration in the industrialized North has been facilitated by rapid progress in technology and communication, countries in the industrializing South also, in the wake of the collapse of the socialist Eastern bloc, began to embark on trade and investment liberalization as part of their structural adjustment programs.

The longstanding conventional argument would hold that increased globalization—which in this chapter is defined in a narrow and specific sense of movements toward freer international trade and capital investments—boosts the national output and, therefore, the accumulation of wealth in the country. Greater openness to global markets has, however, also had its downside. It will be argued here that many developing countries have meagerly benefited from globalization and have, in some instances, been harmed with the consequence of rising domestic inequality.

This chapter evaluates the positive and negative effects of globalization in theoretical and empirical perspectives. The analysis, in particular, seeks to compare the welfare effects of globalization in the industrialized North and the industrializing South. For analytical purposes, the North comprises the group of countries that export capital to the South. The economic implications of openness to trade and investment are analyzed for the North and the South from the theoretical perspective. This chapter then reviews empirical evidence. This review is followed by a summary of the findings and policy implications in the concluding section.

IMPACTS OF GLOBALIZATION ON THE NORTH

It is widely held that increased globalization of economic relations, particularly, when accompanied by rapid technological progress, boosts efficiency in production, thereby raising national output. Among other advantages of globalization for the industrialized North, the domestic producers can avoid the traditional concern about factory bottlenecks by being able to procure materials worldwide at competitive prices. Companies also save the cost as inventory buildups play smaller roles. This new dynamic is expected to unfold throughout the economy in tandem with the process of globalization. Global economic integration, in addition, enhances the welfare of domestic consumers as they benefit from increased choice of products, better quality, and lower prices.

Not everyone, however, accepts the argument that global integration has been all beneficial. There have been many dark sides of globalization. One important aspect with which this chapter is mainly concerned is disequalizing trends in industrialized countries. New concerns relate to the sharing of the benefits of economic growth, which is considered to have been very uneven across different socioeconomic classes. Capitalists are too often pitted against laborers and, within the working class, skilled workers against unskilled.

The widening income gap between capitalists and laborers is caused by increased global competition, which induces the domestic corporations to seek access to low-wage labor pools in developing countries, thereby forcing down domestic wages, especially for unskilled domestic workers (Bluestone and Harrison 1982; Koster and Ross 1988; Bluestone 1990). The outsourcing of production, which weakens domestic labor's position, is, of course, facilitated by the ease in transnational capital mobility.[1] The consequence of globalization has, thus, been rapidly rising profit income relative to wage earnings.

The second aspect of inequality relates to the domestic labor market. Faced with increasing global competition, manufacturers are forced to seek new technologies, which tend to be labor-saving and to raise demands for highly skilled workers at the expense of unskilled ones (Wood 1995). Moreover, the shift in consumer demand toward high-value, differentiated products away from standardized goods also discriminates against use of unskilled labor in production. As the shortage of talent in terms of both geographical areas and skill intensity emerges, the wage disparities between skilled and unskilled labor increase. The consequence, widely observed in the industrialized world, has been increased concentration of employment in high-wage, professional occupations and gradual diminution of blue-collar positions, which are replaced only by low-wage services.

The effects of globalization on the labor market are illustrated in Figure 2.1. To begin with, the labor market is assumed to be divided into

Figure 2.1
Effects of Globalization on the Labor Market in the North

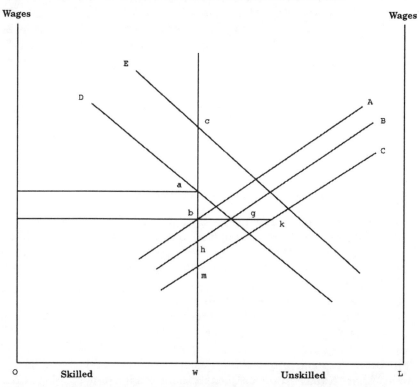

two sectors, producing outputs using skilled labor and outputs using unskilled labor. The skill-intensive sector may be considered as represented by the knowledge-intensive, high-tech industries, and the unskilled sector by manufacturing branches producing standardized products. The supply of workers in the short run is given at the *OL* amount, with the units of skilled workers indicated by distance *OW* and those of unskilled by *WL*.

The curves *D* and *A* represent labor demand, respectively, in the skilled and unskilled sector. The vertical axis measures the real wage rate. We assume that, over the short run, the labor market is rigidly segmented. The initial wage gap, as shown by distance *ab*, is obtained as the difference between skilled wages *aW* and unskilled wages *bW*. The labor demand curve represents productivity of labor. Thus, technology that improves the efficiency of skilled workers will cause an upward shift of its demand. Alternatively, increased demand for knowledge-intensive products similarly causes a shift to the right of labor demand curve *D* to curve *E*. As a result, real wages for skilled workers rise to *c* from *a*. On the other hand, the decline in consumer demand for standardized products—which may result from increased import penetration from global competitors—causes a downward shift in the unskilled labor demand. This is shown by the B curve. Now, if the unskilled real wage rate is assumed as rigid, there will be increased unemployment by bg units. If the wage rate is flexible, it will fall from Wb to Wh, thereby widening the initial wage gap between skilled and unskilled workers. Finally, as capital moves from the North to the South, the demand for unskilled workers in the North will further decline. This effect is shown by a downward shift of the labor demand curve from B to C. Unemployment could rise to as much as bk units in the case of a rigid labor market, or unskilled wages could fall to Wm in a flexible labor market with the resulting wage gap rising to cm amount.

IMPACTS OF GLOBALIZATION ON THE SOUTH

In theory, as the developing country dismantles the protective shield and receives more foreign capital, it should grow faster. As will be shown in the next section, there is, however, a growing body of evidence to indicate that increased globalization has not always been beneficial to a number of countries in the South.

Figure 2.2 illustrates the growth effects in the South of global integration. The initial possibilities of producing exportable and importable goods on a per capita basis are shown by the transformation locus ZZ. We start with the consequence of import substitution for a country in transition to global integration. The tariff-ridden, relative domestic price of importables in terms of exportables under import substitution is indicated by the absolute slope of line DD, which is drawn flatter than the international free trade price line PP. Domestic production is shown to take place at point a, where the production possibilities frontier is tangential to the domestic relative price line DD. Equilibrium consumption, indicated at b, is established at the point of tangency between the domestic price line $D'D'$ and an indifference curve, and also at the point on the international terms of trade line $P'P'$. When trade is liberalized, production and consumption shift to points e and c, respectively. The economy reaches a higher level of indifference curve. This is the essence of the conventional view on the gains from trade.

In reality, however, the benefits from opening to trade have been very uneven across the countries in the South. The logical shortcoming of the conventional analysis is that it overlooks and underestimates the complexity and difficulties involved in the transition from an inward-oriented to an outward-oriented regime in a new global environment. The regional economies in Latin America and Africa, as well as the former socialist economies in Central and Eastern Europe, initiated rather an abrupt transition from import substitution to global integration beginning at different times over the past decade or so. These countries were ill

Figure 2.2
Real Income Effects of Trade Liberalization in the South

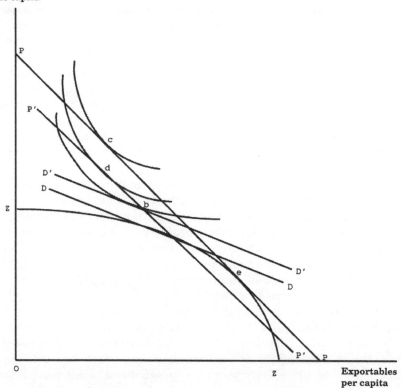

Importables
per capita

Exportables
per capita

prepared to open up their economies, as the consequence of long periods
of indiscriminate import substitution had too often resulted in an inefficient industrial sector. Moreover, the undue emphasis in the past on
importable consumer products—frequently based on the importation of
cheap capital and intermediate goods—discouraged domestic manufacture of capital and intermediate goods. As a result, a competitive export
sector has not yet been developed in these countries. They continue to
depend on the good will of foreign investors to share capital and technology
for long-term development of the economy.

The consequence of rigidities in production structure that inhibit the
economy from capturing the full potential benefits from the openness of
the economy is illustrated in Figure 2.2. Starting with the case of full
benefits from free trade, the open economy will be producing at point *e*
on the domestic production frontier *ZZ* and consuming at point *c*, where
the ratio of international price of export good to import good is given by
the slope of the line *PP*. At point *c*, the slope of the international price
line is drawn to be equal to that of an indifference curve.

The country under import substitution, when it opens to trade, will have a different starting point. Since the price of importable products facing both domestic producers and consumers under protection is higher than that under free trade, the relative domestic price of importables, shown by the slope of the line *DD*, is drawn flatter than the international price line. Given the domestic price line *DD*, the economy will produce at point *a*. The international price line P'P', drawn parallel to the line *PP*, must pass through the domestic production point *a*. Consumption will take place at point *b* on the line *P'P'*. At *b*, the slope of the domestic price line *DD* is also equal to the slope of an indifference curve.

The opening of trade is now shown to result in the new consumption point d on the price line *P'P'*. The assumption made here is that openness to trade fails to increase domestic production of exportables on a per capita basis. The new equilibrium at *d* lies on a lower indifference curve than the one that is at point *c*, indicating the possibility of limited gains from trade.

If the terms of trade deteriorate with the opening of the economy, it is even conceivable to have the Bhagwati type of "immiserizing growth." This can be shown graphically—although it is not shown in Figure 2.2—as a counterclockwise rotation of the international price line *PP* so that the new consumption equilibrium will be at a lower indifference curve than the one that is at point *b*.[2]

Turning to capital and labor markets in the South, we start with the assumption that capital is highly mobile across national boundaries, whereas domestic labor is not. It is well known that many developing countries, denied access to international loans with the debt crisis throughout the 1980s, have turned to foreign direct investment. Recent upsurges in investments abroad have also been stimulated by increasing ease in international communications, as well as liberalization of financial and capital markets in developing countries.

The benefits to capital inflows to the South in such a context are obvious, but the South's labor also has a large stake. Figure 2.3 illustrates how the enlarged economic pie brought about by foreign investment will be shared among the participants—foreign investors and the host country's labor and capital.

In the figure, curve *A* shows the initial schedule of rates of return on capital, which is assumed to display the diminishing returns on investment. Curve *D* is the domestic supply of capital and curve *S* the supply of the total capital stock, which is obtained by including the foreign supply curve. Graphically, the foreign component can be shown as the horizontal distance between two curves, *S* and *D*. Suppose that initially, at the rate of return given at distance *OF*, the total capital stock is divided by the *Od* units owned by domestic capitalists and the *ba* units owned by foreign capitalists. The initial division of gross domestic product (GDP) is indicated by area *WFe* as wage earnings, area *OFhb*

Figure 2.3
Globalization Effects on the Capital Market in the South

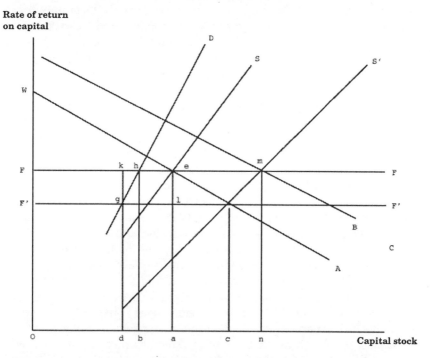

as income accruing to home capitalists, and area *hbea* as income accruing to foreign investors.[3]

The financial liberalization, generally in the form of deregulation in foreign investment and equal treatment of foreign and domestic capital, has resulted in substantial cost reductions in investment transactions in the host countries of the South. This has promoted inflows of foreign capital. For illustration, the inducement effect of capital inflow is shown as a downward shift of the foreign capital supply (curve *S'*). As a result, the rate of return on capital falls to *OF'* and the *db* units of domestic capital are replaced by foreign investment. The domestic capitalists lose income by shaded area *F'Fhbdg*, while foreign capital income rises to a larger rectangular area *dgfc*. The winners in this case are domestic labor. Their gains are shown by area *FF'fe*.

The replacement by foreign capital must not be considered as the final effect. If multinational corporation products produced in foreign subsidiaries are reexported, as would be more likely in a multilateral free trade system, the capital demand curve will also shift to the right, as shown by the new curve *B*. The induced expansion of domestic production could make domestic capital share part of the income gains. The net outcome to domestic capital depends on the relative strength of the replacement and the demand effects. The case when the demand effect exactly offsets the replacement effect is shown graphically at equilibrium point m, where the augmented demand curve B intersects with the supply curve S'. Although the quantitative magnitudes of gains and losses must be calculated in the context of each specific country, it stands to reason to conclude that increased globalization unequivocally benefits the capital-exporting North and host country labor, whereas the net outcome for host country capital is not all that clear.

As for the impact on domestic labor, it is important to note that the term "labor" referred to in the above analysis was defined in aggregate terms. In reality, as shown by Figure 2.1, the developing country labor market is also segmented by skill intensity. Conventional trade theory asserts that freer trade raises demands for the country's relatively abundant factor, which would be unskilled labor in the case of most developing countries, while it contracts demands for the relatively scarce factor, which would be skilled labor. This is seen as resulting in the narrowing of the wage gap between skilled and unskilled workers as wages of the former are lowered and those of the latter raised.

In the context of today's global economy, however, the conventional theory is challenged by the recent empirical evidence that reveals rising wage inequality in some regions of the developing world.[4] Theoretically, there are two factors that can be considered as contributing to wage inequality. First, there have been discernible changes in technology, which is increasingly biased against use of unskilled workers (Robbins 1996). Unlike in the 1960s, when the East Asian countries could find comparative advantage in low-skill, labor-intensive products, recent technical progress is generally labor replacing and is biased toward specific skill and knowledge use. The spread of technology globally raises the demand for more skilled and better-trained labor, even in labor-rich countries, since the use of technology is often more cost-effective.

Second, openness to trade forces the firms to move into high-value, sophisticated consumer products, the production of which requires use of labor with some skill intensity. This will be particularly the case with multinational investment abroad, because the products produced by their subsidiary plants are largely to be reexported in highly competitive global markets. They will have to hire reasonably skilled yet lower-wage (relative to the Northern workers) workers in the South. Unskilled or illiterate workers who have literally no training would be of little use in today's globally linked production network. Moreover, increased global competition induces multinational corporations to invest in the selected sectors or geographical areas—for example, in urban agglomerates— where host country workers tend to be better educated and skilled and where physical infrastructure for production and marketing is more adequate. The working poor in the South are mostly located in the low-value, traditional sectors, including the subsistence rural economy.

Since the work force in these backwater sectors is likely to remain unaffected by globalization, its impact can be seen as leading to increased wage inequality within the country.

In this context, it has been observed that the widening of the wage gap between skilled and unskilled labor is more conspicuous for the middle-income countries, where the ratio of skilled-labor endowment to unskilled labor typically is higher compared to low-income, labor-rich countries (Robbins 1996). Moreover, as explained by Wood (1995), the entry of labor-rich China and other Southeast Asian countries into the global market has further reduced the demand for unskilled workers in middle-income countries such as those in Latin America. As exports of goods of low-skill intensity from labor-abundant China, India, Indonesia, and other South and Southeast Asian countries expand, the comparative advantage of middle-income countries shifts to goods of intermediate-skill intensity. Thus, for the middle-income countries, the faster expansion of the sectors of intermediate-skill intensity additionally contributes to the rise in relative wages of skilled workers.

SOME EMPIRICAL EVIDENCE

In much of the industrialized North, recent years have seen increases in inequality in earnings between capital and labor as well as in wages among workers of different skill intensity (Wood 1994; Bloom and Brender 1993). First of all, the income losses of the workers at large tend to be offset by the gains of wealth holders. In stark contrast to the stagnant earnings of rank-and-file employees, there has been a drastic rise in wealth accumulation by the owners of capital, as well as in the level of compensation for chief executive officers (CEOs) of large corporations. This seems to be the case in more neoliberal economies such as the United States and the United Kingdom.[5] Of course, to the extent that capital is socialized by increased holdings of mutual funds, stocks, and bonds by workers, part of profit gains must be considered as raising labor's share. In reality, however, less-skilled worker incomes are accounted for predominantly by wage sources.[6]

Furthermore, the expansion of trade, combined with the advance in laborsaving technology, has caused deeper segmentation of labor markets in industrial Europe and North America. Recent studies (Wood 1995; Batra 1993) reveal that, in the industrialized North, not only have the employment shares of less-skilled production workers fallen, but the absolute numbers of structurally unemployed in this group have also increased. The expansion of trade with developing countries is seen as the main cause of both the decline in wages of low-skilled workers and the rise in wage inequality (Sachs and Schatz 1996). This phenomenon appears to be more conspicuous for the de-industrialized countries which have cumulative trade deficits. For example, in the United States, import penetration, in particular from the newly industrializing developing countries, has displaced the traditional industries producing standardized products, which resulted in laying off the workers with fewer skills.

Figure 2.4 shows the current and projected unemployment rates in the selected Organization for Economic Co-operation and Development (OECD) countries. Although the historical patterns of intercountry differences in the open unemployment rate have changed little, over the past decade or so, the unemployment rate in most European OECD nations increased by more than 50 percent. Joblessness has, thus, become almost an endemic feature in the North, with the discernible exceptions of Switzerland and the countries with a more flexible labor market—such as the United States—where the unemployment rate in

Figure 2.4
Current and Projected Unemployment Rates in Selected OECD Countries

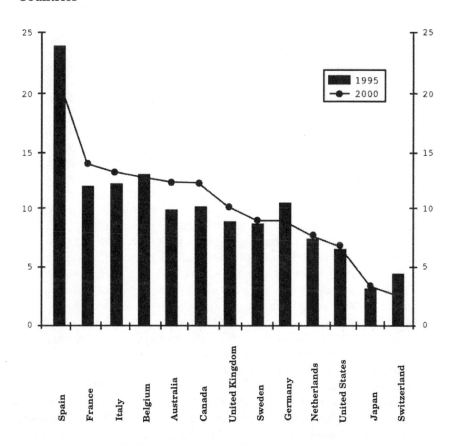

Source: International Labor Organization (1995).

the mid-1990s has been slightly lower than the peak rate in the 1980s. However, as already noted, lower unemployment rates in these countries are generally accompanied by stagnant or even falling real wages. For several OECD nations, including Germany, Italy, France, Canada, and Australia, the double-digit unemployment rates are projected to stay at least until the end of this century. Also, in nine out of the thirteen countries shown in the figure, the unemployment rate is projected to rise.

The problems of unemployment and stagnant wages in the North are related to sharply diminished roles played by organized labor unions. For instance, in the United States, the number of workers represented by unions, as a percentage of the total, declined from a third to about 15 percent over the past two decades. As companies shift—and sometimes threaten to shift—their domestic production to low-wage countries to set up nonunion operations abroad, they could easily undermine the local union's wage-benefit packages. Labor unions have, thus, become more amenable to settling strikes under pressure from companies. Table 2.1 reveals that the frequency of labor unrest in Europe, Japan, and the United States has indeed plummeted over the past two decades.

Turning to the South, Figure 2.5 compares the growth effects of global integration. Measured in per capita GDP growth rates, the results show very uneven performances by different regions. During the first half of the 1990s, increased openness to trade continued to benefit the already export-successful East Asian countries, while economic growth remained elusive in most of the other transition economies in Latin America, Eastern Europe, and Africa. In the case of Africa and Eastern Europe, growth rates in per capita income have been meager or have even fallen.

Table 2.1
Working Days Lost to Strikes in Selected Industrialized Countries, 1975–94

Country	Hourly Wages and Benefits	Work Days Lost Per 1,000 Employees		
	1994	*1975*	*1990*	*1994*
United States	$17.10	226	55	45
Canada	15.68	1,303	296	62
Germany	27.31	3	15	3
France	17.04	227	36	21
Japan	21.42	221	3	2

Source: U.S. Bureau of Labor Statistics.

Figure 2.5
Per Capita Real GDP Growth Rates by Regions, 1991–95

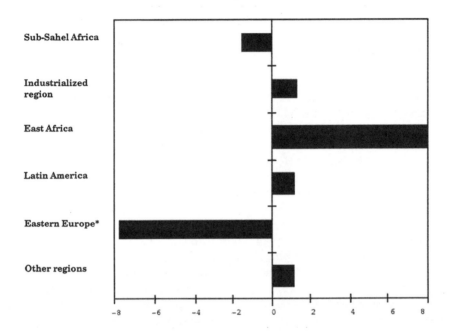

Source: World Bank data and estimates.

* Includes Central Europe and Central Asia.

Of particular significance is the case of sub-Sahel Africa. These African countries have been projected to have a further economic deterioration as global trade liberalization under the auspices of the new General Agreement on Trade and Tariffs (GATT) unfolds (Goldin et al. 1993). Figure 2.6 shows the recent OECD projections of African export revenues as the existing tariff preferences for the continent erode under multilateral liberalization. Specifically, sub-Sahel Africa's net annual losses are estimated to reach $2.6 billion in the period to 2002. In contrast, the industrialized world reaps $135 billion or 64 percent of total annual gains in world income from the new GATT. Food-importing African countries are projected to be particularly severely impacted by higher world food prices, which will be brought on by reductions in agricultural subsidies for European exporters. Also, the failure to bring the Multi-Fibre Agreement under the GATT discipline will cause many African countries to experience reductions in growth rates of textile exports.

There is also some evidence to indicate that, in a number of developing countries, income inequality and poverty persist despite the economic expansion. The regional variations in income distribution and poverty incidence over the past several years are compared in Table 2.2.

Figure 2.6
Projections of Annual Trade Balance to Year 2002

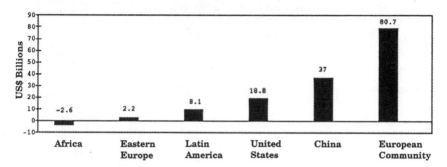

Source: U.N. Department of Public Information (1993/1994).

Among the developing regions, East Asia as a whole has done better in reducing the relative and absolute deprivation, although there are variations among the selected countries (Table 2.2A). For instance, over the 1980s, Malaysia, Indonesia and Singapore made significant progress in reducing inequality and poverty while inequality rose in Thailand and China.

In contrast to the East Asian experience, income inequality and poverty rose in the transition economies in Central and Eastern Europe, sub-Sahel Africa, and a large number of Latin American countries. Most of these countries have already embarked on market opening and reforms, and several countries have been experiencing some economic growth. The general picture that emerges, however, indicates that no visible improvements have been made in the distribution of income or in the alleviation of absolute poverty. The data in Table 2.2 reveal evidence on this. The rise in inequality and poverty is more drastic in the transition economies of Russia and Bulgaria than in the Czech Republic, Hungary, and Poland, which have had more stabilization and faster economic growth (Table 2.2B).[7] For sub-Sahel Africa, the region has remained at a very low level of income since the early 1970s. Although the level of inequality for the regional economies is not any higher than other developing regions, real incomes in the eleven sampled countries, except Uganda and Nigeria, either fell or stayed stagnant over the period from 1987 to 1994 (Table 2.2C).

In several regional economies of Latin America which have been successful in macroeconomic stabilization, increased foreign investment has boosted economic growth throughout the mid-1990s.[8] As noted earlier, the problem with Latin America's recovery, as would be the case with other transition economies, is that because of high-import dependency on capital and intermediate goods along with technology, continued capital inflow remains critically vital for sustained economic growth.

Table 2.2
Income Inequality and Poverty

A. The Asia-Pacific Region			
Country	Period	Head Count Poverty (%)[1]	Gini Coefficient
China[2]	1990–92 (rural)	11.6–10.8	.299–.321
Singapore	1982/83–87/88	14.1–8.3	.291–.264
Thailand[3]	1988–90	42.4–36.1	.439–.471
Malaysia	1984–89	12.6–6.1	.508–.486
Indonesia	1984–90 (rural)	45.7–26.6	.293–.264
Philippines	1984–90 (urban)	34.0–28.9	.334–.347

Sources: U.N. Economic and Social Commission for Asia and the Pacific, 1991; Asian Development Bank data for 1993; and World Bank data (OECD, 1996).

1. Poverty incidence is measured as the proportion of the population earning below per capita monthly income of US$30, which is adjusted to purchasing power parity.
2. Poverty line is defined by the local standard.
3. Poverty line is defined at per capita monthly income of US$60.

B. Central and Eastern Europe			
Country	Gini Coefficient (1993)	Increase from 1987/88	Poverty Incidence 1987/88–1993	
Russia	0.48	0.14–0.24[1]	—	0.38
Poland	0.30	0.05	0.06	0.12
Hungary	0.23	0.02	0.01	0.02
Czech Republic	0.27	0.08	0.00	0.01
Slovania	0.28	0.04	0.00	0.01
Estonia	0.39	0.16	—	0.23
Bulgaria	0.34	0.11	0.02	0.33

Source: World Bank data.

1. The range of the increase estimated by different sources.

C. Sub-Sahel Africa

Country	PPP GNP Per Capita (US = 100)		Gini Coefficient[1]
	1987	1994	
Rwanda	3.8	1.3	0.29
Tanzania	2.6	2.4	0.38
Uganda	5.0	5.4	0.41
Nigeria	4.3	4.6	0.38
Zambia	4.1	3.3	0.46
Ghana	7.9	7.9	0.34
Mauritania	6.4	6.1	0.42
Zimbabwe	8.7	7.9	0.57
Senegal	7.3	6.1	0.54
Ivory Coast	8.3	5.3	0.37
Lesotho	14.4	14.4	0.56

Source: World Bank data.

1. Different survey years between 1990 and 1993.

D. Latin America[1]

Country	Gini Coefficient	
	Period	Change
Argentina (urban)	1980–89	.410–.478
Bolivia	1986–89	.518–.528
Brazil[2]	1979–89	.599–.638
Colombia	1988–91	.531–.513
Costa Rica	1981–89	.475–.461
Honduras	1986–89	.553–.595
Mexico	1984–89	.508–.591
Panama	1979–89	.409–.568
Paraguay (urban)	1983–90	.453–.399
Uruguay	1981–89	.436–.424
Venezuela	1981–89	.430–.442

Sources: ECLAC (1994) and World Bank data.

1. Income is measured by a multiple of the respective per capita poverty line. The low income stratum represents the bottom 40 percent and the high income the top 10 percent.
2. For 1990.

This explains why the majority of Latin American countries that have not been targeted by foreign investors have failed to gain much from openness to trade.

This far-from-automatic relationship between globalization and growth has another implication. While economic recovery may have been spurred by external financing in some countries, gainful employment and real wages for the working poor have been stagnant or even falling. As shown by Table 2.2D, in the majority of countries—including, in particular, the big economies of Brazil, Mexico, Argentina, and Venezuela—the distribution continues to deteriorate.[9] This points to our earlier observation that growth by itself in a new laissez-faire global environment does not automatically result in equity. This seems to be more the case with the middle-income countries that pursued an inward-oriented industrialization strategy. As noted by Robbins (1995 and 1996), the effects on wage inequality of increased openness, which have occurred at different time periods over the past few decades in developing countries, are more discernible for the middle-income countries of Latin America— including Argentina, Chile, Uruguay, Colombia, Costa Rica, and Mexico—than for the low-income, labor-rich countries elsewhere. Foreign investment in the middle-income countries is seen to raise the demand for skilled labor relative to unskilled. This is because these countries are well endowed with skilled workers relative to low-income countries and are able to find a new comparative advantage in more skill-intensive industries. Furthermore, the shift in the line of comparative advantage is expedited by the thrust into global markets of labor-intensive products coming from low-wage, newly industrializing countries in the Southeast and China (Wood 1997).

It must be pointed out, however, that wage inequality is also likely to increase even in the low-income countries in Asia and Africa. There is some evidence to suggest that growing inequality, for example, in China (Rahman et al. 1992; Adelman and Sundings 1987)[10] and Thailand (Tinakorn 1995; Kim and Voraspontaviporn 1989), is caused by trade. The working poor in the subsistence rural sector are shown as hardly affected by globalization of the economy. Foreign capital invested in developing countries simply does not seek out cheap, illiterate, unskilled workers (Pissarides 1997). New technologies brought with it would need some minimal level of training and skill intensity. Hence, although economic integration may not necessarily hurt the poor, it can go hand in hand with increased inequality, even in low-income countries.

Thus, while global economic integration provides new opportunities for economic growth, its downside in the context of rapidly evolving technological change has been growing inequality and poverty in most developing countries. The exceptional case is East Asia's newly industrialized countries, which had different departure points and strategies in adjusting to the global economy. The difference is that the East Asian governments, while giving deliberate attention to economic stabilization and the globalization process, have pursued specifically targeted, antipoverty social adjustments and measures to develop a broadly based human capital stock (Goodno and Miller 1996; World Bank 1996).

CONCLUSIONS

This chapter has identified the economic benefits and liabilities of global integration of the domestic economy from both the theoretical and empirical perspectives. While the findings support the conventional view that globalization, which is seen today as the most powerful force transforming a national economy, will continue to boost economic growth widely across industrialized countries, the benefits of growth, however, will likely be very uneven across developing countries. Moreover, global integration will likely lead to rising inequality and poverty in countries both in the North and the South, insofar as their governments decide to overlook the need to reach out to the lower ends of the economic scale. In a globally integrated, laissez-faire economy, the link from growth to reductions in inequality and poverty is not automatic; on the contrary, increased openness further widens the already existing gaps between capital and labor and among the workers with different educational backgrounds and skill intensities. The real winners would be the capitalists, in particular of the North, with the losers being mostly the working poor in both the developed and developing nations.

In this regard, this chapter points to the importance of the public sector's role in alleviating the absolute and relative deprivations in society. Given that globalization is no longer an option, the adjustment strategy must aim at reducing the liabilities while obtaining the maximum benefits from an integrated world. For this, the state needs to take actions rather than passively embracing the dictates of free trade. In a new global environment, the conventional theory of comparative advantage must be understood in a vigorous dynamic context where the development of high-value, technology-intensive products, the speed and types of investment flows, economic management, and strategic alliance with foreign partners are more important in export success. Over the long run, sustainable international competitiveness will be assured only by developing innovative technologies, management skills, and competitive export industries. In this context, the appropriate role of the state will be critical to success in the South. For example, the state can be involved in supporting research and development efforts, development of cluster industries, joint ventures for technology transfer, and human capital development.[11]

Moreover, the problem of international competitiveness must be tackled in ways that reduce domestic poverty and economic inequality. While the state must have comprehensive programs to develop human capital, to manage the dislocations caused by international changes, and to provide safeguards for the victims, it must also be understood that poverty or inequality reductions cannot take place without direct involvement in their own affairs by the underprivileged themselves. To achieve this goal, the state must expand the poor's access to basic education and training, health care, and other income-producing activities. As a first step, political reforms can be aimed at increasing the poor's participation in economic decision making.

Finally, since the openness to trade and international capital causes the state to lose the political clout to discipline domestic capital, the task of setting the domestic economy on a sustainable, low-inequality growth path would call for a close coordination with other nations.[12] To avoid an excessive and harmful international competition which could turn into "a race to the bottom" for the domestic workers and a worldwide degradation of ecology, there must be a range of international agreements and understanding concerning workers' rights, exploitation of labor, and preservation of the environment. These adjustment issues are meant to be suggestive, and the details are beyond the scope of this chapter.

NOTES

1. The ease in transnational capital mobility has caused labor unions to become more amenable to settling strikes under pressures from companies. This is evidenced by the recent plummeting in the frequency of strikes in Europe, Japan, and the United States. *Wall Street Journal*, March 25, 1996.

2. Even when some countries can receive foreign investment in sufficient amounts to expand exports, the case of immiserizing growth is still possible if the repatriation of profits from foreign firms is taken into consideration (Johnson 1967).

3. For the original analysis of the welfare effects of foreign investment, see MacDougall (1960).

4. For details, see the next section.

5. The American CEOs receive compensation in the form of options to purchase company stock. Their total compensation was 149 and 212 times that of an average American worker in 1993 and 1995, respectively. In 1960, their compensation was only forty times that of the worker. In Japan, the heads of major corporations earned only thirty-two times as much as their workers (Folbre 1995).

6. According to Wolff (1995), in 1992, only one-half of 1 percent of the U.S. population (half a million U.S. households) owned 39.3 percent of all wealth assets, which was twice that in England, the country considered as the most unequal in Western Europe.

7. The strategy of the latter group of countries has generally been to proceed on the reform process cautiously and gradually to minimize abrupt impacts on unemployment and inequality.

8. In the case of Latin America, capital inflows from the North (mostly from the U.S.) more than offset the continent's total current account deficit, which amounted to 2 percent of the regional GDP in 1995 (Economic Commission on Latin America and the Carribean 1996).

9. In Latin America, over the decade of the 1980s, almost forty million people were added to the ranks of officially defined poor, and the region's poverty rate rose to 43 percent by the end of the decade (World Bank 1996); in Brazil alone, the poverty incidence rose from 24 to 39 percent with the number of Brazilian poor reaching more than ten million. In Mexico, the poverty rate increased from 40 percent in 1980 to 54 percent in 1987 (Kim 1993).

10. China has expanded at dazzling rates of growth, frequently at a double-digit rate since 1976, when full-scale economic reform started. Its development strategy, which centered on urban-based growth poles, especially along selected coastal areas, has contributed to a growing urban-rural gap, as well as regional inequality. For instance, the rural income, as a percentage of urban income, plunged from 58 percent in 1985 to 39.4 percent in 1993 (*The Nikkei Weekly*, June 5, 1995).

11. For articulation of this point, see Porter (1990).

12. For example, it would not be any easier for the government to reduce interest rates, as this could induce outflows of domestic capital. Nor would it be effective to rely on the fiscal policy to raise taxes, since domestic businesses could seek lower taxes or tax havens abroad.

REFERENCES

Adelman, I., and D. Sundings. 1987. Economic policy and income distribution in China. *Journal of Comparative Economics* 11(3):444–61.

Batra, R. 1993. *The Myths of Free Trade*. New York: Charles Scribner's Sons.

Bloom, D. E. and A. Brender. 1993. *Labor and the Emerging World Economy*. NBER Working Paper 4266. Washington, DC: National Bureau of Economic Research.

Bluestone, B. 1990. The great u-turn revisited: Economic restructuring, jobs, and the redistribution of earnings. In *Jobs, Earnings, and Employment Growth Policies in the United States*, edited by J. D. Kasarda. Boston: Kluwer Academic Publishers.

Bluestone, B., and B. Harrison. 1982. *De-industrialization of America*. New York: Basic Books.

Economic Commission for Latin America and the Caribbean (ECLAC). 1994. *Social Panorama of Latin America, 1994*. Santiago, Chile.

———. 1996. *Preliminary Overview of the Economy of LA and the Caribbean*. Santiago, Chile.

Folbre, N. 1995. *The New Field Guide to the US Economy*. New York: The New Press.

Goldin I., O. Knudsen, and D. van der Mensbrugghe. 1993. *Trade Liberalization: Global Economic Implications*. Washington, DC: OECD/World Bank.

Goodno, J. B., and J. Miller. 1996. Which way to grow? Notes on poverty and prosperity in Southeast Asia. In *Real World International*, edited by M. Breslow et al. Somerville, MA: Dollars and Sense.

International Labor Organization (ILO). 1995. *World Employment 1995 Report*. Geneva.

Johnson, H. G. 1967. The possibilities of income losses from increased efficiency or factor accumulation in the presence of tariffs. *Economic Journal* 77(305):151–54.

Kasarda, J. D., ed. 1990. *Jobs, Earnings, and Employment Growth Policies in the United States*. Boston: Kluwer Academic Publishers.

Kim, K. S. 1993. An alternative strategy for equity with growth—case of Mexico. *Hitotsubashi Journal of Economics* 34(1):45–66.

Kim, K. S., and P. Voraspontaviporn. 1989. International trade, employment, and income: The case of Thailand. *Developing Economies* 27(1):60–74.

Koster, M. H., and M. N. Ross. 1988. *The Quality of Jobs: Evidence from Distributions of Annual Earnings and Hourly Wages*. Washington, DC: American Enterprise Institute.

MacDougall, D. 1960. The benefits and costs of private investment from abroad: A theoretical approach. *Economic Record* 36(1):13–35.

Pissarides, C. A. 1997. Learning by trading and the returns to human capital in developing countries. *The World Bank Economic Review* 11(1):17–32.

Porter, M. 1990. *Competitive Advantage of Nations*. London: Macmillan.

Rahman, A., K. Griffin, C. Riskin, and R. W. Zhao. 1992. Household income and its distribution in China. *China Quarterly* 1(132):1029–61.

Regional Employment Program for Latin America and the Caribbean (PRE-ALC). 1990. *Informal Sector*. Working Paper 349. Santiago, Chile.

Robbins, D. 1995. *Trade, Trade Liberalization, and Inequality in Latin America and East Asia: Synthesis of Seven Country Studies*. Discussion Paper. Cambridge, MA: Harvard Institute for International Development.

———. 1996. *Evidence on Trade and Wages in the Developing World*. OECD Development Centre Technical Paper 119. Paris: Organization for Economic Development and Co-operation.

Sachs, J. D., and H. J. Schatz. 1996. U.S. trade with developing countries and wage inequality. *American Economic Review* 86(2):234–39.

Tinakorn, P. 1995. Industrialization welfare: How poverty and income distribution are affected. In *Thailand's Industrialization and Its Consequences*, edited by M. Krongkaew. London: Macmillan.

United Nations. 1993/94. *Africa Recovery*. Geneva: UN Department of Public Information.

Wolff, E. N. 1995. *Top Heavy: A Study of the Increasing Inequality of Wealth in America*. New York: Twentieth Century Fund Press.

Wood, A. 1994. *North-South Trade, Employment, and Inequality: Changing Fortunes in a Skill-Driven World*. Cambridge, U.K.: Oxford University Press.

———. 1995. How trade hurt unskilled workers. *Journal of Economic Perspectives* 9(3):57–80.

———. 1997. Openness and wage inequality in developing countries: The Latin American challenge to East Asian conventional wisdom. *The World Bank Economic Review* 11(1):33–58.

World Bank. 1996. *Social Dimensions of Adjustment*. Washington, DC: The World Bank.

3
Unemployment Dynamics in Transition

Fabrizio Coricelli

The appearance of unemployment in previously centrally planned economies (PCPEs) cannot be considered a surprise, given the fact that PCPEs started reforms from a situation of full employment and were affected by a sharp fall of output at the outset of reforms. Nevertheless, there were puzzling aspects, such as the heterogeneity of the country experiences, the dynamics of unemployment, and its relation to other macroeconomic variables, especially output. Table 3.1 contains average rates of unemployment during the period 1989–95 for most PCPEs, and it clearly shows the large differences in rates of unemployment across countries. As countries started reforms at different dates, the last column in Table 3.1 reports average unemployment for the first three years of reforms in the various countries. Even after adjusting for different starting dates of reforms, unemployment rates display a high variability across countries.

Figure 3.1, where the behavior of the rate of unemployment during the period 1989–95 is plotted against the change in real gross domestic product (GDP), shows a positive, albeit weak, correlation. It is worth noting that countries undertaking faster and broader-based reforms (mainly the Central European countries) show higher rates of unemployment than lagging countries (generally those of the former Soviet Union). However, as unemployment could also contain a component linked to short-term output behavior, a more informative indicator is the rate of unemployment in relation to the deviation of output from its full-employment level (for simplicity, the prereform level). Assuming as starting point the prereform level of output, the change in GDP represents a deviation from full-employment. If the rate of unemployment is divided by the output index, it emerges even more clearly that more

Table 3.1
Unemployment during Transition

Country	1989	1990	1991	1992	1993	1994	1995	Average 1989–94	Average First 3 Years of Reforms
Albania	1.9	7.6	11.7	30.3	22.4	19.2	13.0	15.5	21.5
FYR Macedonia	NA	NA	18.0	19.0	19.0	19.0	NA	18.8	18.7
Bulgaria	0.0	1.5	11.5	15.6	12.8	12.8	10.5	9.6	14.5
Croatia	0.0	9.3	15.5	12.9	12.8	12.8	13.4	11.0	13.7
Slovak Republic	0.0	1.5	11.8	10.3	14.8	14.8	13.1	8.8	12.2
Slovenia	2.9	4.7	8.2	11.6	14.4	14.4	13.9	9.4	11.4
Poland	0.1	6.1	11.8	13.6	15.7	16.0	14.9	10.6	10.5
Hungary	0.3	1.9	7.5	12.3	12.1	10.9	10.4	7.5	7.2
Romania	0.0	0.0	3.0	8.1	10.2	11.0	8.9	5.4	7.1
Armenia	1.0	1.0	3.5	3.5	6.2	5.6	8.0	3.5	5.1
Lativa	0.0	0.0	0.1	2.3	5.8	6.5	6.6	2.5	4.9
Estonia	0.0	0.0	0.1	0.9	5.0	5.1	5.0	1.9	3.7
Czech Republic	0.0	0.8	4.1	2.6	3.5	3.2	2.9	2.4	3.4
Lithuania	0.0	0.0	0.3	1.3	4.4	3.8	6.2	1.6	3.2
Belarus	1.0	1.0	1.0	0.5	1.5	2.1	2.8	1.2	1.4
Russia	0.0	0.0	0.1	0.8	1.1	2.1	3.2	0.7	1.3
Tajikistan	0.0	0.0	0.0	0.3	1.1	1.7	NA	0.5	1.0
Kazakhstan	0.0	0.0	0.1	0.5	0.6	1.6	2.4	0.5	0.9
Moldova	0.0	0.0	0.0	0.7	0.8	1.2	NA	0.5	0.9
Azerbaijan	0.0	0.0	0.1	0.2	0.7	0.9	NA	0.3	0.6
Ukraine	0.0	0.0	0.0	0.3	0.4	0.4	0.6	0.2	0.4
Kyrgyzstan	0.0	0.0	0.0	0.1	0.2	0.7	NA	0.2	0.3
Uzbekistan	0.0	0.0	0.0	0.1	0.2	0.4	0.4	0.1	0.2
Georgia	0.0	0.0	0.0	5.4	8.4	NA	NA	2.8	NA

Source: Boeri (1995).

Figure 3.1
Unemployment Dynamics

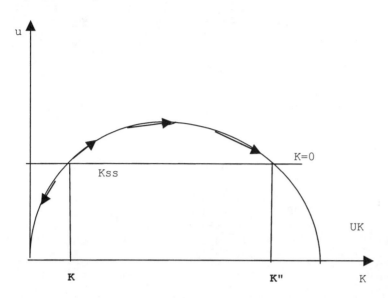

radical reformers display a much higher ratio of unemployment, scaled by the behavior of output (Table 3.2).

Thus, a first stylized fact appears to be that unemployment during the transition did not merely reflect short-term movements in output. The nature of the economic transformation, that is, the extent of restructuring and reallocation of resources across sectors and different policies and institutional arrangements affecting the labor market, played a key role.

In order to assess the nature and the role of unemployment during the transition, it is useful to analyze briefly some of the main characteristics of unemployment. Irrespective of the rate of unemployment, transition economies display small flows in and out of unemployment (Boeri 1995; Blanchard et al. 1995). In the early stages of transition, unemployment can thus be defined as a stagnant pool. Although net changes in employment were very large, gross separations were smaller than in market economies (Table 3.3). This suggests that transition is a phenomenon that differs significantly from normal, steady-state behavior of market economies in which labor markets are characterized by high turnover and small net changes. The fall in employment in transition economies is staggering. The fall is concentrated in the old state sector. In contrast, new private sectors have developed quickly, absorbing a large number of workers. Thus, another feature of transition is the sharply asymmetric behavior of different firms and sectors. Outflows from unemployment were very small, even if compared with Western

Table 3.2
Ratio of Unemployment Rate and GDP Growth

	1989	1990	1991	1992	1993
Slow reformers	0.00	−0.10	−0.57	−0.47	−1.20
Without Russia	0.00	−0.10	−0.57	−1.23	−8.31
Fast reformers	0.11	−0.69	−0.74	−2.30	−15.76

Source: Boeri (1995).

Table 3.3
Turnover of the Unemployment Pool, 1992 (percentage of labor force)

Country	Monthly Inflows[1] UR	LFS	Monthly Outflows[2]	Monthly Outflows to Jobs[3]	Unemployment Turnover[4]
Bulgaria	1.6	1.7	0.8	0.2	2.4
Czech Republic	0.6	0.6	0.8	0.6	1.4
Hungary[5]	0.6	0.9	0.6	0.3	1.2
Poland	0.7	0.9	0.6	0.3	1.3
Slovak Republic	1.1	1.0	1.3	0.6	2.3
East Germany	1.7		1.6	0.6	3.4
West Germany	1.1		1.0	0.4	2.1
Austria	1.5		1.4	0.9	2.8
France (1991)	1.4		1.3	0.5	2.6
Norway (1991)	1.6		1.6	0.8	3.3
UK (1991)	1.3		1.1	NA	2.4

Source: Boeri (1995).

Average monthly unemployment inflows and outflows.

1. UR denotes unemployment register; LFS stands for labor force survey.
2. The 1992 average monthly outflows from unemployment to the average yearly labor force.
3. The 1992 average monthly number of vacancies filed through the intermediation of the public employment service to the average yearly labor force.
4. Column 1 + column 3.
5. Administrative data on inflows and outflows refer only to unemployment benefit recipients.

European countries that were characterized by a high degree of persistence of unemployment. Despite the recovery in output during the period 1993–95, outflows from unemployment remained low, especially in Poland. Consequently, unemployment quickly became a long-term phenomenon. Furthermore, labor-force participation rates, traditionally high in the centrally planned period, declined sharply to levels that in some cases were lower than the OECD average (Boeri 1995). The exit from the labor force has implied, in most countries, a sharp increase in social expenditures, especially for pensions. The unemployment pool has been differentiated not only in terms of duration of unemployment spells, but also in terms of skill characteristics of the unemployed. The stagnant pool of unemployed has been composed mainly of low-skill workers whose reemployability was problematic. Without neglecting the complexity of the phenomena characterizing the dynamics of unemployment during transition, it is nevertheless useful to stress a few stylized facts and to attempt to put them in a simple analytical framework.

The typical pattern of transition in "fast reforming" countries has been a large drop in employment in the state sector, a buoyant private sector, and, with the exception of the Czech Republic, rapidly increasing unemployment. This process has been accompanied by initially generous unemployment benefits and early retirement schemes that have given rise to budgetary pressure. In "slow reforming" countries, unemployment has been much lower, despite a larger fall in output. The reallocation of labor across firms has been consequently smaller. Outside options for state workers have been very low or, in some cases, nonexistent. Unemployment benefits have been well below subsistence levels. Maintenance of employment in state firms has been achieved by a combination of explicit and implicit subsidies to state firms and through large cuts in real wages, often through wage arrears.

Transition can be seen as a process of massive reallocation of resources across sectors and firms. The dynamics of the economy crucially depend on the changing size of the various sectors. State firms shed labor and transfer assets to new private firms. Furthermore, with varying extent and speed across countries, state firms are being privatized. Although it is a rough simplification, the adjustment following the initial output fall in economies in transition can be interpreted as the asymmetric dynamics of declining and growing sectors. Although the recovery of state firms deserves attention, in some cases (most notably Poland), the distinction between private and state sectors captures a large part of the process.

Unemployment arises from the process of restructuring. As initially the growing sector is small, the outflow of labor from the declining state sector is not fully matched by hirings in private firms. Thus, unemployment may arise during the process of reallocation of resources from state to private firms. That unemployment is an inevitable by-product of market reforms is unlikely to be controversial. However, more controversial is the role that unemployment plays during the transition. Even if one accepts the inevitability of a certain level of unemployment, the market may lead to rates of unemployment that are either too high or too low. Furthermore, it should be emphasized that the Czech Republic stands out as an exception to the view that associates unemployment with restructuring, and it indicates that restructuring can be effected even with low unemployment.

A BRIEF SURVEY OF THE THEORIES

Three main simple models have been put forward to tackle the dynamics of unemployment during transition. All the models share a common view: unemployment during transition is not simply the result of short-term changes in output; rather it reflects the deeper structural change in the economy. Furthermore, not only is unemployment a symptom of restructuring of the economy, but it also plays a crucial role in that process.

Search Models

Search models assume there are frictions in the labor market. There is a process of matching between job seekers and firms that takes time. Rather than a well-defined labor demand (stock concept), what matters is the flow of people in and out of unemployment. In its simplest form, this approach points to the factors affecting long-run unemployment. Applying this model to PCPEs, Burda (1993 and 1995) concludes that a combination of demand and supply shocks, in addition to institutional changes (unemployment benefits, severance pay, increased union power), led to an increase in the long-run equilibrium unemployment rate. Although the framework is useful because of its emphasis on the role of changing labor market institutions, the dynamics of unemployment that emerge are not very interesting. Indeed, unemployment monotonically moves from zero to a positive long-run equilibrium level. The whole issue of transition, and possibly transitional unemployment, is not addressed.

Extending the model to introduce an on-the-job search and fiscal constraints leads to more interesting dynamic effects. Indeed, with these extensions, multiple long-run equilibria can arise. In the benchmark model, only the unemployed search for jobs. Thus, there is an increasing relationship between unemployment and job searches. However, if there is a fraction of workers that search on the job, the positive relationship between unemployment and job searches may disappear, at least for certain ranges of unemployment. Indeed, this is the case if one assumes that the intensity of on-the-job searches (i.e., the fraction of workers who search for jobs while working) is a decreasing function of the rate of unemployment. This can give rise to multiple equilibria. A perhaps more interesting point stressed by Burda is the potential for multiple equilibria arising from the fiscal implications of unemployment. He assumes that governments in PCPEs face a tight flow budget constraint. This may arise because of lack of access to credit markets or because of external constraints, such as agreements with the International Monetary Fund (IMF) within a stand-by program.

The first model to consider is a simple one. Assume there is an exogenous separation rate s and that the labor force is constant and normalized to be equal to 1. Thus, employment equals $1-u$, where u denotes unemployment (which is equal to the rate of unemployment, just as the labor force is equal to 1). Hirings occur through a matching process between job seekers and firms. The matching function depends on the rate of unemployment, u, and on vacancies, v.

$$u = s(1-u) - x(u, v) \tag{3.1}$$

In steady state:

$$s(1-u) = x(u, v) \tag{3.2}$$

From the above equation, one can derive the locus of points in the (u, v) space consistent with stable long-run unemployment. The other side of the labor market is characterized by firms posting vacancies. Firms face a flow cost in posting vacancies. Because of frictions in the labor market, the number of vacancies is obtained as an investment decision on the part of the firm. The firm compares the present value of having a worker employed (J) and the present value of an unfilled vacancy (V). The difference between these two values gives the net gain from filling a vacancy. The following arbitrage conditions apply to the present discounted value of an occupied job (J) and to the present discounted value of expected profit from a vacant job.

$$rJ = y - w - s(J - V - F) \tag{3.3}$$
$$rV = -k + h(\theta)(J - V) \tag{3.4}$$

where F denotes severance costs, y output per worker, w the wage rate, k is the flow cost of posting a vacancy, and h the ratio of x and vacancies (the hiring rate in proportion of vacancies). Job seekers compare the value of being unemployed (denoted by U) with that of obtaining a job (E). The following arbitrage conditions hold:

$$rU = b + 1 + f(\theta)(E - U) \tag{3.5}$$
$$rE = W - s(E - U - T) \tag{3.6}$$

where $b + 1$ is the return to being unemployed; $f(\theta)$ is the ratio of hiring x to the pool of unemployed; and T is a severance benefit received by the employees when they lose their jobs. Because of the presence of frictions in the labor market, when job seekers and firms are matched, there is a surplus from the match; $J–V$ for the firms and $E–U$ for the workers. Wage setting determines the way the surplus is split between workers and the firm. The standard solution adopted in the literature is to assume a Nash-bargaining, according to which wage setting maximizes the total surplus (the product of the net gain for the firm and for the workers), attributing certain weights to the relative shares going to the players according to their bargaining power. Burda's model assumes myopic players. As a result, wage setting is independent of the conditions of the labor market. However, the more general version of Pissarides (1990) implies that the solution of the Nash-bargaining yields a wage rate that depends on the tightness of the labor market and, thus, on unemployment.[1]

An important extension of the model is obtained by considering the fiscal implications of unemployment. In particular, interesting results arise when taxation is concentrated on firms, with distortionary effects on employment and output. If the government faces a flow budget constraint, it has to finance unemployment benefits through taxes on firms. Assuming linear technology, taxing output or employment is equivalent. Thus, let us assume that taxes fall on employees. The following government budget constraint holds:

$$\tau(1-u) = bu \tag{3.7}$$

Assuming exogenous unemployment benefits *(b)*, the tax rate is endogenous and a function of unemployment:

$$\tau = (1-u) \tag{3.8}$$

Burda shows that, in this case, the *VS* curve is nonlinear and depicts a bell-shaped curve. Thus, multiple equilibria arise, with a low- and a high-equilibrium unemployment. The intuition is rather simple. The effects of unemployment on the supply of vacancies is ambiguous. There is a positive effect through the increased probability of finding a match for the firm. However, higher unemployment implies higher taxation, which, in turn, reduces the supply of vacancies. Consequently, two different ranges may arise—one in which the positive effect dominates and the other in which the negative fiscal effect dominates. Burda does not analyze the dynamic properties of the model. The two equilibria can be interpreted as different expectational or self-fulfilling equilibria. Indeed, if firms are optimistic, supply of vacancies will be higher, job creation will be higher, and, hence, unemployment and taxation will be lower. In contrast, if firms are pessimistic, supply of vacancies will be lower and unemployment and taxation higher.

Despite its simplicity, the model illustrates a few important results. First, it attributes an important role to unemployment. Unemployment is not simply a cost paid by reforming economies, but it serves an important supporting role for restructuring. Indeed, there is an optimal rate of unemployment, generally different from zero.

Second, there is an important role for labor market policies and labor market institutions. Such policies and institutions affect the shape and characteristics of the matching function $x(.)$. The more efficient is a matching process, the lower is the rate of unemployment consistent with labor market turnover.

Despite its interesting findings, this type of modeling has several shortcomings. The model emphasizes frictions in labor markets but neglects heterogeneity of the labor force and explicit investment as a precondition for job creation. Furthermore, the model lacks a dynamic analysis, that is, a crucial aspect of a transition process, an obvious out-of-steady state process. We next review some of the contributions that attempt to overcome these shortcomings.

Speed of Reforms and Unemployment

Aghion and Blanchard (1993) tackle issues similar to those examined by Burda but use a different setting. In the simplest version of their model, state firms are exogenously closed. Wages in private firms are set according to an efficiency wage mechanism that gives rise to an equilibrium rate of unemployment. The reallocation of labor across sectors takes place in a similar way as the Harris-Todaro model. Workers that depart from the declining state sector become temporarily unemployed. New private firms randomly hire workers from the pool of unemployed. As in Burda, the long-run equilibrium of the system is crucially affected by fiscal feedbacks. In the following paragraphs, we give a sketch of the model and of its main conclusions.

The economy is populated by two sectors—the state and the private— with the latter more productive than the former. The state sector shrinks as a result of reforms. The rate at which the state sector declines is a policy variable. Moreover, wages in the state sector absorb all the revenues (the wage rate equals the average product of labor) net of tax payments. The latter assumption implies that state firms face hard budget constraints. The change over time of employment in the state sector is simply:[2]

$$dE/dt = -s \qquad (3.9)$$

All the action is in the private sector, where employment is determined according to the choice of profit-maximizing firms. The change in employment in private firms depends on current profitability if firms are myopic. Alternatively, if private firms are forward-looking, the change in employment depends on the present value of net profits, that is, the value of the firm. Given a linear technology, the value of the firm corresponds to the value of a new private job. To account for an interesting interaction between unemployment and the reallocation of labor across sectors, wages are assumed to be set according to an efficiency wage mechanism:

$$w = b + c \, (r + H/U) \tag{3.10}$$

where b is exogenous unemployment benefits, c the premium of the value of a private-sector job over the value of being unemployed, r the real interest rate, H the flow of hirings in the private sector (dN/dt), and U the stock of unemployed. Assuming a random selection of workers from the pool of unemployed, H/U represents the probability of getting a job in the private sector when unemployed. Furthermore, as in Burda, it is assumed that the government faces the flow budget constraint of equation (3.7):

$$\tau(1-u) = bu$$

Finally, the labor force is assumed to be constant.

Myopic Firms. The case of myopic firms is rather simple. Job creation in private firms is proportional to current profits.[3]

$$dN/dt = a(y-w-\tau) \tag{3.11}$$

Substituting in the above expression the value of wages from equation (3.10) and using the government budget constraint, one can obtain the dynamics of N as a function of the rate of unemployment:

$$dN/dt = a(U/(U+ca))[y-rc-(1/(1-U))b] \tag{3.12}$$

The above expression can be graphically represented by a bell-shaped curve. As the total labor force is constant, stable rates of unemployment arise when the inflow into unemployment from the shrinking state sector is exactly matched by the outflow from unemployment through job creation in the private sector. Two long-run equilibria can emerge, as shown in Figure 3.1. It is easy to show that the low-unemployment equilibrium is stable, while the high-unemployment equilibrium is unstable. The intuition for the multiplicity of equilibria is analogous to the one discussed for Burda's model.

The main result of the model is that there is a maximum rate of contraction of the state sector(s) consistent with equilibrium. Moreover, faster transition implies higher-equilibrium unemployment. However, because of the different levels of productivity in the two sectors, there is an optimal rate of unemployment. The dynamics of unemployment are rather trivial. As the economy starts typically from low unemployment, it converges monotonically to the steady-state rate of unemployment.

Forward-Looking Firms. New private firms are likely to take into account, not only current profits, but also future profitability of their activity. Indeed, because of the presence of frictions in the labor market, job creation represents an investment decision. Thus, the creation of private jobs depends on the value of the new job. The dynamics of this version are much richer than that of the myopic case, and it is summarized in Figure 3.2. There are still two equilibria—the low-unemployment equilibrium is saddle-path stable, while the high-unemployment equilibrium is either a sink or a node, depending on parameter values. Two different equilibrium paths are admissible—one consistent with successful restructuring, the other with failed restructuring, with transition ending with high unemployment and no private sector. Expectations play a key role in determining convergence to one of the two equilibria. Thus, successful transition requires not only a high value of new jobs, but also expectations of its continuous increase in the future.

Summing Up the "Flow Approach." The "flow approach" put forward by Burda and by Aghion and Blanchard leads to two main results. First, there is the possibility of multiple equilibria due to fiscal feedbacks. Second, the speed of transition, summarized by the rate at which the state sector shrinks, matters for the final outcome of reforms from a welfare point of view. From the perspective of the existence of a long-run equilibrium with successful restructuring, there is a maximum rate of feasible decline of the state sector. The welfare analysis is more compli-

Figure 3.2
Unemployment and Income Distribution

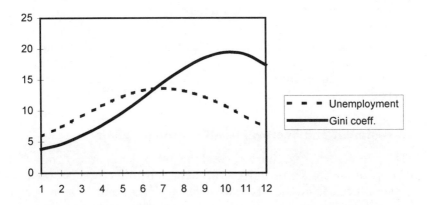

cated. Assuming that productivity is higher in private firms, the reallocation of labor from state to private firms has ambiguous effects on welfare. Indeed, growth of the more productive private firms implies higher unemployment and, thus, a loss of output resulting from the unemployment of those who were previously employed productively in state firms. The total effect on welfare depends on the relative strength of the increased productivity associated with new private jobs and the loss of productivity associated with unemployment. Aghion and Blanchard show that results are ambiguous: the market solution could lead to either too high or too low a speed of restructuring. In a similar model, Gavin (1993) obtains the result that the market solution tends to lead to too high a speed of restructuring.

The models of Burda and of Aghion and Blanchard also have important implications for labor market policies. Unemployment benefits play a key role, and the higher the unemployment benefits, the higher the equilibrium rate of unemployment. Burda, by explicitly analyzing the matching process between job seekers and firms, stresses the importance of policies that improve the efficiency of such matching. According to this model, active labor market and incomes policies may significantly improve the functioning of the labor market. Burda and Boeri (1995) find empirical support for such views.

REFORMS, INVESTMENT, UNEMPLOYMENT, AND INCOME DISTRIBUTION

Chadha and Coricelli (1995) have developed an approach that shares many of the results discussed above. However, a few main innovations are introduced:

- Explicit modeling of investment in the private sector, which allows for an analysis of the dynamics of the system.

- Costs of adjustment are assumed larger in capital than in labor markets.

- Finally, and more important, restructuring is an endogenous process, determined by the choices of workers in state firms. Policymakers can influence such decisions through tax-subsidization policies but do not control directly the rate of decline of state firms.

Investment and Sectoral Reallocation of Labor

The state sector is characterized by labor-dominated firms. The coalition of workers maximizes the expected difference between its members' income and the alternative income if they left the state sector. This alternative income is a weighted average of unemployment benefits and the private-sector wage, with the weights given by the probability of remaining unemployed and the probability of obtaining a job in the private sector. Assuming risk neutrality and thus a linear utility function of the workers, the objective function of the workers' coalition can be expressed as follows, as in Calvo (1978):

$$V_t^{\ 1} = L_t^{\ 1} [W_t^{\ 1} - (\delta_t^{\ B} + (1-\delta_t))W_t^{\ 2}] \tag{3.13}$$

where $L_t^{\ 1}$ denotes employment in the state sector, $W_t^{\ 1}$ the wage in the state sector, $W_t^{\ 2}$ the wage in the private sector, and B unemployment benefits; δ represents the probability that a worker laid off from the state sector remains unemployed, and $(1-\delta)$ represents the probability that he obtains employment in the private sector.

Production in the state sector is assumed to arise from a Cobb-Douglas production function, with labor as the only variable factor:

$$Q_t^{\ 1} = F(L_t^{\ 1}) = (L_t^{\ 1})b \qquad where \ 0 < b < 1 \tag{3.14}$$

If workers appropriate all the revenues from the firm, wages will be equal to the average product of labor, net of the tax that the government can impose. In that case, maximization is subject also to the zero profit condition:

$$(1-\tau))PQ_t^{\ 1} - W_t^{\ 1}L_t^{\ 1} = 0 \tag{3.15}$$

where τ is the tax (or subsidy, if negative) paid to the government and P is the price of the state-sector output expressed in terms of the private-sector good, assumed as numeraire.

With a Cobb-Douglas production function, the average product of labor is just a multiple of the marginal product. Thus, assuming that wages are equal to the marginal product of labor does not change the results of the model. If one adds an arbitrage condition stating that workers will leave the state sector until the wage in that sector is smaller, the expected alternative income (the second term in brackets in equation (3.10)), one obtains the following employment rule (which would have been arrived at by maximizing equation (3.9) subject to the constraints of (3.10) and (3.11)):

$$F(L_t^{\ 1})^{\beta-1} = 1/((1-\tau)P) [\delta_t B + (1-\delta_t)W_t^{\ 2}] \tag{3.16}$$

Equation (3.16) states that employment in the state sector decreases with taxes and with the probability of remaining unemployed, while it increases with the relative price, unemployment benefits, and wages in the private sector and with the probability of being employed in the private sector. In the state sector, there is no investment in physical capital and no technological progress and workers' effort is constant.

Private Sector

Output in the private sector is produced by a Cobb-Douglas technology, with labor measured in efficiency units and capital as a production factor:

$$Q_t^{\ 2} = K_t^{\ 1-a} \, [E(W_t^{\ 2} - B, U_t) L_t^{\ 2}] \alpha \qquad (3.17)$$

where K denotes the capital stock and $E(.)$ the effort function, which is increasing in the premium of wages over unemployment benefits and in the rate of unemployment.

Profit maximization by the firm leads to the following conditions, from which wages and employment in the private sector can be derived:

$$(\delta E(W_t^{\ 2} - B, U_t) / \delta W_t^{\ 2}) * (W_t^{\ 2} / E(W_t^{\ 2} - B, U_t)) = 1 \qquad (3.18)$$

which is the so-called Solow condition, which implies that the elasticity of effort with respect to the real wage is unity. From that condition one can derive the following signs of derivatives:

$$\partial W_t^{\ 2} / \partial U_t < 0, \ \partial W_t^{\ 2} / \partial B > 0$$

The level of employment in efficiency wage models is on the labor demand curve of the firm, which is:

$$L_t^{\ 2} = ([\alpha K_t]^{1/1-\alpha} [E(W_t^{\ 2} - B, U_t)]^{\alpha/1-\alpha}) / [W_t^{\ 2}]^{1/1-\alpha} \qquad (3.19)$$

Using (3.18), wages can be eliminated in (3.19) to obtain:

$$L_t^{\ 2} = L^2[W^2(U_t; B), U_t, K_t, B] = L^2(U, K, B) \qquad (3.20)$$

with $\partial L^2 / \partial U > 0$; $\partial L^2 / \partial K > 0$; $\partial L^2 / \partial B < 0$.

Labor Market Equilibrium for a Given Capital Stock

Assuming that the private sector randomly selects workers from the pool of people who are not employed in the state sector, the probability that a worker abandoning the state sector becomes employed in the private sector is:

$$1 - \delta_t = L_t^2 / (L_t^{\ 2} + U_t) \qquad (3.21)$$

Using (3.17) we can derive employment in the state sector as:

$$L_t{}^1 = L^1\ (U_t,K_t;(1{-}\tau)P,B) \tag{3.22}$$

All the effects can be signed except those associated with a change in B which has ambiguous effects on state-sector employment.

Equilibrium in the labor market requires that the sum of employed and unemployed people be equal to the labor force, which we normalize to be equal to 1.0. Thus;

$$L_t{}^1 = (U,K,(1{-}\tau)P,B) + L_t{}^2\ (U,K,B) + U_t = 1 \tag{3.23}$$

Equation (3.23) yields a relation between unemployment and the stock of capital, the *UK* curve discussed in the text.

Private-Sector Growth

Most papers on transition have emphasized the presence of adjustment costs, or search costs, in the labor market. Assuming a difference in the level of productivity in state and private sectors, they then derive results on the optimal speed of movement of labor from state to private firms. We emphasize explicitly the forces affecting the growth of the private sector and the accumulation of capital, both human and physical, as the driving force of transition. To stress the central role of capital accumulation, we abstract from the presence of adjustment or search costs in the labor market.

Several models of investment, both in human and physical capital, can be considered. Chadha and Coricelli (1995) and Chadha (1994) analyze different models of investment. If one considers K in the production function of the private-sector good as human capital or a generic technological factor that grows exogenously over time, transition takes place inevitably. Following Chadha (1994) consider in equation (3.17) H_t instead of $K_t{}^{1-a}$. Assume that H grows over time at a constant rate. This implies that total factor productivity in the private sector is continuously shifting over time. The system travels along the bell-shaped curve *UK* of Figure 3.1. Economic policy can affect the shape of the curve and thus the level of unemployment during transition. However, whatever policies are implemented and whatever is the initial level of human capital or technology, the economy eventually reaches its final equilibrium with all labor employed in the private sector.

More interesting are the cases in which the process of growth of the private sector is endogenously determined. For instance, human capital can grow through a process of learning by doing. As in Lucas (1988), the growth of human capital is an increasing function of the number of workers employed in the private sector. Chadha (1994) has shown that this implies the presence of two distinct equilibrium paths. The two paths are separated by a critical value of initial level of human capital in the private sector. The economy still travels along the *UK* curve. However, to the left of the critical value of human capital, transition fails and the economy gets stuck in an equilibrium dominated by state sector firms—one myopic and the other forward-looking. In contrast, starting to the right of the critical value of human capital allows the economy to move toward specialization in the private sector good.

The case of investment in physical capital leads to similar, although richer, results. Chadha and Coricelli (1995) analyzed a model in which forward-looking firms in the private sector invest in physical capital. Investment takes place according to a standard, text book like specification (Blanchard and Fischer 1988). Firms maximize the present discounted value of profits, and investment is subject to installation costs. The resulting dynamics of the system display two steady-state equilibria—one with low capital and the other with high capital in the private sector (Figure 3.1). There is still a threshold level of initial capital to be used in the private-sector which ensures that transition will succeed. However, transition may crucially depend on expectations of private sector firms. Indeed, even when the initial capital stock would be sufficient to place the economy on a successful path, if expectations on future returns on investments are pessimistic, restructuring will not take place. Similarly, if expectations are optimistic, restructuring can take place even when the initial capital stock in the private sector is very low. Thus, transition does not depend only, in a deterministic fashion, on inherited capital, but it crucially depends on expectations. This implies that policies also have important effects through their impact on expectations. Another important aspect of the model is that initial conditions highlight a trade-off between the initial level of capital in the private sector and the rate of unemployment. Indeed, the lower the initial capital stock usable in the private sector, the higher is the unemployment rate consistent with successful transition.

The presence of multiple equilibria and of a highly nonlinear adjustment path gives an important role to economic policies. Two main policy issues stand out: first, privatization policies that can affect the initial stock of capital available to the private sector; second, the fiscal constraints on restructuring and the relation between fiscal policy and the speed of transition. Indeed, while several authors have identified, as a main policy instrument, the closure of state firms, the indirect effects on the dynamics of state firms due to taxes and subsidies appear more relevant.

Fiscal Constraints and the Speed of Transition

Given the assumptions on taxation, the budget balance is simply the difference between tax revenues from state firms and unemployment benefits:

$$D_t = \tau P(L_t{}^{-1})\beta - Bu_t \qquad (3.24)$$

In Chadha and Coricelli (1995), it is shown that the relation between unemployment and the tax rate, for a given budget balance, is nonlinear and that it follows a hump-shaped curve. One can thus compute a second relation between unemployment and the tax rate from the labor market equilibrium condition of equation (3.19). That relation is monotonic and increasing (Chadha and Coricelli 1995). The effects of different constraints on the budget balance can thus be studied by shifting the two curves. The main result is that when unemployment is high, tightening the budget constraints implies reducing taxation on state firms (or increasing subsidies to them). When unemployment is low, tightening the budget is consistent with higher taxation of state firms and with faster restructuring.

Thus, the relation between budgetary developments and the characteristics and speed of restructuring reduces the informational role of the budget. Indeed, budget deficits may result from a strong commitment toward fast and far-reaching market reforms, rather than from a populist attitude, or from the maintenance of the status quo via large subsidies (Kornai 1992; Tanzi 1993). These views provide a useful framework for interpreting fiscal variables during the transition.

Speed of Reforms and Fiscal Accounts

With the notable exception of the Czech Republic, reforms in Central and Eastern European economies (CEEs from now on) have been invariably associated with worsening fiscal balances. In view of the large fall in output that took place across the region, such a deterioration is not surprising. However, there seems to be a very weak correlation between output behavior and the budget. Thus, more structural sources seem to be at work. The pace of restructuring, unemployment and the relative dynamics of state and private firms are likely to have had an impact on the budget, somehow independent of the behavior of aggregate output. Moreover, the sharp increase in unemployment and falling real wages have put pressure on social expenditures. The latter, traditionally high in the previous regime of universal social protection, even increased in some cases.

Adopting the classification suggested by the European Bank for Reconstruction and Development (EBRD) and the World Bank, we group CEEs into "fast" and "slow" reformers. This classification proves useful in identifying some key differences in fiscal developments and in fiscal policies. Consistent with our analytical model, we find that (*ceteris paribus*) fiscal pressures become stronger while the transition progresses, and they are more acute in the fast-reforming countries. Thus, demands on governments to slow down restructuring mount, as well as demands for compensating transfers to groups affected by reforms.

Governments face an important trade-off. Excessively tight budget constraints may yield perverse effects, as they may slow down restructuring. Indeed, a fast decline of state enterprises would lead to adverse fiscal effects by increasing unemployment expenditures and, simultaneously, reducing the tax base. These effects are particularly strong when the taxation is concentrated on state firms, while private firms largely escape taxation. Together with pressures arising from increasing income inequality and lobbying from specific interest groups, such as pensioners, fiscal constraints more than likely played a major role in the reform cycle observed in many CEEs and especially in determining the asymmetry between economic and political cycles. Examples of change over time in the speed of reforms are given by the continuing delay of privatization. More generally, the widespread electoral successes of parties originating from former communist organizations testify to the pressures for changing the pace of reforms.

To sum up, fast reformers began the transition by putting strong pressure on state firms by reducing subsidies drastically and, in most cases, raising effective taxation. As transition progressed and unemployment increased, there was pressure for slowing down transition in high-unemployment countries. The loosening of the fiscal pressure came about through the tolerated growth of tax arrears and, in the case of Poland, the reduction of the dividend tax and the excess wage tax. Thus, the slowdown of the pace of restructuring was associated not only with the political cycle, but also with the perverse effects coming from tight fiscal constraints. This view is consistent with the analytical model put forward by Dewatripont (1992) and Dewatripont and Roland (1992).

Income Inequality and Attitudes Toward Reforms

Along the transition path, income distribution follows dynamics of the Kuznets type. Inequality increases initially and persists for a while before falling at later stages of transition when the private sector has become the dominant sector of the economy. Two aspects of the dynamics of income distribution stand out. First, income inequality keeps increasing beyond the turning point of the aggregate output in the economy and of unemployment. The second aspect concerns the speed of the reform and the inequality of income.

Consider the model of Chadha and Coricelli (1995) outlined above for the case in which growth of the private sector is driven by exogenous factors (technological change or accumulation of human capital). The effects of the sectoral reallocation of labor on income distribution can be analyzed by measuring the evolution over time of the Gini coefficient. When the process of reallocation of labor starts, income is fairly equally distributed among the population. The proportion of people employed in the state sector is very large, while the unemployment rate is low. At the end of the reallocation process, income is again equally distributed. The economy is only comprised of private-sector workers, and there is no unemployment.

The key issue is to analyze the change in income distribution during the transition. Two main forces affect such evolution over time. The first deals with the changes in the sectoral composition of employment. Employment in the state sector shrinks continuously while employment in the private sector expands continuously. Second, the ratio between the private-sector and the state-sector wages follows a nonlinear pattern. As employment in the state sector declines, wages rise because the marginal product of labor in the state sector rises. The behavior of wages in the private sector mirrors the path of unemployment, as private-sector wages are a decreasing function of the unemployment rate. In the early stages of the reallocation process, as unemployment increases, wages fall. After unemployment peaks, wages in the private sector begin to rise.

Inequality in income distribution reflects both the changes in the sectoral composition of employment, as well as changes in relative wages. In the early stages of development, the inequality unambiguously widens for two reasons. Unemployment grows as an increasing share of the labor force is laid off from the state sector. The unemployed receive unemployment benefits that are always lower than state-sector wages. Simultaneously, the private sector expands. In the early phases of restructuring, private-sector wages are higher than in the state sector. These two mechanisms tend to increase inequality in income distribution.

The dynamics of the restructuring process imply that inequality must narrow after a critical stage. Again, there are two main channels at work. The first is related to the dynamics of the reallocation of labor across sectors. Private (state) employment monotonically increases (decreases). An increasing share of workers are employed in the same sector, getting the same wage. Unemployment is declining, and there are a declining number of people who get unemployment benefits. The second is due to the evolution of wages. While the state-sector wage is always increasing along the development path, the private-sector wage follows a "U-pattern." Thus, over time, the gap between private- and state-sector wages narrows. This dampens the effects on income inequality associated with the shift of workers from the state sector to the private sector.

Figure 3.2 puts together all the elements and illustrates the evolution over time of income inequality, measured by the Gini coefficient. It is apparent that the path of income inequality describes a Kuznets curve. The important finding of the model is that income inequality tends to increase even after unemployment has reached its peak. The asymmetry between the two curves during transition points to the limits of unemployment as a measure of underlying pressures on governments (see Rodrik 1995 for a similar point).[4]

Indeed, focusing only on unemployment leaves unexplained the puzzling result of the fading of support for reforms in countries well beyond the turning point of output recovery. The synchronized dynamics of output, unemployment, and income distribution may offer an explanation of such a puzzle. Of course, the relation between income inequality and political support for reforms is complex. One extreme view could be that income distribution does not matter in democracy, because the observed income distribution always reflect the preferences of at least the majority of the population. A similar, though less extreme, view is that increasing inequality is inevitable during the shift from central planning to a market economy and that tolerance for inequality increases during the transition to a market economy. The latter is a manifestation of Hirschman's "tunnel effect," according to which people will not be unhappy if other people get richer, as they see in the success of other people the signal of their own future success. However, it is hard to reach any general conclusion. Our analysis simply suggests that income inequality may represent an obstacle to sustaining reforms. We do not discuss welfare implications or the optimal path of income distribution. Nevertheless, the model implies a clear trade-off between income inequality and restructuring of the economy. Policies may have an important role in the process.

The main results are that a reduction of the tax burden on state firms, or an increase in subsidies, tends to reduce inequality in the short run, at the cost of a slower restructuring. A larger pressure on state firms, via higher taxation, increases the speed of restructuring. This implies higher unemployment. Inequality increases initially, although it declines faster in the medium run. As in the discussion of unemployment dynamics, changes in unemployment benefits have ambiguous effects. In particular, higher unemployment benefits may either increase or reduce inequality, depending on parameter values. The results of tax subsidies on state firms provide a rationale for policy reversals (similar conclusions are reached by Rodrik [1995] in a model with exogenous labor dynamics). Reducing taxes (or increasing subsidies) on state firms reduces income inequality (measured by the Gini coefficient) at least during the initial stages of transition. This reduction implies, as well, a slowdown of restructuring and a lower unemployment in the initial stages.

EMPIRICAL EVIDENCE ON THE DYNAMICS OF OUTPUT, UNEMPLOYMENT, INCOME DISTRIBUTION, AND THE SPEED OF REFORM

Despite its simplicity, the Chadha and Coricelli model yields a few striking results:

1. Unemployment and output are related by a highly nonlinear function. In fact, during the first stages of reforms, unemployment increases together with output growth.

2. The growth of the private sector is associated with higher unemployment.

3. Private-sector growth affects output growth negatively but only for a short initial period. Its effect on output growth turns positive well before it leads to a downturn in unemployment.

Although a robust test of the theory is not feasible, we try to evaluate whether the above three predictions of the model find some empirical support. We consider eighteen reforming countries which form the entire sample of Eastern European economies, with the exception of countries involved in wars. The time period is 1989 to 1994.

Let us first consider the relation between unemployment and output growth. From a simple regression, one can note that output growth is positively correlated to the unemployment rate. In the above model, this would imply that the sample is already in the segment of the bell-shaped curve which comes after the initial negative relation (unemployment starts rising when the economy is in recession). However, if we add the square of output changes, it turns out that the data indicate the presence of a bell-shaped relation between unemployment and growth (Table 3.4A). Similarly, the impact of private-sector growth on output growth turns out to be nonlinear in the sample. Indeed, if we split the sample between low private-sector growth and high private-sector growth and run two separate regressions, we obtain that at low private-sector growth, output declines as the private sector grows (Table 3.4B and 3.4C). However, at high levels of private-sector development, output increases with private-sector growth.

Combining these results on unemployment and growth, and private-sector development and growth, we can derive the impact of private-sector growth on unemployment. Interestingly, as for the relation between unemployment and aggregate growth, the relation between the rate of unemployment and private-sector growth is represented by a bell-shaped curve (Table 3.4D).

Finally, we analyze the role of initial conditions. We can interpret the overall index of liberalization as a proxy of the quality of the initial capital stock, both physical and human. Table 3.5 shows the crucial

Table 3.4
OLS Regression Results, 1989–94

A. Unemployment and Output Change, All Countries		
Variable	**Coefficient**	**T-Statistics**
Constant	0.79	9.42
GDP change	0.47	3.70
GDP change squared	−0.01	−1.88
R^2	0.19	

B. Countries with Low-Level Development of Private Sector		
Variable	**Coefficient**	**T-Statistics**
Constant	−4.80	−2.60
Private sector	−17.08	−2.39
R^2	0.30	

C. Countries with High-Level Development of Private Sector		
Variable	**Coefficient**	**T-Statistics**
Constant	−35.85	−3.33
Private sector	44.26	2.93
R^2	0.30	

D. Aggregate Private Sector Development and Unemployment		
Variable	**Coefficient**	**T-Statistics**
Constant	19.44	2.66
Private sector	78.79	3.45
Private sector squared	−22.23	−2.74
R^2	0.30	

importance of prereform liberalization in determining the success of reforms. We can consider the result as an indirect support to the findings of the model. Interestingly, inserting the prereform liberalization index makes the postreform liberalization index insignificant.

Regarding income distribution, data suggest two main observations (Table 3.6A and 3.6B). First, preferences for more-equal income distribution continued to operate especially in the Czech Republic, while in Poland and the U.S.S.R., inequality indicators jumped above those observed in the United Kingdom in the 1980s. Second, the low inequality

Table 3.5

Regression on Output, 1993–94, Relative to 1989 and Liberalization Indices

Variable	Coefficients	T-Statistics	Coefficients	T-Statistics
Constant	53.6	10.6	69.4	8.2
Cumulative liberalization	9.6	2.5	−2.7	−0.7
Dummy-WAR	−28.6	−2.7	−35.6	−4.7
Prereform liberalization			124.7	4.7
R^2	0.33		0.37	

indices for the Czech Republic suggest that low unemployment can be an effective instrument to reduce inequality.

The empirical work carried out especially at the World Bank highlights three additional features, that prima facie support the findings of our analytical model (Milanovic 1996): (1) inequality increases in the private-sector growth in the initial stages of transition; (2) inequality increases with unemployment; and (3) increased wage differentials are an important determinant of increasing inequality. With the exception of Romania, increasing wage differentials account for a large proportion, generally more than 50 percent, of the increase in the Gini coefficient (Milanovic 1996). Table 3.6B displays the change in the Gini coefficient from the prereform period to the postreform period. The striking fact is the magnitude of the increase in income inequality which has been brought about by the movement toward a market economy. An increase in inequality of such proportions, achieved in such short time intervals, is probably unprecedented. Although the increase in inequality reflects the abandonment of the artificially compressed income distribution structure in the old regime, it is likely that, during the transition, there is an overshooting of the inequality indicators that will prevail at the end of the transition period.

As poverty has reached extremely high levels, even in countries like Poland, considered the "success story" of transition, current levels of income inequality should improve over time. The importance of unemployment as a predictor for poverty in the case of Poland suggests that poverty should decline as unemployment begins to decline. Country studies tend to emphasize the role of restructuring, unemployment, and private-sector growth as determinants of increasing inequality and poverty. Thus, increasing inequality may be the inevitable cost of successful transformation.

Table 3.6
Prereform and Postreform Income Inequality

A. Gini Coefficients		
Country	**1985**	**1993–94**
Czechoslovakia[1]	19.9	20/27
Hungary[2]	20.9	28
Poland	25.3	31
USSR[3]	25.6	36
UK	29.7	

B. Change in Gini Coefficients[4]		
Country	**1987–88**	**1993–94**
Czech Republic	19	19
Hungary	21	23
Poland	26	31
Slovak Republic	20	20
Bulgaria	23	34
Slovenia	24	28
Romania	23	29
All transition countries, including FSU	24	32

Sources: Atkinson and Micklewright (1992:112); and Milanovic (1996).

1. In 1993–94, 20 is for the Czech Republic and 27 for Slovakia.
2. Instead of 1985, the year is 1982 for Hungary.
3. In 1993–94, the figure is only Russia.
4. Gini coefficient is based on income data.

However, cross-country data and, in particular, the comparison between Central and Eastern European countries and the countries of the former Soviet Union (FSU), point to an even larger increase in inequality in countries where reforms proceeded at a slower pace. Slowing down transition does not seem to reduce income inequality. Moreover, countries of the FSU display the highest Gini coefficients and the largest increase in the coefficient after reforms, despite the absence of significant unemployment. Thus, prima facie, the argument we put forward on the basis of our theoretical model seems to conflict with the experience of the FSU.

However, both the Gini coefficients and the unemployment data for the FSU should be taken with caution. The nature of transition in most

FSU countries differed from that prevailing in Central and Eastern European countries. A key difference is due to the role of the provider of social services that firms in the FSU, but not in Central Europe, continued to play. The provision of such benefits implies that recorded income severely understates the income received by workers. In several instances, such as in the case of significant wage arrears, social benefits represent the bulk of income received by workers. Moreover, benefits tend to be equally distributed. Thus, de facto, they flatten the income distribution curve. Because we lack a proper measurement of the market value of these benefits, measured incomes give a misleading picture. The true income distribution should, therefore, be much more even than that revealed by incomes data. As part of the expenditure is directed to these services, even expenditure data may suffer from the above bias.

The role of firms as providers of social services helps explain the low level of unemployment registered in the FSU during the first years of transition. The combination of low unemployment benefits and large benefits associated with a job position in the firm sharply reduces the scope for unemployment. Thus, despite the collapse in output, unemployment rates remain extremely low and restructuring limited.

In sum, a proper measurement of income flows, including social benefits, would likely reduce the indicators of income inequality. This would be consistent with the model that predicts that income inequality will increase with the increase of unemployment. As the income of the unemployed tends to be much lower than that of the employed, increasing inequality implies that a large proportion of the population falls into low-income brackets. Indeed, increasing inequality coincides with increasing poverty.

NOTES

1. This is an important point, because the other two models discussed posit a relation between wages and unemployment. The solution of the Nash-bargaining in a search model is akin to the solution of efficiency wage models. Thus, despite some differences, the particular version of the wage setting chosen does not significantly change results.

2. Gavin (1993) developed a two-sector search model, in which the relative dynamics of shrinking and growing sectors are examined. The sector that was previously protected is bound to decline. Workers can search for a job in both sectors. Gavin shows that the market solution in which protection of the old sector is eliminated through a big bang may be inefficient, as it would lead to a level of quits and transitional unemployment that is excessive from a social welfare point of view. Thus, there is an economic case for gradual reforms.

3. Note that assuming that the absolute change of employment is proportional to per worker profitability is not very realistic. A rate of change specifica-

tion, in which the rate of change of employment is a function of per capita profits, appears more interesting.

4. In the political science literature, Przeworski (1991) identified unemployment as a main source of political difficulties during the transition. His political model assumes an underlying pattern of unemployment and output which is very similar to the one produced by our model.

REFERENCES

Aghion, P., and O. J. Blanchard. 1993. *On the speed of transition in central Europe*. Working Paper 6. London: European Bank for Reconstruction and Development.

Atkinson, A. B., and J. Micklewright. 1992. *Economic Transformation in Eastern Europe and the Distribution of Income*. New York: Cambridge University Press.

Blanchard, O. J., and S. Fischer. 1988. *Lectures on Macroeconomics*. Cambridge, MA: MIT Press.

Blanchard, O. J., K. A. Froot and J. D. Sachs, eds. 1995. *The Transition in Eastern Europe*. Vol. 2. (National Bureau of Economic Research Project Report.) Chicago: University of Chicago Press.

Boeri, T. 1995. *Regional Dimensions of Unemployment in Central and Eastern Europe and Social Barriers in Restructuring*. EUI Working Paper 95/17.

Burda, M. 1993. Unemployment, labor market institutions, and structural change in Eastern Europe. *Economic Policy* 16:101–38.

———. 1995. *The Impact of Active Labor Market Policies: A Close Look at the Czech and Slovak Republics*. London: Center for Economic Policy Research.

Calvo, G. A. 1978. Urban unemployment and wage determination in LDCs: Trade unions in the Harris-Todaro model. *International Economic Review* 19(1): 65–81.

Chadha, B., 1994. *Fiscal Constraints and the Speed of Transition*. CEPR Discussion Paper Series 993.

Chadha, B., and F. Coricelli. 1995. *Unemployment, Investment and Sectoral Reallocation*. CEPR Discussion Paper Series 1110.

Dewatripont, M. 1992. The virtues of gradualism and legitimacy in the transition to a market economy. *Economic Journal* 102:291–300.

Dewatripont, M., and G. Roland. 1992. Economic reform and dynamic political constraints. *Review of Economic Studies* 59:703–30.

Gavin, M. 1993. Unemployment and the economics of gradualist policy reform. Columbia University. Mimeographed.

Kornai, J. 1992. The post-socialist transition and the State: Reflections in the light of Hungarian fiscal problems. *American Economic Review, Papers and Proceedings* 82(2):2–21.

Lucas, R. E. 1988. On the mechanics of economic development. *Journal of Monetary Economics* 22(1):3–42.

Milanovic, B. 1996. *Income, Inequality, and Poverty During the Transition*. Washington, DC: World Bank.

Pissarides, C. A. 1990. *Macroeconomic Adjustment and Poverty in Selected Developed Countries*. Discussion Paper 13. London: London School of Economics and Political Science, Center for Economic Performance.

Przeworski, A. 1991. *Democracy and the Market: Political and Economic Reforms in Eastern Europe and Latin America*. New York: Cambridge University Press.

Rodrik, D. 1995. *The Dynamics of Political Support for Reform in Economies in Transition*. CEPR Discussion Paper Series 1115.

Tanzi, V. 1993. *Fiscal Policy and the Economic Restructuring of Economies in Transition*. Working Paper 93/22. Washington, DC: International Monetary Fund.

4

Employment Effects
of Structural Reforms
in African Countries

Fidel Ezeala-Harrison

Postindependence economic development initiatives in most African countries (ACs) were heavily based on emphasis on government intervention rather than free-market forces. However, by the early 1980s, most of these ACs were, indeed, having very dismal economic performances. Over the period from 1975 to 1985, ACs, on the average, suffered a 15 percent decline in per capita gross domestic product (GDP), together with huge declines in exports, investment, and general economic infrastructure. During these times, though, other non-African developing countries (especially in Asia) that had effected fewer economic controls and had their economies function upon free market-forces were experiencing remarkable economic performance. Therefore, and following from this, the need for structural reforms in African economies became even more apparent.[1]

Most ACs are still engaged in the difficult task of reforming their economies: greater use of, and reliance on, the free-market mechanism in resource allocation and distribution of income and wealth in their societies. This change is often referred to as economic liberalization, and applied to ACs specifically, it encompasses the mix of policies toward greater deregulation, privatization, trade liberalization, dismantling of rigid controls, and reversal of agricultural-sector terms of trade in the economy. It is presumed that such a regime would ultimately result in higher economic growth and expanded employment opportunities for the population. This policy of structural (adjustment) reforms, largely mentored and promoted by the World Bank and the International Monetary Fund (IMF), is believed to be absolutely necessary as a general recourse for enabling ACs to experience some resurgence of economic growth.

This chapter examines the potential labor market impacts of these reforms in Africa. It seeks to address the incipient problems of unemployment, poverty, and overall macroeconomic ramifications of the liberalization drive within the labor markets of ACs. As Jones and Kiguel (1994) report, those ACs who instituted the most extensive economic reform policies (around the 1981–91 decade) did achieve median GDP per capita growth of about 2 percent by 1993, while those that did not adopt the reforms had their median GDP growth decline by about 2.6 percent. This evidence appears to suggest that, given their ongoing precarious economic situations, these countries should aim to further increase their reform efforts and reevaluate their adjustment strategies with a view to undertaking more deep-rooted reforms.

However, as the ultimate success or failure of any economic restructuring must be judged by the extent to which it improves or fails to improve income distribution and the standard of economic well-being of the labor force, it is important to have a complete understanding of the full effects of such reforms on such key labor market parameters as employment, productivity, and earnings. In a study that stresses the need for a more active government role in promoting greater use of markets, Ghanem and Walton (1995) argue that effective government policy is not only required to achieve growth through liberalization, but it is also crucial in ensuring that workers reap the economic benefits of the reforms (apparently through a mixture of expanded employment opportunities and higher earnings).[2]

This chapter also gives an account of the basis for the large-scale adoption of the reform programs seen among African economies. The chapter shows that these reforms were necessary at the times when they were undertaken and argues that the reforms were, in fact, the only credible recourse for these countries.

The labor market impact of the structural reforms is then analyzed. This section enables us to shed light on what potential prospects the reform exercise has for major labor market parameters, namely, employment and productivity, earnings, income maintenance and the distribution of income, in poor African countries. Finally, the chapter assesses the recent experiences of the ACs under reform and provides some perspectives for the direction of policy in the future.

THE POLITICAL ECONOMY OF STRUCTURAL REFORMS IN AFRICA

Africa's perennial economic decline has been a subject of much inquiry and research in recent times. Despite experiencing more rapid economic growth during the late 1960s through the early 1970s, most ACs have receded into rapid decline since that period.[3] Domestic policy inadequacies have been seen as the main factors responsible for poor economic performance in ACs in general. In a bid to redress these policy inadequacies and tackle the massive economic retrogression and the resulting chronic mass poverty, most ACs have acquiesced to structural adjustment programs (of economic reforms). This has often been done reluctantly under severe pressures exerted by the sponsoring agencies, namely, the World Bank and IMF. Unfortunately, however, since their introduction in the mid-1980s, these reforms seem to have failed in their attempt to propel economic growth and development in these countries.

In a number of studies designed to gain insight into the pace of reforms and their prospects for success in ACs, the World Bank (1994a, 1994b) compared the policies and performance of twenty-nine ACs over two separate periods. The first, covering the period of economic crisis in these countries, spans 1981 to 1986. The second, coinciding with the period of economic reform started in 1987, ended in 1991. In attempting to explain why many countries which took the path of adjustment still continued to experience economic decline, the World Bank and the IMF have argued that such countries have been unable to implement the reforms in a sustained fashion and that this inability accounts for these countries' lack of growth through economic liberalization (Jones and Kiguel 1994). It was stated in the later part of the 1980s and early 1990s that governments pursuing strong adjustment programs clearly outperformed those which failed to fully implement adjustment programs.

This finding is complemented by Husain (1994), who found that even among those ACs which seemed to be genuinely committed to the reform program, none strictly adhered to the tenets of economic liberalization in full, nor did any of these countries actually put a stable macroeconomic framework of adjustment fully in place. This brings to the fore the central question: What exactly needs reforming in African countries? The search for answers to this question has been the focus of immense attention in the international economic development literature of late.[4]

Targets of Sectoral Reforms

Table 4.1 shows the state of structural diversities in the world's regional economies by population (and its geographical compositions), the proportion of the labor force engaged in primary economic activities for their livelihood, and the share of agricultural production in GDP in the world's regions and subregions. There is a striking difference between the proportionate size of Africa's agricultural population (75 percent) and, say, South Asia's (63 percent). These structural differences are indicative of the factors that have helped shape the present rich-poor dichotomy in the world economic situation concerning which African countries are attempting to "restructure" their economies. In particular, Africa is among the poor regions that have the highest populations, the

Table 4.1
Structural Diversities in World Regional Economies, 1994

Region	Population (millions)	% Urban Population	% Rural Population	% Agricultural Labor	% Agricultural in GDP
World LDCs	5420	43	57	45	
South Asia	1682	28	72	63	33
East Asia	1386	34	66	51	21
Africa	654	30	70	75	32
S. America*	453	70	30	32	10
All LDCs	4196	34	66	66	17
DCs					
Former USSR	284	66	34	20	—
Europe	511	75	25	9	7
Japan	124	77	23	11	3
N. America	283	75	25	5	2
All OECD	18.2	89.4	3.1		

Source: Caluclated from World Bank, *World Development Report*, 1994; and *World Population Data Sheet*, Washinton, DC, 1994.

* Including Central America and Caribbean.
LDCs = Less developed countries.
DCs = Developed countries.

greater majority of which dwell in the rural sector and are employed in agriculture.

Table 4.2 highlights Africa's precarious situation (relative to the other developing regions of the world) in terms of income, GDP growth, and inflation rate. The region's high inflation rate and meager GDP growth rate spell a dismal economic picture. Contributing to the poor economic situation are a mix of internal and external factors. In Ezeala-Harrison (1995d), it is argued that although a number of external factors feature very strongly in constraining the development efforts in ACs, the combination of domestic policy ineptitude and bad governance appears to be much stronger in perpetuating poverty and underdevelopment in ACs.[5] A similar conclusion emerges from the works of Campbell and Clapp (1995), who argue, in the case of Guinea, that external impediments and domestic policy flaws equally combine to explain the poor economic situation.

Table 4.2
Indicators and Relative Performance in Developing Regions, 1994

Region	% of World Population	% of World Income	Average % GDP Growth	Average % Inflation
Asia	59.2	5.2	6.7	7.2
Africa	13.1	1.7	0.12	38.6
S. America*	9.5	3.7	2.5	28.8
All LDCs	81.7	34.0	5.2	12.5

Sources: Calculated from *International Financial Statistics*, 1995; World Bank, *World Development Report*, 1994; and *World Population Data Sheet*, Washington, DC, 1994.

* Including Central America and Caribbean.

Among Africa's major sectoral and macroeconomic policy reforms with important employment and other labor market implications, those that are particularly worthy of attention are to be found in the areas of agricultural revival, policies on import-substitution industrialization, public-sector participation, and the exchange rate. We now examine each of these in turn, in order to better portray their employment ramifications.

Agricultural Rediscovery

Most ACs tended to operate their economies with blatant anti-agricultural bias. The labor markets of these countries indicate the overwhelming relative dominance of agricultural occupation in the labor force (on average about 76 percent), as against the relative smallness of nonagricultural (including industrial manufacturing) employment (on average about 19 percent).[6]

The economies of most ACs during their much—acclaimed period of buoyancy—the decade spanning the mid-1960s to mid-1970s—were strongly agrarian. In these times, many ACs were not only self-sufficient (up to 80 percent on average) in food production, but many were also leading exporters of some of their produce. Examples were palm produce (Nigeria), cocoa (Ghana, Ivory Coast), and coffee (Uganda); other major African cash-crop exports included cotton, groundnuts, timber, rubber, hides, and skins. Agricultural exports alone accounted for about 78 percent of total exports of ACs around 1980. Unfortunately, however, in 1994, they accounted for about 39 percent.

Prior to the onset of economic declines in ACs, economic policies favored the urban and industrial sectors of the economy, creating rural-urban and agricultural-industrial imbalances in investment, infrastructural development, employment, productivity, and earnings. Continued neglect of the agricultural sector, while the policy of industrialization was prioritized, amounted to misplacement of emphasis in most ACs' economic development efforts. The result of this has been the unceasing waves of agricultural to industrial and rural to urban migration and massive open and disguised unemployment. The severe manpower losses for the agricultural sector, as the rural-urban income disparity was not narrowed, has led to huge shortfalls in domestic food and raw material supplies. This has been one key factor that made the economies of most ACs highly vulnerable to incessant global shocks and international commodity price fluctuations.

In pursuit of their urban/industrial bias of fostering development, ACs' governments tended to levy heavy taxes on the agricultural sector: marketing boards (statutory monopolies that buy cash crops below market prices from domestic producers for export at higher world market prices) were established and used as mechanisms whereby governments could effectively tax agricultural producers. African farmers are, on average, taxed about 70 percent more than farmers in other regions of the world. This has led to massive "abandonment" of the farms and resulted in low agricultural output. A recent study by Khan and Khan (1995) indicates that agricultural output grew at only 1.9 percent per year during 1965–80 and 1.7 percent during 1980–92 (compared to, say, China's 3 percent and 5.4 percent for these two respective periods).

Industrial Reorientation

The policies of industrial development in postindependence ACs have been slanted toward the inward-oriented, import-substitution posture driven by widespread tariff and import/export license barriers. This basically eliminated external competition, especially in manufacturing, and encouraged the operations of weak and technically inefficient industrial conglomerates.

In most countries, state-owned industrial projects were established under tariff protection. Direct foreign ventures were subjected to rigid controls in bids to "indigenize" the economy, and many foreign-owned enterprises were nationalized. African development policymakers of the time strongly believed that industrialization was the best strategy to achieve economic development.[7]

The first attempts were to set up import-substitution industries to produce previously imported manufactured goods. The potential economic benefits of this were obviously enormous: domestic employment expansion and higher market demand for locally produced raw materials and increased savings of foreign exchange. It turned out, however, that many of these industries came to be dependent on imported raw materials as domestic sources proved inadequate. Moreover, the market demand for the industries' produce was limited in the face of the low-income character of the general population. Consequently, the industrialization effort proved disappointing as the countries came to be saddled with balance of payments problems and a network of broken-down and fragmented industries.

Reforms of Public-Sector Enterprises

Public-sector enterprises include the provision of socioeconomic infrastructure and direct public sector investment in economic ventures. Most ACs' governments tended to commit themselves to public-sector provision of social overhead capital (infrastructure and public utilities), which are necessary requirements for economic development. This policy in itself seemed economically astute.

However, notwithstanding their having to operate with huge state subsidies, the overwhelming economic importance of these social overhead capital industries required that they be maintained at highly efficient and adequate levels. As natural monopolies (characterized by economies of scale and economies of scope), their most socially optimal operations fall upon the state sector. Therefore, any reform policies by way of their privatization or deregulation in the name of liberalization are apt to be uneconomical.

Apart from the social overhead capital sector, state enterprises in other sectors, such as transportation, banking, insurance, and even manufacturing industries, became rife in ACs and mostly proved highly inefficient. As government companies became devoid of profit incentives and rife with corruption, nepotism, inept management, and unaccountability, these enterprises came to epitomize the gross inefficiency and wanton misallocation of scarce resources witnessed in most ACs.

In manufacturing, many of the state enterprises were established as import-substituting industries: mainly domestic monopolies shielded artificially from foreign competition, with high tariff protection.[8] Under such market leverages, these firms produced high-cost goods from inefficient, ill-equipped, and overmanned factories. Lacking the requisite managerial skills, their operations were shored up by state adoption of controlled prices, often resulting in disequilibrium conditions in the markets for these manufacturers. The state enterprises simply failed to ever operate efficiently, and the situation called for massive reorientations.

Financial-Sector Reforms

Huge government presence tended to dominate the banking sector in most ACs. Real interest rates were often fixed, and the central banks exerted considerable influence on the trading of the country's currency and the determination of its international exchange rate. Overvaluation of the national currency often resulted, fueling overimportation through undue cheapening of foreign goods.

Massive government borrowing and overspending and excessive military expenditures, as well as support of inefficient public sector enterprises, created huge budget deficits. These accumulated into huge domestic and foreign public debts, jeopardizing the inflow of foreign investment while encouraging capital flight.

LABOR MARKET IMPACTS OF STRUCTURAL REFORMS

Given this study's special focus, of particular interest is the impact of the reforms on the dynamics of labor demand, productivity, earnings, and incomes, with implications, of course, for general working conditions and job security within specific sectors of the macro economy. In this regard, one is immediately struck with the feeling that widespread economic liberalization might expose workers to the harsh realities and mercy of "cold market forces."

Ghanem and Walton (1995) analyze the potential labor market gains that a country could reap through widespread adoption of a market-driven regime. As markets expand and the economy grows due to economy-wide expansion in output and rising labor productivity, firms compete for workers with offers of higher wages and better working conditions. Anything short of this sequence, following a regime of economic liberalization, could only amount to distortions in the labor market and will not likely result in economic growth.

In a recent study, Schadler (1996) observed that labor market rigidities have been addressed only to a limited degree in the structural reform programs of most less developed countries (LDCs). This observation is made on the grounds that real wages in these countries have not been very responsive to existing labor market conditions. Notwithstanding, the various ways in which structural reforms could give rise to growth (and greater employment creation) have been analyzed in a number of other recent studies. Adjustments that involve privatization of public sector firms, efficient administration of public utilities, investment on social and economic infrastructure, maintenance of appropriate monetary, fiscal, and tax rate targets, and overall dismantling of rigid controls are all especially viable.

Dornbusch (1993) explains that for at least three reasons, privatization is a very important and useful step in economic restructuring. These reasons are that, in the first place, the public sector lacks the managerial capacity and incentives to administer major sectoral enterprises in a cost-effective fashion. Further, the public sector does not have the requisite level of investment resources that are needed for adequate provision of all public services; and, besides, the government needs reliable sources of (tax) revenues in order not to engage in (destabilizing) deficit financing and public debt creation.

Drawing upon the foregoing paradigms, the following analysis is offered to illustrate the mechanism of transmission of growth through employment generation as adjustment and reforms are undertaken. We provide a structural model that applies straightforward analytical techniques to explore the conditions under which economic liberalization and reforms would propel expansion in employment and greater economic growth.

We consider an aggregate production function, stating the determinants of the economy's total output (GDP), Y, as the available labor force, L; existing capital resources, K; the amount of natural resource acquisition, R; and the state of knowledge and institutional settings, ψ:[9]

$$Y = \psi.Y(L,K,R) \tag{4.1}$$

Following Dornbusch (1993), we posit growth in this production function according to the tradition of the Solow-Dennison growth accounting model, as:

$$(\partial Y/\partial t)/Y = (\partial \psi/\partial t)/\psi + \alpha.(\partial L/\partial t)/L + \beta.(\partial K/\partial t)/K + \gamma.(\partial R/\partial t)/R \tag{4.2}$$

where:
α, β, and γ are respectively, the factor shares of labor, capital, and natural resources.

This represents the time growth path of national output, in terms of the growth rates of the various inputs and their productivities.[10] The importance of this specification for the present study lies in the fact that it can be used to highlight the crucial aspects of factor inputs in general, as in Dornbusch (1993), and labor input, in particular, which is our central concern in the present study. These are the available supply of labor in the economy, the level of utilization of the given existing labor supply, and the efficiency with which this existing supply is allocated. The last two of these aspects represent the key indicators of the employment impact of adjustment and reforms and are used here as proxies for measuring the labor market effects which we seek to determine.

To capture these labor market effects of economic restructuring, we let:

$\mu L=$ Index of the level of utilization of available labor supply (which we may term the employment effect)

$\xi L=$ Index of the level of efficiency with which the available labor supply is allocated (which we may term the productivity effect) φ L= Index of the extent to which distortions in the allocation of labor impair efficiency of allocation and general productivity (which we may term the unemployment-drag effect)[11]

In terms of these parameters, the growth equation (4.2) can be written as:

$$(\partial Y/\partial t)/Y = (\partial \psi/\partial t)/\psi + (\partial \mu L/\partial t)/\mu L + (\partial \xi\ L/\partial t)/\xi L - (\partial \phi L/\ \partial t)/\phi\ L +$$
$$\alpha.(\partial L/\partial t)/L + \beta.(\partial K/\partial t)/K + \gamma.(\partial R/\partial t)/R \qquad (4.3)$$

Thus, besides depicting the various sources of growth through economic restructuring, this relationship also highlights the potential labor market effects. The sources of growth are shown as technological progress, capital intensity, natural resource discovery, efficiency of allocation, and the level of utilization (of all resources). As we are focused on the labor market, the expressions for the employment effect, productivity effect, and unemployment-drag effect are respectively:

$$(\partial \mu L/\partial t)/\mu L = (\partial Y/\partial t)/Y - [(\partial \psi/\partial t)/\psi + (\partial \xi L/\partial t)\ /\xi L - (\partial \phi L/\partial t)\ \phi L +$$
$$\alpha.(\partial L/\partial t)/L + \beta.(\partial K/\partial t)/K + \gamma.(\partial R/\partial t)/R] \qquad (4.4)$$

$$(\partial \xi L/\partial t)/\xi L = (\partial Y/\partial t)/Y - [(\partial \psi/\partial t)/\psi + (\partial \mu L/\partial t)\ /\mu L - (\partial \phi L/\partial t)\ \phi L +$$
$$\alpha.(\partial L/\partial t)/L + \beta.(\partial K/\partial t)/K + \gamma.(\partial R/\partial t)/R] \qquad (4.5)$$

$$(\partial \phi L/\partial t)\ \phi L = (\partial \psi/\partial t)/\psi + (\partial \mu L/\partial t)\ /\mu L + (\partial \xi L/\partial t)\ /\xi L +$$
$$\alpha.\ (\partial L/\partial t)/L + \beta.\ (\partial K/\partial t)/K + \gamma.(\partial R/\partial t)/R - (\partial Y/\partial t)/Y \qquad (4.6)$$

These expressions are not only indicative of how growth would result from restructuring; they also give the measure of the various impacts on the labor market. Further, they reveal the major factors that contribute to growth as restructuring occurs, namely, capital formation, resource utilization, efficiency of utilization, and total factor productivity.[12]

The effect of economic liberalization policies such as deregulation, privatization, trade liberalization, dismantling of rigid controls and reversal of agricultural-sector terms of trade adversity can be represented as a gain in productivity, (Easterly 1989). This is achieved because these policies would directly lead to more efficient use of resources, growth in total factor productivity and increased earnings and per capita income. These are long-term gains and must be matched against the short-term (unemployment) shocks ($\phi L > 0$) that are imminent as the reform measures are administered.

To capture the aggregate labor market impact of such measures, and thereby determine measures for the absolute quantitative effects of reforms, we follow a methodology akin to Dornbusch's value-added approach and respecify the production function of total final output in terms of the potential amount of total final labor input.[13] In this formulation, we depict a model that places importance on the variety of intermediate products (similar to Romer 1989) and simulate from it the total amount of labor requirement, which gives the impact on employment.

For simplicity, we assume that all other inputs enter into production as intermediate goods and that it takes one unit of labor to produce a unit of intermediate good. The production function of final output can then be given by the Cobb-Douglas type:

$$Y^* = \psi L^\alpha \sum_1^N (Ti)1-\alpha, \quad i = 1,2 \ldots N \qquad (4.7)$$

where:

Y* = volume of total final output
T = quantity of each intermediate good
N = total number of intermediate goods

Assuming there are *s* intermediates, then the total amount of labor required for intermediates is:

$$LT = sT$$

Thus,

$$L^* = L - LT$$

is the amount of labor required for final goods production. The aggregate output of final goods (equation 4.7) can then be rewritten as:

$$Y^* = \psi(L{-}LT)^\alpha \left\{ \sum_1^N (Ti) \right\}^{1-\alpha}$$

whose time growth path can be written in the generalized Cobb-Douglas form:

$$Yt^* = \psi e^{\sigma t}(L_t{}^*)^\alpha \; N_t{}^{1-\alpha} \; T_t{}^{1-\alpha} \qquad (4.8)$$

where:

t = time
σ = rate of growth of technological progress

Under our simplifying assumptions, the aggregate production function simply reflects the total amount of labor utilization in the economy required for the production of both total intermediate and final goods. The growth rate of this function (equation 4.8) would be analogous to the growth rate of labor utilization, which amounts to the rate of expansion of employment (because the rate of the economy's labor utilization is taken as a close proxy for the rate of the economy's aggregate labor demand shifts).

If we depict the economy's total labor utilization as Lf, the growth rate of final output can be found as:

$$(\partial Y \partial t)/Y = \sigma + \alpha .(\partial Lf/\partial t)/L_f + (1-\alpha) . (\partial N/\partial t)/N + (1-\alpha) . (\partial T/\partial t)/T$$

from which we may then express the growth of total labor utilization as:

$$(\partial L_f/\partial t)/L_f = \frac{1}{\alpha} .[(\partial Y/\partial t)/Y - \sigma - (1-\alpha) . (\partial N/\partial t)/N - (1-\alpha) . (\partial T/\partial t)/T]$$

or

$$(\partial L_f/\partial t)/L_f = \frac{1}{\alpha} .[\{(\partial Y/\partial t)/(Y-\sigma)\} - (1-\alpha \frac{1}{\alpha} .[(\partial N/\partial t)/N + (\partial T\partial,t)/T\}]$$
$$(4.9)$$

Given that this result is derived from the Dornbusch-Romer-Easterly value-added approach that specifies the production function of total final output in terms of the potential amount of total final labor input) equation (4.9) aptly captures the aggregate labor market impact of restructuring (the measures for the absolute quantitative effects of reforms). This is because the reform policies would directly lead to more efficient use of resources, growth in total factor productivity, and increased earnings and per capita income.

Thus, equation (4.9) indicates that a number of factors impinge upon the employment effects of reforms. Among these, the most prominent are the productivity of labor ($\alpha = (\partial Y/\partial L)/(Y/L)$), the productivity of the other (cooperant) resources ($1-\alpha$), growth rate of technological progress (σ, an index of total factor productivity), the aggregate output (GDP) growth rate ($(\partial Y/\partial t)/Y$), and the degree or depth of the reforms (the combined effects of $(\partial N/\partial t)/N$ and $(\partial T/\partial t)/T$). While these inferences seem quite obvious, further deductions, particularly those relating to the size and variety of intermediate goods (sectors) and the sectoral quantity or magnitude of each intermediate variety, are quite intriguing.

For purposes of our inquiry, what these imply is that the employment impact of reforms would depend on both the intensity and extensiveness of the reform program. For example, a larger and more open market (achieved through, say, liberalization of the agricultural sector or free-trade reform) and expanded sectoral composition and production variety (achieved through, say, more extensive privatization and deregulation) would pave the way for increases in labor productivity, total factor productivity, and the GDP, all of which then combine to enhance employment expansion. As noted by Dornbusch (1993:45), a larger and more open market increases the aggregate output directly through its opening of the way for the production of a larger variety of specialized inputs (labor included).

The next section focuses on the policy guides that emanate from the foregoing framework. We draw from existing case experiences in ACs to examine the extent to which the outcomes and performances of economic liberalization and reform packages in ACs may or may not be vindicated by the predictions of this model. Based on the emerging findings, the labor market impacts of economic liberalization programs in ACs may then be viewed in their more correct and proper perspectives.[14]

POLICY ANALYSIS AND LESSONS FROM RECENT TRENDS

The World Bank's (1994a and 1994b) studies of the restructuring experience among twenty-nine ACs examined two major facets: the degree to which these countries' originally intended restructuring drives were actually carried out (intensity and extensiveness of reform) and the relative macroeconomic impacts over the two periods of reform, that is, 1981–86 and 1987–91. On the first aspect, the study concluded that only six of these ACs achieved relative successes.[15] On the second, the degree of success appears to have been limited during the second period (1987–91), when the commitments to the programs appear to have waned.

In their study of the rising unemployment problems in the transition economies of Eastern Europe, Blanchard, Commander, and Coricelli (1994) observed that in the process of economic restructuring, unemployment may be expected (initially) as the natural outcome of the process of massive resource reallocations that are involved. This is because the introduction of economic restructuring amounts to administering macroeconomic shocks upon the economy. Job losses through layoffs, attrition, early retirements, and job sharing are the necessary results of the processes of privatization of state enterprises, deregulation of public utilities, and removal of state subsidies and tariff protections.

In Africa, the short-run unemployment fallouts from restructuring have been far more devastating than in Eastern Europe. The data in Table 4.3 reveal that the European transition economies did experience rising unemployment rates following the onset of reforms, although their rates are much lower than those of the ACs. Looking at these comparative numbers, one may fear that the sheer size of the immediate employment shocks of restructuring would be apt to discourage African governments from total commitment to reforms.

Table 4.3
Short-Run Unemployment Shocks in Restructuring Economies (%)

	1988	1989	1990	1991	1992	1993	1994
Eastern Europe[1]							
Bulgaria			1.6	11.9	14.0	15.5	16.1
Czech Republic			0.7	4.2	2.6	3.2	3.7
Hungary			1.5	7.8	14.1	13.7	12.5
Poland			6.1	11.5	15.5	15.0	16.0
Romania			—	3.0	8.3	9.5	10.1
Russia			—	—	1.1	1.4	2.1
Slovak Republic			1.5	6.6	11.4	14.4	15.7
African Countries[2]							
Burkina Faso	21.0	23.5	26.0	18.8	19.0	19.5	19.2
Gambia	27.5	32.0	29.8	28.4	29.5	29.1	29.3
Ghana	24.8	25.2	24.0	22.1	20.9	17.0	17.0
Nigeria	32.6	36.2	30.5	26.8	29.0	29.5	27.0
Tanzania	26.2	25.5	25.0	28.2	28.0	26.5	26.7
Zambia	22.0	22.4	22.5	23.5	24.0	24.5	24.2

Sources: 1. Blanchard, Commander, and Coricelli (1994); 2. Field research data and African
Development Bank.

Table 4.3 clearly indicates that the restructuring program that is
necessary to fully liberalize the economy would, indeed, exacerbate the
unemployment situation in the short run. This is the unemployment-
drag effect represented by $\phi L > 0$ and modeled in equation (4.6). Beyond
this, however, it is believed that more extensive liberalization would
result in lower unemployment in the long run, presumably, as the
agricultural sector recovers.

Despite the negative short-run employment effects, the overall economic impacts of reforms in ACs seem to have been mildly positive,
although the reforms lack sustainability, as a recent study by Lall (1995)
indicates. Jones and Kiguel (1994) state that those ACs which instituted
the most far-reaching macroeconomic reforms during the period 1986–
91 generally appear to have achieved some concrete payoffs, albeit a
rather moderate one, in the form of per capita GDP increases of about
2 percentage points, in addition to growths in exports and industrial

expansion. Those that did not seriously undertake reforms suffered GDP growth declines of about 2.6 percent.

As already noted, in most cases, reforms and adjustments have meant the onset of strict austerity measures that always translate into protracted stagnation, at least in the short run. The immediate socio political repercussions of such conditions have often limited the abilities of most ACs to implement the reform packages to the fullest. Thus, structural adjustment programs in ACs have faltered.

Clearly, most ACs have not implemented the liberalization programs to the extent at which their full labor market impact would materialize. In such circumstances, the expected long-run, positive employment effects, according to the predictions of our theoretical model, would be limited. Therefore, it is necessary that there be consistency in the implementation of the complete package of the restructuring. In this regard, particular stress must be placed on the degree of macroeconomic intensity and extensiveness of liberalization mentioned earlier. These involve wider openness of the market through free trade and greater liberalization of the agricultural sector, and expansion of sectoral composition and production variety through more extensive deregulation and privatization. It is through the greater labor and total factor productivities that these would yield that expanded employment and GDP would result.

In ACs, there is no question that these potentials are latent. As existing evidence shows, agriculture, particularly, has responded the most to reforms. According to the Jones and Kiguel (1994) study, total agricultural value-added in African countries that implemented tax cuts on their major export crops jumped by about 2 percentage points. Countries that failed to sufficiently review "tax penalties" on their farmers experienced about 1.6 percentage point declines in their agricultural output.

Particular restructuring initiatives impinging upon the labor market in Africa are worthy of special analysis. The region's labor supply is dominated by rural-urban migrants from smallholder agriculture and school-leavers. The former automatically benefit from any reforms that put an end to forcing them to sell their farm produce at low official prices. The latter benefit from privatization and deregulation that allows for small-scale enterprise development through expansion of self-employment opportunities coupled with greater demand in the informal sector.

Further employment impacts of reforms become imminent as devaluation enables local food producers to become more competitive against previously artificially cheap imports. Presumably devaluation should also benefit export producers, as it makes them more competitive.[16] Dismantling price controls on food prices and removing food subsidies act as incentives for rural farmers to raise food production and earn higher incomes. In Zambia, though, the World Bank (1994b) study found that this has not been the result. This appears to be because private monopsonistic middlemen continued to buy at very low prices after removal of controls. However, it is envisaged in this Zambian case that as the market becomes more liberalized, more buyers will enter and draw producer prices upward.

As for overall employment creation, restructuring can involve labor-intensive public works in infrastructural development. This may be complemented by other income-generating activities that could absorb laid-off public- sector workers and unemployed graduates through re-training schemes, counseling and guidance, and credit and small-scale entrepreneurial promotions. The advantages are manifold: creation of unskilled jobs and of a network of labor-intensive, small-scale enter-prises capable of being the agents for ultimate maintenance and reha-bilitation of public infrastructure in the future (see Mwase 1993).

In certain ACs, some attempts have been made to address the (short-run) inevitable unemployment effects (such as those highlighted by Blanchard et al. 1994) that go with restructuring. Marc, Graham, and Schacter (1994) carried out a study to evaluate the so-called safety nets designed to control the deterioration in the living standards due to liberalization. These include the social action programs (SAPs) and social funds (SFs) to protect the poor and other vulnerable groups.[17]

In Africa, the SFs and SAPs have been operational in Burundi, Cameroon, Chad, Ethiopia, Ghana, Guinea-Bissau, Madagascar, Senegal, Uganda, and Zambia. Marc et al. found that the employment cushioning effects of these programs have been limited in these ACs due to a combination of structural and technical factors, some of which include the policy errors that necessitated the reforms in the first place. For example, most of the SFs and SAPs have been urban based, with the usual excuses that the rural sectors are too remote, involving supervision difficulties and lack the microenterprises (such as adequate infrastructural facilities) capable of carrying out the works. However, Marc et al. cite some success cases as well. In the case of Senegal, for example, they provide a very interesting account of a model involving local government, communities, and small-scale contractors and arti-sans. These were involved in a public works and employment project that created 11,103 employment positions with an average duration of one month each. While the program had low management costs, it involved many small-scale construction companies, which were the ones that were usually excluded from benefiting from standard implementa-tion of public works. This represents a clear indication that a seriously designed and executed program of reforms and liberalization package can be used to attain the desired objectives in ACs, if only the human factor aspect of policy implementation is met.

CONCLUSIONS

Although the principal focus of this study is the labor market, one major strand of argument that has consistently featured itself has pointed to the need for greater commitment toward more economic reform and liberalization in the drive for containment of poverty and lack of economic growth in ACs. Upon greater reflection, it becomes clear that this would involve not only the need to implement more reforms and liberalization per se, but also the need for pursuing reforms quite differently. By differently is meant extending reforms and liberalization to include both social and political liberalization. This would have pervasive impacts across all sectors of the economy, including the labor market.

Such reforms include land reform that liberalizes land ownership; provision and maintenance of social overhead capital (infrastructure such as access roads, clean water sources, health-care facilities, and post and telecommunication facilities); promotion of political stability; accountability and dedicated political leadership; and the like.

It is reported that land reform in Ethiopia resulted in returning vastly inefficient, state-held farmlands to peasant farmers who converted them to more productive agricultural holdings, with noticeable effects in employment and income.[18] But at the same time, these positive effects are hampered by poor surrounding conditions: as lack of good access roads prevents about 80 percent of Ethiopian farmers from delivering and selling their produce to urban dwellers, higher crop prices scarcely have the desired effects on employment and incomes.

Reforms of educational and health systems are crucial. There is the need to shift any necessary public expenditures away from military spending and the running of massive government bureaucracies to the building and maintenance of health facilities (rural health clinics, hospitals, medicinal drugs, and paramedical equipment) and educational development. Education should be reoriented away from its current misplacement of curricula in ACs onto an optimal trajectory of its purported economic, cultural, and pedagogic (ECP) sequential agenda.[19]

Employment generation through restructuring is often promoted by foreign entrepreneurs and firms that may be attracted by Africa's cheap labor. This calls for maintenance of well-functioning legal and financial institutions. In many ACs, the rule of law must be more strictly adhered to, especially by the political rulers. Entrenched military and quasi-military dictatorships that exist across the region must be disengaged to ensure a proper socioeconomic and political climate conducive to attracting foreign investors.

ACs must seek measures designed to revamp intraregional trade. World Bank data indicate that intraregional trade accounts for only about 5 percent of all international trade among all ACs. Most international trade still goes along former colonial trade routes and links, mainly to Europe. Trade liberalization is not apt to truly materialize along the one-way "exploitative" arrangement of trading raw materials at give-away prices for expensive manufactured goods with the industrialized countries. Reform toward greater intra-African trade in manufactured goods, agricultural food, and raw materials, as well as services, all at their real values, will be mutually beneficial to ACs.

The role of the international agencies, especially the World Bank and the IMF, and to a significant extent the Organization for Economic Co-operation and Development countries in influencing the success or failure of reform and liberalization in Africa cannot be overlooked. In this connection, these agents ought to show greater goodwill to ACs by way of less stringent requirements of debt servicing and devaluations. Uganda, for example, which has been noted as genuinely committed to liberalization, is handicapped by being obliged to devote over 50 percent of its total annual export earnings to servicing its foreign debt. Nigeria, another committed reformer, devotes about 35 percent of its total annual foreign exchange earnings for debt servicing. About half of Africa's external debt is owed to (rich) OECD governments (which can choose to write it off if the will exists).

Economic liberalization in Africa will not result in greater employment or income in the region unless it is supported by the external economic agents in OECD countries and, particularly, the international financial institutions, including the IMF and World Bank—or at least not jeopardized, by the quasi-hostile, stringent conditions imposed on it by these external agents. These institutions should be more troubled by the fact that since the ACs adopted the liberalization reforms sponsored by them, their economic records have not met the expectations envisaged.

On its own, the failure of ACs to pursue the adopted reform packages fully can hardly sufficiently explain the woeful economic outcomes of these programs so far. Rather, we must look more closely at some external factors, notably, the methods of implementing the reforms, as well as the conditionalities dictated and imposed by the external financial and governmental institutions. In their case study of Guinea, Campbell and Clapp (1995) noted that such inhospitable external conditions have been largely responsible for the weak contributions of the agricultural and mining sectors' reforms to the wider economy. This, in turn, acted to slow down the government's implementation of further reforms, which then caused the international financial and governmental institutions to restrict funding and support to drive further liberalization and reforms.

One might presume that the inadequate implementation of the reform packages in ACs could only have acted to slow down the overall rate of economic growth rather than causing overall declines in growth.

The economic decline that has widely taken place must be attributed to the observed restriction of funding and support by the international agencies, as noted by Campbell and Clapp. Therefore, the World Bank and IMF, as well as the governments and other lending agencies in the OECD countries, must change their attitudes and adopt a more supportive and accommodating posture toward ACs in the bid to sustain liberalization reforms and await their long-term labor market and overall economic benefits.

NOTES

1. These reforms are generally labeled as structural adjustment programs (SAPs) by the World Bank and IMF. This often refers to the package of measures designed to direct an economy away from central planning and control and toward a well-functioning free-market system based on competition, liberalization, deregulation, and an enhanced private sector. For the list of the African countries that adopted SAPs, see Hodd (1992); for some case-analytic studies of SAPs in ACs, see Ezeala-Harrison (1993) for Nigeria and Campbell and Clapp (1995) for Guinea.

2. The role of government lies in ensuring that the direction of the reform points toward meaningful growth by, among other things, promoting workplace standards, income security, union-management harmony, and general (macroeconomic) monetary and fiscal policies which are conducive for the reform program. It is in such an economic environment that productivity growth will be achieved, resulting in higher incomes and expanded employment.

3. For some of the most recent studies on this, see Ezeala-Harrison (1995d), Ezeala-Harrison and Adjibolosoo (1994), DeLancey (1992), and Pickett (1990).

4. Among the most recent of these studies are the works of the World Bank (1994a, 1994b), Jones and Kiguel (1994), Campbell and Clapp (1995), Ezeala-Harrison (1993), Husain (1994), and Hodd (1992). See also a special contribution by Budhoo (1990). These have been preceded by Adedeji (1989) and World Bank and United Nations Development Programme (1989), which represent the earliest attempts to offer an assessment of the reform efforts in Africa, in the light of the international debt crisis.

5. It is argued that whereas the external factors are the short-run development constraints, the internal "bads" represent long-run constraints that would negate any development prospects even when the short-term external factors are largely overcome. Related to this, and specifically on the issue of political and organizational leadership (among sub-Saharan African nations) in economic development, recent research has focused on the topic of the human factor deficiency in Africa. For more on this, see Ezeala-Harrison and Adjibolosoo (1994) and Ezeala-Harrison (1995c).

6. The vast majority of ACs' agricultural dependents are self-employed, family-farming units of the subsistence type. The sector provides means of livelihood for about 65 percent to 70 percent of the labor force and over 70 percent of the population, although self-employment in non-agricultural sectors is also very prominent. A structural model that addresses employment and labor

productivity in Africa's agricultural occupation is found in Ezeala-Harrison (1994).

7. Agricultural development was seen rather as a complement to industrialization and, thus, was not given much attention beyond mere lip-service pronouncements, nor was it emphasized in most development plans.

8. In this case, the familiar arguments against the policy of establishing and operating import-substituting industries come to mind (an exhaustive account of this can be found in Ezeala-Harrison 1996).

9. The parameter ψ, representing a shift parameter in the production function, is an index of technology and a measure of the total factor productivity in the economy. As the state of knowledge and institutional settings, ψ could be seen as encompassing technological know-how, the state of socioeconomic and political institutions, and, most important, the state of human factor parameters (as alluded to in note 5). As the index of total factor productivity, it is a measure of the economy's state of global competitiveness with the rest of the world (see Ezeala-Harrison 1995b).

10. Note that the factor shares of the respective inputs are defined by the ratios of their marginal productivities to average productivities:

$$\alpha = [\partial Y / \partial L] / [Y / L], \ \beta = [\partial Y / \partial K] / [Y / K], \ \gamma = [\partial Y / \partial R] / [Y / R]$$

11. We must realize that these efficiency and utilization indexes do not apply solely to labor; they are common to all inputs and, as such, the production function can be written as:

$$Y = \psi . Y(\mu L \xi L \phi L L, \ \mu K \xi K \phi K K, \ \mu R \xi R \phi R R)$$

which, upon assumption of linear homogeneity, becomes:

$$Y = \psi . \mu L \xi L \phi L L . \ \mu K \xi K \ \phi K K . \ \mu R \xi R \phi R . Y(L, K, R).$$

See Dornbusch (1993).

12. The ultimate and targeted labor market objective of the economic restructuring and liberalization program is to have $\mu L = 1$ (maximum employment impact), $\xi L = 1$ (maximum productivity impact), and $\phi L = 0$ (minimum unemployment impact). Thus, the closer μL and ξL are to 1 and ϕL is to 0, the more successful the program would be in the labor market.

13. Dornbusch's (1993) approach is addressed to the analysis of the effects of improved resource allocation on growth, brought about through trade liberalization or deregulation. In a similar study cited by Dornbusch, Romer (1989) placed emphasis on the size of the market in sustaining the profitable production of specialized intermediate goods. We adapt Dornbusch's model here and use it to analyze the total employment impact of restructuring.

14. Time series data could be employed toward an empirical analysis that computes the trend values of $(\partial Lf/\partial t)/Lf$, using equation (4.9), which would then indicate the labor market impact of the program over the appropriate periods. This methodology, however, is not followed here, as it lengthens the study beyond the scope envisaged.

15. The six ACs which were able to implement fundamental restructuring were Burkina Faso, Gambia, Ghana, Nigeria, Tanzania, and Zambia. The study found that as a result, on average, there were improvements in industrial

output, exports, savings, and earned income per capita among the six countries. The employment picture among these countries was not indicated.

16. These points about the benefits of devaluation are, however, valid only if the export and import goods are manufactured products (having elastic demand in both foreign and domestic markets, respectively). The exports of ACs are mainly agricultural primary products (having inelastic demand in export markets), while their imports are mainly manufactured consumer goods and capital equipment (having relative inelastic demand in the domestic market). Due mainly to this situation, the case for devaluation is highly flawed for most ACs. It may be argued, however, that devaluation provides a means of enabling the economy to avoid distorted production incentives (presumably in favor of the domestic agricultural sector). But this argument overlooks the fact that the greater proportion of ACs' domestic (agricultural) output ends up in foreign markets. Indeed, the inclusion of devaluation within the restructuring package (along with the insistence of the World Bank and the IMF to that effect) appears to have been one of the major reasons why the reforms have failed to yield economic growth in ACs.

17. Social funds are designed to fund local organizations (public or private) to operate in a more flexible and transparent manner than regular government ministries. They are demand-driven and respond to funding requests from local agencies. Social action programs are designed as regular investment projects. For detailed functional and operational mechanisms of these agencies and other "safety nets," see Graham (1994).

18. *The Economist*, March 5, 1994, p. 22.

19. On the analysis of an optimal trajectory of education's ECP agenda in Africa, see Ezeala-Harrison (1995a). The impetus to that study was provided by Serpell's (1993) worthwhile Zambian case study which utilized a grassroots approach toward the analysis and better understanding of the structure and functioning of educational systems in an African society.

REFERENCES

Adedeji, A. 1989. *African Alternative Framework to Structural Adjustment Programmes for Socio-Economic Recovery and Transformation.* New York: U.N. Economic Commission for Africa.

Adjibolosoo, S. 1994. The human factor and the failure of economic development and policies in Africa. In *Perspectives on Economic Development in Africa*, edited by F. Ezeala-Harrison and S. Adjibolosoo. Westport, CT: Praeger.

Blanchard, O. J., S. Commander, and F. Coricelli. 1994. Unemployment in Eastern Europe. *Finance and Development* 31(4):6–9.

Budhoo, D. L. 1990. *Enough Is Enough: Open Resignation Letter to IMF.* New York: The Apex Press.

Campbell, B., and J. Clapp. 1995. Guinea's economic performance under structural adjustment: Importance of mining and agriculture. *Journal of Modern African Studies* 33(3):425–49.

DeLancey, V. 1992. The economies of Africa. In *Understanding Contemporary Africa*, edited by A. A. Gordon and D. L. Gordon. Boulder and London: Lynne Rienner Publishers.

Dornbusch, R. 1993. *Stabilization, Debt, and Reform: Policy Analysis for Developing Countries*. Englewood, NJ: Prentice-Hall.

Easterly, W. 1989. *Policy Distortions, Size of Government and Growth*. NBER Working Paper 3214. Cambridge, MA: National Bureau of Economic Research.

Ezeala-Harrison, F. 1993. Structural re-adjustment in Nigeria: Diagnosis of a severe Dutch disease syndrome. *American Journal of Economics and Sociology* 52(2):193–208.

———. 1994. African subsistence labour allocation: A model with implications for rural development and urban unemployment. In *Perspectives on Economic Development in Africa*, edited by F. Ezeala-Harrison and S. Adjibolosoo. Westport, CT: Praeger.

———. 1995a. Africa's diploma disease: Diagnosis of the non-sequential agenda of education. Paper presented at the conference of the Canadian Association for the Study of International Development, Montreal, June.

———. 1995b. Canada's global competitiveness challenge: Trade performance versus total factor productivity measures. *American Journal of Economics and Sociology* 54(1):57–78.

———. 1995c. Human factor issues in the history of economic underdevelopment. *The Review of Human Factor Studies* 1(1):1–25.

———. 1995d. Over-stretched economic underdevelopment in sub-Saharan Africa. *Briefing Notes in Economics* 14, January.

———. 1996. *Economic Development: Theory and Policy Applications*. Westport, CT: Praeger.

Ezeala-Harrison, F., and S. Adjibolosoo. 1994. *Perspectives on Economic Development in Africa*. Westport, CT: Praeger.

Ghanem, H., and M. Walton. 1995. Workers need open markets and active governments. *Finance and Development* 32(3):3–6.

Graham, C. 1994. *Safety Nets, Politics, and the Poor: Transitions to Market Economies*. Washington, DC: The Brookings Institution.

Hodd, M. 1992. *The Economies of Africa*. London: G. K. Hall and Co.

Husain, I. 1994. Results of adjustment in Africa: Selected cases. *Finance and Development* 31(2):7–12.

Jones, C. and M. A. Kiguel. 1994. Africa's quest for prosperity: Has adjustment helped? *Finance and Development* 31(2):2–5.

Khan, M. H., and M. S. Khan. 1995. *Agricultural Growth in Sub-Saharan African Countries and China*. IMF Papers of Policy Analysis and Assessment 95/7. Washington, DC: International Monetary Fund.

Lall, S. 1995. Structural adjustment and African industry. *World Development* 23(12):2019–31.

Marc, A., C. Graham, and M. Schacter. 1994. *Economic Reforms and the Poor: Social Action Programs and Social Funds in Sub-Saharan Africa*. Findings 12. Washington, DC: World Bank Africa Technical Department.

Mwase, N. 1993. The liberalization and deregulation of the transport sector in sub-Saharan Africa. *African Development Review* 5(2):74–86.

Pickett, J. 1990. *The Low-Income Economies of Sub-Saharan Africa: Problems and Prospects*. Research Paper 12. Abidjan, Ivory Coast: African Development Bank.

Romer, P. 1989. Capital accumulation in the theory of long run growth. In *Modern Business Cycle Theory*, edited by R. Barro. Cambridge, MA: Harvard University Press.

Schadler, S. 1996. How successful are IMF-supported adjustment programs? *Finance and Development* 33(2):14–17.

Serpell, R. 1993. *The Significance of Schooling: Life Journeys in an African Society*. New York: Cambridge University Press.

World Bank. 1994a. *Adjustment in Africa: Lessons from Country Case Studies*. Washington, DC: World Bank.

———. 1994b. *Adjustment in Africa: Reforms, Results, and the Road Ahead*. Washington, DC: World Bank.

World Bank and United Nations Development Programme. 1989. *Africa's Adjustment and Growth in the 1980s*. Washington, DC: World Bank.

5

International Trade and Employment in Greece in the Course of European Integration

Alexander Sarris

Greece formally joined the European Economic Community (EEC; herein the acronyms EC for European Community and EU for European Union will also be used interchangeably) in January 1981. Before that, Greece's trade was conditioned by an association agreement with the EC since 1961. As one would expect, given the small size of Greece relative to that of the EC, accession has had a major influence on trade patterns, the structure of production, and international trade. The purpose of this paper is to study the adjustment of the Greek economy to the changing trade regimes and, particularly, to investigate the resulting changes in the labor market.

Integration of a country with the EC can lead to structural adjustment, defined as the process by which factors of production shift from sectors or branches with stagnant or declining demand to those of better prospects. The trading environment is particularly affected by integration, and hence, changes in the trade structure can have strong implications for both production and employment.

Despite the importance of international trade for Greece, there have been very few studies of industrial and overall trade. Sarris (1988) analyzed the developments of trade and protection in Greece from 1960 to 1980 and showed that, while tariff protection had significantly declined, nontariff protection in the form of other border and internal taxes had not. He also showed that export propensity for several industries had significantly increased, aided by export subsidy policies that were in force before the EC accession. Import penetration, however, had also increased, particularly in sectors that traditionally were export sectors.

Katseli (1990) analyzed the trade patterns and the structure of the Greek economy. She showed that the Greek pattern of trade resembles more that of less developed countries than of developed ones and that protection had declined after accession for the traditional import-competing sectors while it had not for the modern ones. Giannitsis (1988) showed that trade competitiveness had declined in almost all traditional industrial sectors after accession, but had increased slightly in modern sectors and in sectors where protection had increased. Other relevant studies of Greek industrial trade include those of Katsos and Spanakis (1983), Alexakis and Xanthakis (1992), and Mardas (1992). This latter group of studies focused on the intra-industry trade of Greece at the aggregate level. On the other hand, Droucopoulos and Thomadakis (1994) analyze trade at the firm level. They show a rather low level of globalization of Greek enterprises, concentrating mainly in large firms (i.e., those employing over fifty persons). After 1983, however, there are some signs of globalization of small- and medium-scale enterprises, as export growth of these firms is higher than that of larger ones.

The most recent empirical analyses of Greek trade are those of Tsounis (1992) and Sarris, Papadimitriou, and Mavrogiannis (1997). Tsounis explored the structure of protection in the period 1970–80 and the pattern of trade of Greece and the EC in the period 1976–87. He found that the pattern of comparative advantage, as measured by various ex-post measures, was stable in the period 1976–87. He also found that Greek trade with the EC can be adequately explained by relative factor endowments and that Greece exports to the EC products that are relatively labor intensive and imports ones that are relatively capital intensive. Additionally, he found that the overall pattern of protection in Greece declined in the 1970–80 period. His analysis of ex-post effects of EC integration reveals considerable net trade creation (of the order of 4.4 percent of gross domestic product, or GDP), most of which is internal trade creation.

Sarris, Papadimitriou, and Mavrogiannis (1997) explore the intra-industry trade (IIT) of Greece. They show that IIT accounts for a very small portion of Greece's total trade and, hence, that the pattern of trade is explained mostly by the factor content version of international trade, a result consistent with the analysis of Tsounis. They also show that the pattern of IIT in the post accession period has tended to favor lower-quality products, while horizontally differentiated products are a small share of total trade.

Concerning the relation of trade and the Greek labor market, there is a dearth of studies. Katseli (1990) explored the rigidities of the Greek labor market as part of an overall evaluation of rigidities of the Greek economy and showed that these were substantial. The only studies that tackle the issue of labor market rigidities directly are the ones by Glytsos (1994) and Sarris, Papadimitriou, and Mavrogiannis (1997). Glytsos found that there is extensive wage rigidity in Greek manufacturing and, consequently, adjustment takes the form of unemployment. Sarris et al.

find that trade has had a moderate impact on the evolution of industrial employment, with domestic demand factors accounting for the main part of the changes.

In this chapter, we discuss the trends and patterns of Greece's trade and production structure in the post–EC accession period. We then analyze the structure and evolution of the Greek labor market, and explore the pattern of industrial adjustment in the period 1978-87. Following that discussion, we study the relationship between changes in industrial employment and a series of factors including trade. Finally, we summarize our conclusions.

EVOLUTION OF GREEK TRADE, ECONOMIC STRUCTURE, AND PROTECTION

There are three phases that one can distinguish in the process of Greek integration with the EC (Katseli 1990). The first covers the period of the association agreement until accession (1962–80). This period is characterized by rapid growth and gradual elimination of tariff barriers, coupled with active use of domestic policy instruments for the selective protection of industrial activity. The second phase covers the immediate postentry period (1981–86) and is characterized by slow growth, faster dismantling of existing trade barriers, and a simultaneous series of measures aimed at restructuring industrial activity, but also at prolonging protection afforded to selected sectors. The third phase started in 1987 and is characterized by repeated macro-stabilization programs and slow growth, in view of large internal imbalances, elimination of all remaining protection and export-subsidy measures, and liberalization of the domestic financial system, the international capital account, international transactions in services, and public procurement. Many of these liberalization measures were taken in accordance with the schedule for the completion of the Single Market by the EC. The period 1960–96 has witnessed a substantial opening of the Greek economy. The share of exports of goods and services in GDP increased continuously from 5.8 percent in 1960 to 14.2 percent in 1990 and 16.5 percent in 1995. Over the same period, the share of imports of goods and services in GDP increased from 14.6 percent to a peak of 35.7 percent in 1985 and then retreated to 27.4 percent in 1990 and 26.9 percent in 1995. This retreat is to a large extent due to the stabilization programs that, in one way or another, have been in effect since 1986. Over the same period, the deficit in the merchandise trade has grown from about 9–12 percent of GDP in the preaccession period to 13–20 percent in the period after 1980.

The merchandise deficit in Greece is counterbalanced by substantial surpluses in the services and capital accounts. In fact, exports of services are about twice as large as merchandise exports, while imports of services are only about 20–25 percent of merchandise imports.

Table 5.1 indicates the structure of Greek merchandise trade over the period 1960–90 by major Standard International Trade Classification (SITC) sections. It is clear that there have been substantial and rapid structural changes in both Greek exports and imports over this period. In the early 1960s, more than 90 percent of Greek exports consisted of products in SITC categories 0, 1, and 2 (food and live animals, beverages and tobacco and inedible crude materials except fuels, respectively). Only 8.2 percent of exports were in manufacturing (SITC categories 5–8). On the eve of EC accession, this picture had drastically changed. In 1977, the share of manufactures in total exports was about 55 percent, while the share of SITC 0–2 products had dropped to 40 percent. By 1990, ten years after accession, the share of manufactures in total exports increased to 61.8 percent, while the share of SITC 0–2 products had declined to about 27 percent.

Within manufactures, however, certain "low-technology" sectors occupy disproportionately large shares. For instance, articles of apparel and clothing (SITC 84) accounted in 1990 for 89 percent of total exports of SITC section 8, or 19.8 percent of total merchandise exports. Textiles, nonmetallic mineral manufactures, iron and steel manufactures, and nonferrous metal manufactures (SITC 65–68) accounted for 85 percent of trade in SITC section 6, or 20 percent of all merchandise exports. Among them, these five sectors accounted for 74 percent of all manufactured exports.

In 1961, 74 percent of imports consisted of manufactures. This share slightly dropped in 1977 to 69 percent and has increased slightly after accession and reached 70.2 percent by 1990.

Table 5.2 exhibits the share of Greek trade with the other eleven member countries of the European Community before the most recent enlargement with Sweden, Finland, and Austria (to be referred to as EC12). The observed changes over time are much less dramatic than the changes in the overall pattern of Greek trade. The other eleven countries of EC12 had been the destination of 40–54 percent of Greek exports and the source of 45–56 percent of Greek imports before accession, with no marked trend pattern of change. After accession, the share of Greek exports going to EC12 seems to have risen as has the share of Greek imports coming from EC12. The pattern in manufacturing has not been much different from the pattern in overall trade. With the collapse of the communist regimes in Eastern Europe and the opening of these markets to western imports, Greek exports have penetrated considerably in these markets, and the share of total exports (which, in turn, have expanded considerably) that goes to EC12 seems to have gone down by a few percentage points.

Table 5.3 exhibits a comparison of the structure of production and importance of trade in the Greek economy between the years 1980 and 1988. The year 1980 was, of course, the last year before EC accession,

Table 5.1
Structure of Greek Merchandise Trade—Shares of Exports and Imports in Different SITC Categories (percent)

SITC	1961	1967	1972	1977	1985	1990
			A. Exports			
0	24.8	28.5	24.9	25.2	21.3	17.2
1	49.6	39.3	16.0	6.9	4.6	4.7
2	17.3	12.1	14.1	8.0	7.4	4.8
3	0.0	0.7	1.3	4.8	12.0	6.2
4	0.1	3.3	1.5	0.4	2.1	3.6
5	2.6	2.3	7.4	5.8	4.0	18.5
6	3.9	11.4	26.4	31.7	28.8	19.9
7	0.9	0.8	2.3	5.3	2.9	3.6
8	0.8	1.7	6.2	11.8	16.6	19.8
9	0.0	0.0	0.0	0.0	0.2	1.8
Total 0–9	100.0	100.0	100.0	100.0	100.0	100.0
Value of Exports*	340.6	717.5	871.0	2,724.0	4,536.6	9,486.7
			B. Imports			
0	3.9	16.4	10.0	7.7	11.5	13.7
1	0.1	0.1	0.2	0.2	0.8	1.8
2	9.7	9.4	8.7	7.1	5.7	5.4
3	11.7	11.3	9.9	15.2	29.6	8.3
4	1.0	0.2	0.1	0.2	0.2	0.4
5	8.8	9.2	9.8	8.0	8.6	3.5
6	20.5	17.9	17.1	12.9	15.9	23.3
7	41.4	31.8	41.0	45.6	23.7	33.5
8	2.9	3.6	3.2	2.9	4.0	9.9
9	0.0	0.1	0.0	0.1	0.1	0.1
Total 0–9	100.0	100.0	100.0	100.0	100.0	100.0
Value of Imports*	706.8	1,351.2	2,346.4	6,778.2	10,138.9	18,266.1

Source: Computed from OECD data.

* Million current US$.
Legend for SITC sections:
0—food, live animals; 1—drinks, tobacco; 2—raw materials; 3—mineral fuels; 4—animal/vegetable oils; 5—chemicals; 6—manufacturing, classified by material; 7—machinery, transport equipment; 8—misc. manufacturing; 9—commodities not elsewhere classified (N.E.S.).

Table 5.2
Structure of Greek Merchandise Trade—Shares of Exports to and Imports from EC12 in Different SITC Categories (percentages)

SITC	1961	1967	1972	1977	1985	1990
			A. Exports			
0	59.8	59.7	59.4	53.5	64.1	72.7
1	32.9	35.0	43.1	28.5	38.8	49.2
2	40.5	34.9	46.4	42.7	44.9	56.1
3	8.3	29.9	28.1	41.0	47.1	39.6
4	10.2	89.3	87.7	24.4	57.6	80.0
5	31.9	39.8	47.7	47.0	28.8	7.1
6	30.1	56.4	63.9	49.3	48.1	63.2
7	47.6	34.1	52.1	14.6	37.9	53.7
8	13.0	43.5	43.9	71.2	74.3	70.7
9	0.0	0.0	0.0	30.8	65.5	70.3
Total 0–9	40.7	46.5	54.2	48.5	54.2	53.9
Total 5–8	31.1	51.6	57.5	50.5	54.3	64.0
			B. Imports			
0	67.8	26.3	34.9	27.7	79.6	77.3
1	84.1	87.1	76.9	83.1	88.8	87.7
2	29.5	23.2	22.3	21.7	24.0	26.0
3	7.1	10.5	21.4	8.1	2.8	8.2
4	31.6	25.2	58.4	83.7	93.3	83.8
5	71.2	75.1	74.8	78.5	79.9	29.7
6	66.2	65.6	66.2	61.9	73.6	69.7
7	59.6	74.1	66.5	50.9	60.9	66.3
8	66.3	66.8	67.4	66.6	72.7	73.1
9	0.0	20.1	92.0	83.3	68.0	26.6
Total 0–9	53.1	52.4	55.9	44.8	48.2	61.4
Total 5–8	63.1	71.4	67.6	56.8	68.8	69.9

Source: OECD trade data.

Table 5.3
Structure of Production and Trade Performance of the Greek Economy, 1980 and 1988

Sector	Share in GDP	Share in Exports	Share in Imports	Export Propensity	Import Penetration	Average Rate of Import Taxation
				1980		
Agriculture, forestry, fishing	13.7	4.7	4.6	4.7	5.6	12.4
Mining, energy, electricity, water	3.6	7.0	22.7	8.1	32.6	0.4
Manufacturing of food, drinks, tobacco	2.9	11.3	6.8	11.9	9.4	18.3
Manufacturing of other consumer goods	6.7	16.6	5.8	17.5	8.5	20.4
Manufacturing of intermediate goods	5.3	14.0	19.3	16.0	30.1	15.2
Manufacturing of capital goods	3.1	2.5	37.7	3.1	56.4	9.1
Construction	11.5	2.0	0.0	1.9	0.0	0.0
Transport, communications	8.9	22.7	1.8	31.6	4.3	0.0
Trade	13.6	9.1	0.0	9.6	0.0	0.0
Housing services	8.1	0.0	0.0	0.0	0.0	0.0
Health services	1.0	0.0	0.1	0.0	0.9	0.0
Education services	2.3	0.0	0.0	0.0	0.2	0.0
Recreation and tourist services	1.4	5.5	0.8	22.9	4.7	0.0
Other market services	8.1	3.9	0.4	8.1	0.9	0.2
Public services	9.7	0.7	0.0	1.3	0.1	0.0
Total	100.0	100.0	100.0	9.9	12.6	9.5

Table 5.3 continued

Sector	Share in GDP	Share in Exports	Share in Imports	Export Propensity	Import Penetration	Average Rate of Import Taxation
			1988			
Agriculture, forestry, fishing	12.5	6.2	4.5	6.0	6.7	5.7
Mining, energy, electricity, water	3.5	9.0	12.2	13.8	32.0	0.1
Manufacturing of food, drinks, tobacco	3.0	12.9	12.0	10.7	16.5	4.3
Manufacturing of other consumer goods	6.7	23.7	13.8	17.2	17.9	4.2
Manufacturing of intermediate goods	4.6	16.3	23.5	12.9	31.7	3.0
Manufacturing of capital goods	1.6	4.1	25.9	5.5	55.0	3.9
Construction	7.9	0.0	0.0	0.0	0.0	0.0
Transport, communications	6.7	12.4	1.9	24.1	7.3	0.0
Trade	15.3	0.3	0.5	0.2	0.6	0.6
Housing services	11.9	0.0	0.0	0.0	0.0	0.0
Health services	4.3	0.1	0.0	0.3	0.0	0.0
Education services	4.4	0.0	0.0	0.0	0.1	1.9
Recreation and tourist services	4.7	13.2	4.6	24.7	17.0	0.0
Other market services	5.2	1.4	1.0	2.6	2.7	0.0
Public services	7.6	0.2	0.0	0.4	0.0	0.0
Total	100.0	100.0	100.0	8.5	13.7	3.1

Sector	Share in GDP	Share in Exports	Share in Imports	Export Propensity	Import Penetration	Average Rate of Import Taxation
			Differences in Above Shares between 1980 and 1988			
Agriculture, forestry, fishing	-1.2	1.5	-0.2	1.2	1.1	-6.7
Mining, energy, electricity, water	-0.1	2.0	-10.5	5.7	-0.6	-0.3
Manufacturing of food, drinks, tobacco	0.1	1.7	5.2	-1.2	7.1	-14.0
Manufacturing of other consumer goods	0.0	7.1	8.0	-0.3	9.4	-16.2
Manufacturing of intermediate goods	-0.7	2.3	4.3	-3.0	1.6	-12.1
Manufacturing of capital goods	-1.5	1.6	-11.8	2.4	-1.4	-5.2
Construction	-3.6	-2.0	0.0	-1.9	0.0	0.0
Transport, communications	-2.2	-10.3	0.1	-7.5	3.0	0.0
Trade	1.7	-8.8	0.5	-9.3	0.6	0.6
Housing services	3.8	0.0	0.0	0.0	0.0	0.0
Health services	3.3	0.1	-0.1	0.3	-0.9	0.0
Education services	2.1	0.0	0.0	0.0	-0.1	1.9
Recreation and tourist services	3.2	7.7	3.9	1.8	12.3	0.0
Other market services	-2.9	-2.5	0.6	-5.5	1.8	-0.2
Public services	-2.1	-0.4	0.0	-0.9	-0.1	0.0
Total	0.0	0.0	0.0	-1.4	1.1	-6.4

Source: Computed by author from data in unpublished Greek social accounting matrices for 1980 and 1988.

while 1988 represents a year well after the initial adjustment of the Greek economy to the EC transition period. The data in the table derive from detailed social accounting matrices (SAMs) that have been built for Greece for these two years and that have not, as yet, been published (Sarris, Anastassakou, and Zografakis 1995 and Zografakis 1997). The first column in the table exhibits the share of the fifteen sectors in Greek GDP at factor cost. It is apparent that the period 1980–88 has been characterized by considerable adjustment in the productive structure. All goods-producing sectors, with the exception of food and consumer good manufacturing, have declined in importance in the overall economy, as exhibited by declining shares in GDP. Most of the tertiary sectors seem to have expanded in GDP shares, with the exception of transport and communications, other market services and public (namely, non-market) services.

Columns 2 and 3 in Table 5.3 exhibit the structure of exports and imports (including service exports and imports). It appears that over this period, the trade structure of Greece has shifted in favor of goods-producing sectors both in exports and imports. On the export side, this appears to be because of the large relative decline in the transport (mainly maritime) sector, whose national output has moved offshore to convenience flag countries. On the import side, the big relative declines are in the energy (mainly petroleum) and capital goods sectors, as imports of food and other consumer goods expanded rapidly. Export propensity, defined as the ratio of exports to total available domestic supply (production plus imports), seems to have declined for most sectors, especially for transport and trade. The aggregate export propensity of the economy was reduced from 9.9 percent to 8.5 percent.

Over the same period, the aggregate import penetration (defined as the ratio of imports to total domestic-apparent consumption, namely, production plus imports minus exports) has increased from 12.6 percent to 13.7 percent. The main sectors where import penetration has increased are food and consumer goods manufacturing, as well as the tourism sector, all relatively traditional sectors of production. The final column of the table offers some clues concerning these developments. It exhibits the ratio of total import taxes (both tariff-related and other taxes) collected at the border by sector as a share of total import value. This measure is an underestimate of the actual rate of protection, as subsectors that are highly protected will exhibit low imports and, hence, will not be counted completely in total sectoral imports. It is, nevertheless, quite apparent that there have been impressive reductions in trade protection. Between 1980 and 1988, the "realized" aggregate rate of protection declined from an average of 9.5 percent to only 3.1 percent. The largest reductions in protection have been exhibited in the good-producing sectors and especially in manufacturing. It is thus not surprising that import penetration has increased considerably, especially in those sectors formerly heavily protected, like food and consumer goods manufacturing. It appears that the largest adjustment has taken place in manufacturing, where the Greek trade regime had to adapt to the much more liberal EC12 regime.

The evolution of industrial border protection is illustrated in Table 5.4 in further detail, where average real and nominal rates of protection for twenty manufacturing sectors are presented for the 1960–85 period. The average real rate of protection is computed by the following formula:

$$NRRP = 100*\left(\frac{1+tar}{1+dtax-domsubs}-1\right) \tag{5.1}$$

where tar is the aggregate rate of tariffs and other border taxes, dtax is the rate of domestic taxation on products of the sector, and domsubs is the rate of domestic subsidies on the products of the sector. The idea is that there are domestic taxes that might enhance or counteract border taxes. The nominal rate of protection is computed simply from the border taxation.

In almost all manufacturing sectors, there is a significant decline in real nominal protection from 1960 to 1980, namely, throughout the entire preaccession period. The early postaccession period is characterized by declines in border protection of consumer goods and of the traditional sectors, but also by increases in border protection of intermediate and capital goods, as well as of the modern sectors. These are goods and sectors that, for the most part, were not heavily protected (not even taxed) in the preaccession period, as Greece did not produce them in significant amounts.

Other researchers have found similar results. For instance, Tsounis (1992) estimated that the arithmetic average of nominal tariff rates decreased from 25.3 percent in 1970 to 17.5 percent in 1980. He also found that the effective protection rates were highly correlated with nominal tariff rates.

The decline in protection of the traditional sectors of Greece has led to decreases in export propensities, increases in import penetration, and declines in competitiveness of sectors previously protected. Katseli (1990) showed that trade competitiveness, as measured by the Balassa index (namely, the ratio of the absolute value of net exports to the sum of exports and imports), declined in the early postaccession period for all traditional sectors except tobacco and paper and printing. Competitiveness seems to have increased slightly in the modern sectors, namely, those in which protection rose after accession. Similar results are found by Sarris (1988).

The trade performance, as well as the internal adjustment of Greece in the process of adjustment to EC integration, is also conditioned by the degree of similarity of Greece's trade with the trade of its main partners. It is widely accepted that integrating countries with similar

Table 5.4
Evolution of Protection in the Greek Manufacturing Sectors, 1960–85

CCCN Code		Real Nominal Rate of Protection (%)			Nominal Rate of Border Protection (%)	
		1960	*1970*	*1980*	*1980*	*1985*
20	Food	31.7	43.6	31.2	21.7	9.6
21	Beverages	608.8	251.0	101.9	145.9	119.8
22	Tobacco	340.8	69.9	−35.0	9.6	6.5
23	Textiles, yarn	32.9	44.2	45.6	38.7	32.4
24	Shoes, clothing	72.9	60.6	21.8	38.5	35.1
25	Wood, cork	22.7	31.0	46.5	36.9	24.5
26	Furniture	158.1	53.4	25.1	33.3	28.9
27	Paper products	22.5	20.3	15.6	20.0	19.4
28	Printing, publishing	18.6	4.1	3.8		
29	Leather goods	12.7	−2.2	0.4	46.0	33.3
30	Rubber and plastics	22.2	38.0	31.4	32.6	31.9
31	Chemicals	21.3	20.8	13.4	20.0	22.3
32	Refinery products	−32.7	−37.9	12.0	19.6	40.7
33	Nonmetallic minerals	33.2	11.6	19.0	29.4	31.4
34	Basic metallurgy	−10.9	7.4	4.3	26.1	20.5
35	Products of Metal	37.7	31.6	22.0	25.2	24.8
36	Nonelectrical machinery	8.9	−0.7	−2.9	11.6	13.4
37	Electrical machinery	25.1	21.9	16.2	26.3	43.3
38	Transport equipment	21.4	17.3	15.1	26.5	66.3
39	Other manufactures	24.5	20.6	12.3	29.0	32.5
	Consumer goods				30.6	24.8
	Intermediate goods				21.8	25.7
	Capital goods				23.3	41.5
	Traditional (13 sectors)				38.8	33.6
	Modern (7 sectors)				24.5	33.5

Sources: Sarris (1988); and Giannitsis (1988).

trade and production structures are likely to be affected by intra-industry specialization; that is, by specialization within product lines of a given industry without large intersectoral factor shifts. The likely effects are conditioned by the share of intra-industry trade (IIT) of a country with respect to its partners. IIT refers to the simultaneous import and export of similar products (see Greenaway and Milner 1986 and Grubel and Lloyd 1975).

The appropriate measure of intra-industry trade has been subject to some debate in the literature (see Greenaway and Milner 1983 and Vona 1991). The most widely used measure, however, is the Grubel-Lloyd (GL) index, which is defined for an industry i and a given year as follows:

$$GL_i = 1 - \frac{|X_1 - M_i|}{|X_i + M_i|} \tag{5.2}$$

where X_i and M_i are respectively, values of exports and imports in industry i. The GL index for a higher-level industry aggregation, such as an SITC three-, two- or one-digit industry i, can be computed by weighting the GL indices for the five-digit subindustries included in the aggregate by their respective trade shares. In other words, if GL_{ij} is the GL index of a subindustry j within a larger industry group i, computed by the above formula, then the GL for the group i is computed as follows:

$$GL_i = \Sigma \, w_{ij} GL_{ij} \tag{5.3}$$

where the weights w_{ij} are given as follows:

$$w_{ij} = \frac{X_{ij} + M_{ij}}{\underset{j}{\Sigma} \, (X_{ij} + M_{ij})} \tag{5.4}$$

and X_{ij} and M_{ij} are the values of exports and imports, respectively, of sub-industry j of industry group i.

Table 5.5 presents the Grubel-Lloyd index of Greek trade for the main SITC aggregates over the period 1961–90 and for trade with the EC12, non-EC12, and the world as a whole. The indices have been computed using the OECD trade data as available (i.e. four-digit data for 1961 and 1967 and five-digit data for the later years). The first observation is that the share of intra-industry trade in total trade of Greece is much lower than previously computed with aggregated three-digit data. In 1990, after a period of continuous increase in intra-industry trade, only 20 percent of the total trade of Greece with the world and 19 percent of manufacturing trade were of the intra-industry type. This contrasts with figures on the order of 45 percent computed earlier with three-digit data (Greenaway and Hine 1991). It also contrasts with much higher

Table 5.5
Grubel-Lloyd Indices over Time for Greek Trade with the EC12 and the Non-EC12 Countries and the World

SITC	A. Trade with EC12 Countries					
	1961	1967	1972	1977	1985	1990
0	0.018	0.034	0.073	0.061	0.059	0.096
1	0.003	0.014	0.090	0.298	0.141	0.186
2	0.035	0.053	0.061	0.116	0.121	0.070
3	0	0.155	0.116	0.416	0.192	0.598
4	0.020	0.004	0.010	0.143	0.140	0.066
5	0.009	0.077	0.071	0.129	0.102	0.079
6	0.027	0.109	0.156	0.205	0.233	0.212
7	0.015	0.012	0.033	0.026	0.056	0.062
8	0.023	0.116	0.174	0.110	0.168	0.264
9	0	0	0	0.086	0.686	0.090
SITC 0–9	0.018	0.050	0.082	0.082	0.131	0.156
SITC 0–4	0.017	0.035	0.076	0.143	0.093	0.138
SITC 5–8	0.018	0.058	0.084	0.100	0.147	0.164

SITC	B. Trade with Non-EC12 Countries					
	1961	1967	1972	1977	1985	1990
0	0.036	0.058	0.075	0.084	0.066	0.141
1	0.001	0.001	0.025	0.032	0.044	0.229
2	0.051	0.125	0.120	0.164	0.260	0.200
3	0	0.021	0.023	0.040	0.055	0.348
4	0.078	0.014	0.015	0.044	0.008	0.087
5	0.059	0.192	0.205	0.414	0.235	0.215
6	0.186	0.229	0.259	0.230	0.225	0.195
7	0.028	0.060	0.053	0.109	0.084	0.079
8	0.280	0.302	0.170	0.195	0.212	0.200
9	0	0	0	0.620	0.298	0.409
SITC 0–9	0.046	0.083	0.107	0.128	0.177	0.197
SITC 0–4	0.019	0.050	0.069	0.079	0.083	0.249
SITC 5–8	0.086	0.164	0.147	0.170	0.172	0.166

Table 5.5 continued

	C. Trade with the World					
SITC	1961	1967	1972	1977	1985	1990
0	0.030	0.059	0.085	0.098	0.109	0.151
1	0.004	0.007	0.055	0.124	0.135	0.281
2	0.052	0.123	0.138	0.187	0.241	0.178
3	0	0.041	0.071	0.173	0.181	0.446
4	0.060	0.013	0.011	0.169	0.100	0.143
5	0.029	0.166	0.119	0.249	0.197	0.166
6	0.118	0.187	0.242	0.284	0.304	0.260
7	0.022	0.026	0.041	0.072	0.080	0.078
8	0.185	0.240	0.232	0.204	0.202	0.273
9	0	0	0	0.250	0.556	0.210
SITC 0–9	0.040	0.082	0.114	0.157	0.183	0.203
SITC 0–4	0.022	0.054	0.092	0.145	0.164	0.236
SITC 5–8	0.057	0.114	0.127	0.163	0.200	0.188
	GL Adjusted for Trade Imbalance					
SITC 0–9	0.062	0.118	0.211	0.273	0.296	0.297

Source: Sarris, Kordas, and Papadimitriou (1994). Computed from OECD four-digit (1961, 1967) and five-digit (1972, 1977, 1985, and 1990) data.

levels of IIT for the other EU countries calculated with the same type of detailed data. IIT accounted for only 16 percent of total and manufacturing trade with the EU12 in 1990. Similar low shares are observed for trade with non-EU12 countries.

Turning to trends, it is quite obvious that the share of intra-industry trade has increased substantially over the thirty-year period 1960–90. The increase appears to be strong in the postaccession period and particularly so in the nonmanufacturing sectors (SITC 0–4) for the most recent period. This is largely due to the liberalization of such imports from the EU. Table 5.5 shows that IIT in manufacturing (SITC sections 5–8) is generally higher than IIT in primary-product industries (SITC sections 0–4), as one would expect. The difference, however, is not large and, in fact, in 1990, IIT is higher in the SITC 0–4 groups than in the SITC 5–8 groups. This is due to the large increase of IIT in Greek trade with non-EU12 countries after 1985. It is not clear why such a pattern of IIT has emerged.

An interesting finding is that the IIT of Greece with the EU is generally lower than the IIT of Greece with non-EU countries for almost all periods in consideration when total trade is examined and in all periods for the manufacturing trade. This means that, despite the overall increase in IIT, Greece's trade with EU12 was and remains more dissimilar compared with its trade with non-EU12. Thus, integration with the EU does not seem to have created a production structure that tends toward the overall EU pattern. As the non-EU includes the rest of the OECD countries that are together a large trade partner of Greece, it is not clear what this pattern of IIT implies, but it is a topic for further research.

The above results suggest that Greece's trade with the EU is mostly of the inter-industry type and, hence, is most likely to be explained by Heckscher-Ohlin (H-O) type of factor endowment considerations rather than by more "modern" trade theories that emphasize trade in similar products. Indeed, Tsounis (1992) finds that the factor content version of comparative advantage explains adequately the Greek pattern of trade and, moreover, that Greek exports to the EU are relatively more labor-intensive compared to imports from the EU. These results, coupled with the earlier analysis, showed that the declines in protection were mostly the consumer and traditional (and labor-intensive) manufacturing sectors of Greece and suggest that trade liberalisation in the course of EC integration has had important impacts on the labor market.

THE STRUCTURE AND EVOLUTION OF THE GREEK LABOR MARKET

The unemployment rate in Greece increased from about 2 percent in the mid-1970s to over 10 percent in 1995, and this has raised concerns about the functioning of the labor market, as well as other influences on employment. The Greek labor market is characterized by extensive duality and serious structural rigidities. The total labor force amounts to about 4,230 thousand workers (1995 figures), implying a labor force participation rate of about 47 percent (64 percent among males and 33 percent among females). Total employment is 3,824 thousand or about 90 percent of the labor force. Table 5.6 exhibits the structure of employed labor in 1981, 1991, and 1995. The most important characteristics involve the relatively high share of agricultural employment (20.4 percent of total) and the high share of nonwage employment (namely, self-employed, unpaid family members, etc.; 46.1 percent of total). Although the share of self-employed in total employed workers has fallen over time, from 51 percent in 1981 to 46 percent in 1995, when one takes into account the larger unemployment in 1995, the share of self-employed in the total labor force has stayed roughly constant.

In the 1980s and 1990s, the Greek economy was hit by exogenous macro shocks, such as the second oil shock, the fall of communism in Eastern Europe, and the EC accession. Furthermore, the 1980s saw extensive government interference in the labor market, especially in

Table 5.6
Civilian Employment in Greece, 1981–95

	Thousand			Share (%)	Annual Change (%)	
	1981	*1991*	*1995*	*1995*	*1981–91*	*1991–95*
Total civilian employment	3529.3	3623.4	3823.8	100.0	0.3	1.7
By sex						
Male	2423.2	2406.8	2452.2	64.1	−0.2	0.6
Female	1106.0	1225.7	1371.6	35.9	3.5	3.8
By sector						
Agriculture	1082.9	806.5	781.9	20.4	−2.9	−1.0
Industry	1022.8	1000.6	887.1	23.2	−0.2	−3.9
Services	1423.6	1825.3	2154.8	56.4	2.5	5.7
By professional status						
Wage earners total	1699.0	1930.5	2060.1	53.9	1.3	2.2
Agriculture	35.0	30.4	39.3	1.0	−1.4	8.9
Industry	749.3	689.9	608.7	15.9	−0.8	−4.1
Services	914.7	1210.2	1412.1	36.9	2.8	5.3
Wage earners						
Public sector	477.1	567.9	566.1	14.6	1.7	−0.8
Private sector	1221.9	1362.6	1494.0	39.8	1.1	3.4
Nonwage earners	1830.3	1701.9	1763.7	46.1	−0.7	1.2
of which: agriculture	1047.9	776.1	742.7	19.4	−3.0	−1.5

Source: OECD (1996).

regulations involving minimum wages and wage negotiations. The share of agriculture in GDP has declined significantly, leading to a decline in jobs in the primary sector, while the manufacturing sector has begun a protracted period of technological adaptation and has shed a considerable number of jobs, especially in larger-scale industry. The tertiary sector has been the single-largest labor-absorbing sector, with the private sector leading the way. Aggregate employment growth has averaged 0.5 percent annually since 1981, with service-sector employment growing at 3 percent annually.

The changing sectoral composition of production, especially the shift toward services, has contributed to a slowing down of aggregate productivity growth. The presence of large unrecorded activity is facilitated by the large number of self-employed and the small size of enterprises, which average two workers compared to six for the whole of OECD. The development in labor supply has been complicated since the late 1980s by the large influx of illegal aliens from the former communist bloc.

Lianos, Sarris, and Katseli (1996) estimated that the illegal workers amounted to about 14 percent of the Greek labor force in 1995, with the largest share coming from Albania.

The composition of unemployment has become increasingly skewed toward economic outsiders, who are increasingly concentrated at the lower end of the wage distribution, probably signaling the existence of a poorly functioning labor market (OECD 1996). Reinforcing the evidence of market segmentation in favor of insiders, the unemployment rate of heads of households is near 2 percent, and studies by OECD indicate that Greece has the lowest rates of inflow and outflow from the ranks of the unemployed.

A major structural rigidity of the Greek labor market involves the lack of significant responsiveness of wages to productivity differences as well as demand fluctuations. Glytsos (1994), for instance, estimates a wage-response equation and finds no significant relation between wages and productivity or domestic demand. He also finds insignificant impact of real wages on employment determination. Nevertheless, he points out that import penetration has a significant (negative) influence on employment, while exports have a positive influence on employment.

The structure of labor bargaining, which until the early 1990s was heavily centralized, and the tendency for a narrowing of the official wage gap between the lowest-paid, unskilled workers and the skilled workers have led to significant unemployment among the unskilled. Also, the skilled workers have taken up second unreported jobs to supplement their lost real purchasing power. The ratio of average white- to blue-collar workers declined from 1.7 in 1974 to 1.2 in the period 1980-86 before rising to 1.3 in 1995. The ratio of minimum wage to average earnings in manufacturing (including bonuses) is about 60 percent for a married worker with ten years of experience, compared with 50 percent in France, 30 percent in Portugal, and 35 percent in Spain. Moreover, the share of minimum-wage workers in total manufacturing employment is estimated at about 30 percent.

INDUSTRIAL ADJUSTMENT, 1978–87

Given that a great deal of adjustment has taken place in manufacturing, this section attempts to illustrate the magnitude of adjustments in the post-accession period. The analysis is restricted to the years before 1988, because of the availability of compatible production, trade, and employment data. In order to assess the implications of post–EC accession trade performance on industrial adjustment and employment, it is required to analyze domestic production and other data along with trade data. While trade data in Greece are compiled according to the SITC as well as the EC's NIMEXE classification system, industrial data are compiled according to a domestic four-digit classification system which, only recently, has been adapted to the EC's NACE system of industrial classification. No official concordance between domestic production and trade data exists. We, therefore, had to derive our own concordance tables. The resulting classification assigned most manufacturing subindustries of Greece to sixty-four three-digit "industries" and derived the corresponding SITC five-digit products compatible with each "industry" using SITC revision 2. The omitted industries accounted for about 10 percent of total domestic sales of all industries in 1978 and 8 percent in 1987. We also classified the sixty-four manufacturing industries into those with high, medium and low degrees of intra-EC, nontariff trade barriers. This classification has been adapted from the one in Mardas and Varsakelis (1988) and is intended to classify Greek industries according to their potential vulnerability and, hence, sensitivity to EC internal market completion measures.[1] This is the consequence of further EU integration resulting from the Maastricht Treaty, which is supposed to eliminate all remaining intra-EU trade barriers.

In Table 5.7 we exhibit various measures of adjustment and trade for the three industry groups, as well as for all of them together, for 1978, 1985, and 1987. In 1978, the high-sensitivity sectors (twelve industries) accounted for 17.1 percent of total manufacturing production (of establishments with ten or more employees), the medium ones (twenty-three industries) for 37.8 percent and the low-sensitivity ones (twenty-nine industries) for 45.1 percent. If we examine the aggregate employment figures for 1978, it can be seen that the high- and medium-sensitivity sectors accounted for 64.7 percent of total manufacturing employment, which is much higher than their share in total production. They also accounted for 64.6 percent of establishments. Thus, more than half of the Greek manufacturing production, employment, and establishments in 1978 was characterized by a medium to high degree of nontariff barriers with respect to intra-EC12 trade. These are the sectors that are expected to be affected the most under the internal market completion program.

As far as trade is concerned, the high- and medium-sensitivity sectors accounted for 40.3 percent of total manufacturing exports, 52 percent of total manufacturing imports, 46.1 percent of total exports to the EC12, and 60.6 percent of imports from the EC12.

If we turn to changes between 1978 and 1985, it can be seen that while the production of all manufacturing industries increased by 50 percent, manufacturing employment rose by only 18.5 percent and the number of manufacturing establishments increased by 138.5 percent. In other words, it appears that the average size of a manufacturing establishment, both in terms of production and employment, decreased considerably. It is not clear whether this is a real development or is due to the fact that many formerly small establishments increased their

Table 5.7
Production and Trade Developments of High-, Medium-, and Low-Sensitivity Manufacturing Sectors of Greece, 1978–87

	High	Medium	Low	All
Base Year (1978) Data				
Value of production	1613.9	3556.9	4239.7	9410.6
Number of workers	61.2	113.3	95.1	269.6
Number of establishments	872.0	1180.0	1124.0	3176.0
Value of exports	367.2	661.1	1525.7	2554.0
Value of imports	1647.2	1303.8	2723.7	5674.7
Value of exports to EC12	206.3	387.5	691.2	1285.1
Value of imports from EC12	1166.3	730.2	1235.0	3131.6
Average export propensity	0.113	0.136	0.219	0.169
Average import penetration	0.403	0.174	0.227	0.453
Percentage Changes 1978–85				
Real value of production	3.3	45.1	71.9	50.0
Number of workers	25.5	14.6	18.7	18.5
Number of establishments	161.7	119.0	141.1	138.5
Value of exports	44.1	30.5	18.4	25.2
Value of imports	1.6	38.2	−18.4	0.4
Value of exports to EC12	59.9	29.7	−17.7	9.1
Value of imports from EC12	6.6	87.0	−1.8	22.0
Average export propensity 1985	0.158	0.124	0.190	0.161
Average import penetration 1985	0.442	0.224	0.157	0.343
Percentage Changes 1985–87				
Real value of production	16.7	1.4	−17.2	−6.4
Number of workers	1.8	0.4	−2.0	−0.1
Number of establishments	3.5	−4.9	1.7	0.0
Value of exports	9.9	26.0	−13.9	0.8
Value of imports	23.4	35.3	9.7	21.8
Value of exports to EC12	25.2	48.3	45.2	41.6
Value of imports from EC12	16.6	27.1	−5.2	13.4
Average export propensity 1987	0.145	0.142	0.183	0.160
Average import penetration 1987	0.423	0.263	0.166	18.3

Table 5.7 continued

	High	Medium	Low	All
Percentage Changes 1978–87				
Real value of production	20.6	47.2	42.4	40.5
Number of workers	27.7	15.0	16.3	18.3
Number of establishments	170.9	108.2	145.3	138.5
Value of exports	58.3	64.5	1.9	26.2
Value of imports	25.3	87.0	–10.5	22.3
Value of exports to EC12	100.1	92.4	19.6	54.5
Value of imports from EC12	24.3	137.6	–6.9	38.4

Source: Sarris, Papadimitriou, and Mavrogiannis (1997), computed from OECD and Greek manufacturing census data.

For 1978, the value of sales is available and is used instead of production. All values are in million 1978 US$; employment in thousand persons; establishments in absolute numbers.

employment above the threshold level of ten and, hence, are now included in the statistics. Production in the highly sensitive sectors was only marginally above their 1978 value, while production in the medium- and low-sensitivity sectors grew at about the same or higher rates than the total. Interestingly, while production grew only marginally in the highly sensitive sectors, employment in those sectors grew at a higher-than-average rate, and the opposite occurred in the medium- and low-sensitivity sectors.

Total manufacturing exports and imports appear to have grown between 1978 and 1985, at much smaller rates than domestic production, with imports having been virtually the same as those of 1978. This is due, to a large extent, to large declines in imports of the ship-repair industry (which is classified as a low-sensitivity sector). If this industry is excluded, imports would appear to have grown by about 17 percent. Exports to EC12 grew much less than total exports, while imports from EC12 grew much more than total imports. This could very well be the consequence of the liberalization of Greek–EC trade that took place after accession. The highly sensitive sectors, despite nontariff trade barriers with the EC12, appear to have increased their total, as well as their EC12 exports, by much more than the increases in aggregate manufacturing exports to the EC12 or the world. The low-sensitivity sectors have experienced reduced total and EC12 exports in 1985 compared to 1978. The medium-sensitivity sectors are inbetween.

As far as imports are concerned, it is interesting to contrast the experiences of the three groups. The highly sensitive sectors experienced import growth roughly in line with that of total imports. The medium-sensitivity sectors, however, experienced much higher import growth, while the low-sensitivity sectors faced import declines. If the ship-repair industry is excluded from the low-sensitivity sectors, then imports in that sector exhibit a marginal decline in 1985.

If we turn to changes between 1985 and 1987, it must be noted that 1987 was a year in which the Greek economy was in the middle of a macrostabilization program. Such austerity programs usually reduce the average propensity to import due to the decline in disposable income. In Table 5.7, the percentage changes between 1978 and 1987 are shown, as well as the cumulative percentage changes between 1978 and 1987. Although aggregate manufacturing production declined between 1985 and 1987, the employment and the number of establishments remained unchanged.[2] Exports appear to have stayed unchanged between 1985 and 1987 but, contrary to what one would expect from the stabilization program, total imports increased substantially. Exports to EC12 increased much more than total exports, while imports from EC12 grew much less than total imports.

When we examine the total changes across groups of industries, we note the substantially different evolution of changes in production. Sectors that are highly sensitive experienced increased production in the course of stabilization, and the medium ones stayed unchanged, while those of low-sensitivity experienced a very large decline in production. Employment seems to have followed the same pattern, but the differences are much smaller. Exports and imports in the sensitive sectors also appear to have increased more than average, while in the less sensitive sectors, they grew by much less than average. It thus appears that the brunt of the adjustment was borne by the sectors that were more open to EC12 trade.

When the short-term changes between 1985 and 1987 are superimposed on those between 1978 and 1985, it can be noticed that, while the production of all manufacturing industries increased by 40.5 percent between 1978 and 1987, manufacturing employment increased only by 18.3 percent. It is interesting to note that the 1978–85 growth in production within the highly sensitive sectors was much slower than that recorded for 1985–87. Over the same time comparison, employment increased considerably more relative to the medium- and low-sensitivity sectors. In these highly-sensitive sectors, employment increased faster than output between 1978 and 1987.

When we examine the trends in trade, it can be noticed that there is an enormous difference in the overall behavior of exports and imports of the highly sensitive sectors compared to those of low sensitivity. In the highly sensitive sectors, exports and imports exceeded the increase in production, while the opposite happened in the low-sensitivity sectors. The latter are characterized by an absolute decline in the real value of imports. The same pattern applies to exports and to imports from the

EC12. The conclusion is that, in the postaccession period, employment and trade appear to have expanded mostly in sectors deemed sensitive (both highly and moderately) to intra-EC12, nontariff trade barriers (NTBs), while they expanded very little in low-sensitivity sectors.

A caveat is in order in interpreting the above results, which refer only to group totals and not group means. When the three groups of industries are considered as different statistical populations, with each industry being a sample in the population, then we can conduct t-tests for the differences between the group means. For none of the variables reported in Table 5.7 did we observe a statistically significant difference between the group means of the three groups reported. This implies that the total differences indicated in Table 5.7 are characterized by large variances in individual industry behavior. Hence, it is, at best, precarious to talk about the "typical industry" within each group. It turns out that there are very few industries within each group that account for the bulk of the observed group changes. Since the degrees of freedom are rather small, it could be that the forces that drive these few industries are of a special nature and are not necessarily related to trade factors.

It thus appears that the sectors that fared better in terms of both trade and employment in the early post accession period were the ones that were most protected and most sensitive to liberalization of intra-EC NTBs. These sectors are likely to bear the brunt of the adjustment in the process of the internal market completion in the 1990s, presumably with more liberalization. The Greek manufacturing sector is bound to face major adjustment and competitiveness problems in the course of EU internal market completion.

INDUSTRIAL ADJUSTMENT AND TRADE PERFORMANCE

In order to relate the postaccession trends in employment indicated in the previous section to trade performance, we first present here an accounting decomposition of changes in the sixty-four Greek manufacturing industries we have been studying. The technique we use follows the one outlined by Hine, Greenaway, and Milner (1994). Employment for industry i in a given year can be written as the ratio of domestic production (equal to the sum of apparent consumption and net exports) and average labor productivity:

$$N_i = \frac{DD_i + X_i - M_i}{PRV_i} \tag{5.5}$$

where DD denotes domestic demand, X is exports, M is imports and PRV is average labor productivity. The employment change between two periods, Dn_i, can be broken into a part that is due to changes in domestic output and a part due to changes in productivity, $DNPRV_i$:

$$\Delta N_i = \Delta N Q_i + \Delta NPRV_i \qquad (5.6)$$

The output effect on employment is defined as the change in domestic production divided by the average labor productivity of the two periods:

$$\Delta N Q_i = \frac{2(Q_{i,t_1} - Q_{i,t_0})}{(PRV_{i,t_1} + PRV_{i,t_0})} \qquad (5.7)$$

The productivity effect is defined residually as the difference between the total employment change and the output effect. Since output can be written as the sum of domestic demand and net exports, the output effect in equation (5.7) can be broken down into a part due to change in domestic demand and one due to change in net exports, by writing the difference in the numerator of equation (5.7) as the sum of the change in domestic demand and the change in net exports. Finally, as the change in net exports can be written as the difference between the change in exports and imports, the trade component of the employment change can be broken into a part due to changes in exports and one due to changes in imports.

Table 5.8 presents the accounting analysis of employment changes for all Greek manufacturing industries, as well as for the intra-EC12 NTB sensitive groups, for the periods 1978–85, 1985–87, and the total interval 1978–87. Between 1978 and 1987, manufacturing employment (in the sixty-four industries considered) increased by 49.5 thousand people or 18.3 percent. Almost all of this increase was accomplished in the pre-stabilization and early postaccession period from 1978 to 1985. There appear to be two opposing influences on employment, however, stemming from production and productivity developments. If productivity had stayed the same, manufacturing employment would have grown by much more, in fact—about 2.5 times the actual growth. Productivity changes appear to have led to a substantial downward pressure on manufacturing jobs, as they accounted for a loss of 82.2 thousand jobs. If output had not grown, manufacturing employment would have actually declined over the period.

The output-induced manufacturing job expansion is, to a larger extent, due to trade developments rather than to domestic demand expansion. This is the result of changes in the ship-repair industry (classified as a low-sensitivity one). This industry accounted, during 1978–87, for 0.4 to 1.1 percent of total manufacturing sales and 3.3 to 5.5 percent of total industrial employment. It experienced, however, substantial import reduction over the period, which translates via the accounting method into a very large, positive contribution to domestic

Table 5.8
Accounting Analysis of Manufacturing Employment in Greece, 1978–87

	1978–85		1985–87		1978–87	
	All Industries					
Total Employment Change	49.9	(50.5)	−0.4	(0.6)	49.5	(51.1)
Productivity Effect	−68.9	(−54.2)	−16.7	(−17.1)	−82.2	(−68.4)
Output Effect	118.7	(104.7)	16.3	(17.7)	131.6	(119.5)
Domestic Demand	31.8	(102.3)	29.6	(39.5)	54.4	(143.2)
Trade	86.9	(2.3)	−13.4	(−21.8)	77.2	(−23.7)
Exports	28.2	(28.4)	25.3	(25.6)	52.0	(52.5)
Imports	58.7	(−26.0)	−38.7	(−47.4)	25.2	(−76.2)
	High-Sensitivity Industries					
Total Employment Change	15.6		1.4		17.0	
Productivity Effect	−3.4		−7.7		−10.2	
Output Effect	19.1		9.1		27.2	
Domestic Demand	17.8		18.2		35.9	
Trade	1.2		−9.1		−8.7	
Exports	10.2		7.2		17.2	
Imports	−9.0		−16.3		−26.0	
	Medium-Sensitivity Industries					
Total Employment Change	16.5		0.5		17.0	
Productivity Effect	−29.9		−5.7		−35.0	
Output Effect	46.4		6.1		52.0	
Domestic Demand	48.1		11.6		57.5	
Trade	−1.7		−5.4		−5.5	
Exports	7.3		8.5		16.9	
Imports	−9.0		−13.9		−22.4	
	Low-Sensitivity Industries					
Total Employment Change	17.8	(18.4)	−2.3	(−1.2)	15.5	(17.2)
Productivity Effect	−35.5	(−20.8)	−3.4	(−3.8)	−37.0	(−23.2)
Output Effect	53.3	(39.2)	1.1	(2.5)	52.5	(40.3)
Domestic Demand	−34.1	(36.4)	0.0	(9.8)	−38.9	(49.9)
Trade	87.4	(2.8)	1.2	(−7.3)	91.4	(−9.5)
Exports	10.7	(10.8)	9.6	(9.9)	17.8	(18.3)
Imports	76.7	(−8.0)	−8.4	(−17.1)	73.6	(−27.9)

Source: Sarris, Papadimitriou, and Mavrogiannis (1997).

All figures in thousand employees; figures in parentheses exclude the industry involved in ship repairs.

employment and tends to swamp the effects of all other industries. If we exclude this industry from the accounting analysis (and it is an industry heavily regulated by the state), as indicated by the figures in the table inside the parentheses, then trade and, in particular, import expansion contribute negatively to changes in postaccession Greek manufacturing employment, and it is mainly domestic demand that has maintained industrial employment.[3]

When the analysis is decomposed by NTB sensitivity groups, the pattern of employment changes appears quite similar. This is especially so when the ship-repair industry is excluded. In this context, the trade effect appears to account for a small or negative impact on employment in all groups, while the domestic demand effect appears to account for positive employment growth in all industries. The substantial fall of imports in the ship-repair industry can reverse this conclusion in the low-sensitivity sectors. The trends in that industry are governed by domestic subsidy policies, as well as the general worldwide decline of shipping in the early 1980s, and cannot be related to EC accession and attendant trade developments.

The accounting method clearly does not allow for inferences concerning causality or even correlation between employment changes and trade performance. In particular, it assumes that productivity developments are independent of trade developments. To avoid these problems we employ a cross-section regression analysis. The question we investigate is whether post–EC accession industrial employment changes in Greece are related to trade performance and trade structure. The model we employ seeks to relate changes in employment to three classes of variables. The first class is intended to reflect trade structure. We use the average export propensity (EP) in the beginning and ending years and the average import penetration (IP) as proxies for trade structure.

The second group of variables reflects trade performance. For this we employ two variables. The first is the A index of marginal intra-industry trade (MIIT) (Brulhart 1994). This index measures the extent to which the change in trade in an industry between two periods is of the intra-industry rather than the inter-industry type. The A index is given by the following formula:

$$A_i = 1 - \frac{|\Delta X_i - \Delta M_i|}{|\Delta X_i| + |\Delta M_i|} \tag{5.8}$$

where DX_i and DM_i denote the change in exports and imports, respectively, of an industry i between two periods. This index, like the GL index, varies between 0 and 1. A value of 0 indicates that the MIIT in the particular industry is completely of the inter-industry type, while a value of 1 indicates that the MIIT is entirely of the intra-industry type. The index shares all the statistical properties of the GL index (a comprehensive description of these can be found in Greenaway and Milner 1986). The A index can be summed, across industries of the same level of statistical aggregation, with appropriate weights just like the GL index. The A index is expected to have a positive influence on employment changes.

The second variable of trade performance that we use is the ratio of the difference between the changes (between the two periods) in exports and imports to the sum of the absolute values of the same changes. This index is the B index of trade performance of Brulhart (1994), and it ranges between −1 and +1.

Our third class of variables involves domestic developments. We employ the change in domestic apparent consumption (DD) and the change in productivity ($DPROD$). Since we are not sure whether there is an influence of trade and domestic demand on productivity, we estimate equations both with and without the productivity variable.

Our preliminary results show that the export propensity and import penetration variables are strongly correlated with the changes in domestic consumption, albeit uncorrelated between them. We also found that all the other regressors were uncorrelated between them. Hence, we estimated regressions where we included either the change in domestic demand or the export penetration and import propensity variables.

Table 5.9 illustrates the results of regressions of employment changes between 1978 and 1985, as well as between 1978 and 1987. The results suggest a significant influence of trade-related variables on employment changes, irrespective of the use of productivity variables. They also suggest more robust relations in the regressions for 1978–85 changes than in those for 1978–87. This was expected for the reasons discussed earlier. From the regression for 1978–85, it appears that the coefficients of domestic demand, productivity, marginal IIT (A index), and trade performance (B index) are all of the expected sign and are significant. When the change in domestic demand is excluded, it turns out that export propensity emerges as a very significant determinant, while productivity is insignificant. While in the accounting method it was seen that the exclusion of the ship-repair industry affected the results considerably, there is no such difference in the regression results.

CONCLUSIONS

There have been significant adjustments in the Greek economy in the post–EC accession period since 1980. Concurrently, there has been an extensive trade liberalization with attendant expansion of imports, especially in the previously protected sectors. This appears to have involved substantial industrial restructuring and productivity growth.

Our accounting analysis of employment changes in the post–EC accession period suggested that domestic demand changes and produc-

Table 5.9
OLS Regression Results for Determinants of Post–EC Accession,
Sectoral Changes in Greek Industrial Employment

	All	High Sensitivity	Medium Sensitivity	Low Sensitivity
	Employment Changes between 1978–85			
Constant	0.057	0.028	0.060	0.048
A	0.340**	0.372**	0.458**	0.460***
B	0.128***	0.099**	0.010	0.010
Δ D	0.417***	0.305***		
Δ PROD	−0.296***		−0.082	
EP			0.350***	0.348***
IP			−0.057	−0.064
Corr. R^2	0.493	0.343	0.341	0.327
	Employment Changes between 1978–87			
Constant	0.046	−0.034	−0.038	−0.041
A	0.246	0.359*	0.315	0.319
B	0.126*	0.070	−0.074	−0.075
Δ D	0.397***	0.340***		
Δ PROD	−0.264**		−0.009	
EP			0.775***	0.774***
IP			−0.023	−0.023
Corr. R^2	0.466	0.397	0.222	0.222

Source: Computed by the author.

Dependent variables $\Delta L = 2 (L_t - L_{t0}) / L_t + L_{t0}$. The Δ D and Δ PROD variables are defined as the absolute changes in consumption or productivity, divided by the average (beginning and end periods) consumption and productivity, respectively. The EP and IP variables are defined as the simple averages of beginning and ending year EP and IP values.

*   significance at 10 percent level.
**   significance at 5 percent level.
*** significance at 1 percent level.

tivity effects had the most significant influence, with trade factors making negative contributions. The regression analysis verified this initial finding but nevertheless revealed that trade performance is an important determinant of Greek industrial employment changes.

The analysis covered medium and larger industries, namely, those included in the annual industrial surveys and industrial censuses. A large proportion of Greek industrial enterprises are small, however, and are not covered by these surveys. In the course of adjustment, there was a significant increase in the number of small establishments and an increase in the underreported activities. It is not clear to what extent this development has counteracted the decline of the "official" industrial sector, but the topic merits further research.

The results of this chapter raise some policy issues. Trade performance appears to be more important for employment adjustment in the low-sensitivity sectors, while domestic demand performance is more significant for the high- and medium-sensitivity sectors. The completion of the EC internal market, which is expected to affect mostly the trade performance of the sensitive sectors, could potentially be counteracted by favorable domestic policies that would boost domestic demand. The planning of such policies, however, could stumble upon restrictive convergence targets placed by the Maastricht Treaty. Consequently, Greek economic policy in the medium run is bound to be difficult, because it will have to cope with conflicting objectives.

NOTES

1. The complete list of industries and correspondences with the EC NACE classification is indicated in Sarris, Papadimitriou, and Mavrogiannis (1994).

2. This, to a large extent, can be attributed to the rigidities prevailing in the Greek labor market. See Katseli (1990) for an extended analysis of this issue.

3. A similar conclusion has been drawn by Droucopoulos and Thomadakis (1994), who investigated the impact of globalization on job creation in Greek small- and medium-sized enterprises.

REFERENCES

Alexakis, P., and M. Xanthakis. 1992. Export performance of Greek manufacturing companies: Export subsidies and other factors. *Economia Internationale* 45(2):143–52.

Brulhart, M. 1994. Marginal intra-industry trade: Measurement and relevance for the pattern of industrial adjustment. *Weltwirtschaftliches Archiv* 130(3):600–613.

Droucopoulos, V., and S. Thomadakis. 1994. Globalisation of economic activities and small- and medium-sized enterprises development. Department of Economics, University of Athens. Mimeographed.

Giannitsis, T. 1988. *Accession to EEC and Effects on Industry and Trade: Foundation of Mediterranean Studies (Idryma Mesogeiakon Meleton)* (in Greek). Athens, Greece. Mimeographed.

Glytsos, N. P. 1994. Greek labour market adaptability in the EC integration. In *Participation, Organizational Effectiveness and Quality of Work Life in the Year 2000*, edited by L. Nikolaou-Smokoviti and G. Szell. Frankfurt, Germany: Peter Lang.

Greenaway, D., and R. C. Hine. 1991. Intra-industry specialization, trade expansion and adjustment in the European economic space. *Journal of Common Market Studies* 29(6):603–22.

Greenaway, D., and C. Milner. 1983. On the measurement of intra-industry trade. *The Economic Journal* 93:900–908.

——. 1986. *The Economics of Intra-Industry Trade.* Oxford: Basil Blackwell.

Grubel, H. G., and P. Lloyd. 1975. *Intra Industry Trade.* London: Macmillan.

Hine, R. C., D. Greenaway, and C. Milner. 1994. Changes in trade and changes in employment: An examination of the evidence from UK manufacturing industry, 1979–87. University of Nottingham. Mimeographed.

Katseli, L. T. 1990. Economic integration in the enlarged European community: Structural adjustment of the Greek economy. In *Unity with Diversity in the European Economy: The Community's Southern Frontier,* edited by C. Bliss and J. B. de Macedo. Cambridge: Cambridge University Press for the Centre for Economic Policy Research.

Katsos, G., and N. I. Spanakis. 1983. *Industrial Protection and Integration.* Athens: Center for Planning and Economic Research.

Lianos, T., A. Sarris, and L. Katseli. 1996. Illegal immigration and local labour markets: The case of northern Greece. *International Migration* 34(3):449–84.

Mardas, D. 1992. *The Consequences of the Unified Market on Greek Export Trade: An Intra-Industry Analysis* (in Greek). Athens: Greek Center for European Studies (EKEM).

Mardas, D., and N. Varsakelis. 1988. Greece in commission of European communities: "The cost of non-Europe" basic findings. *European Economy.*

Organization for Economic Co-operation and Development (OECD). 1996. *Economic Surveys, 1995–96.* OECD.

Sarris, A. H. 1988. Greek accession and EC commercial policy toward the south. In *European Trade Policies and the Developing World,* edited by L. B. M. Mennes and J. Kol. London: Croom Helm.

Sarris, A. H., Z. Anastassakou, and S. Zografakis. 1995. *Social Accounting Matrix of the Greek economy for the year 1980* (in Greek). Research Report to the Greek General Secretariat for Research and Technology. Athens: University of Athens.

Sarris, A. H., G. Kordas, and P. Papadimitriou. 1994. Intra-industry trade of Greece in the course of European integration. Department of Economics, University of Athens. Mimeographed.

Sarris, A. H., P. Papadimitriou, and A. Mavrogiannis. 1997. Intra-industry trade and industrial adjustment of Greece under European union membership. *OIKONOMIKA* (Forthcoming).

——. 1994. Manufacturing trade, specialization and adjustment of Greece in the course of European integration. Department of Economics, University of Athens. Mimeographed.

Tsounis, N. K. 1992. The effects of European economic integration on the Greek economy and the pattern of Greek international trade. Ph.D. Diss., University of Manchester.

Vona, S. 1991. On the measurement of intra-industry trade: Some further thoughts. *Weltwirtschaftliches Archiv* 127:678–700.

Zografakis, S. 1997. Economic policy and impacts on the distribution of income in Greece: Analytical approach with the use of a computable general equilibrium model. Ph.D. Diss., University of Athens.

6
Economic Liberalization and Unemployment in Chile

Luis A. Riveros

An extensive economic liberalization has taken place in Chile since the early 1970s. After a long tradition of state intervention in economic matters, including price fixing and widespread market intervention, as well as macroeconomic instability and policies aimed at closing the economy to international trade and financial flows, Chile stands today as an example of liberalization, stabilization, and structural adjustment. This achievement required radical changes with regard to traditional economic practices, in addition to a deep reduction in the economic size of the state, a profound opening up to trade and capital flows, and an across-the-board liberalization of markets and prices. In order to achieve this, policy reforms acted upon tariffs, wages, privatization, reducing the government intervention in a broad range of economic topics, and promoting competition in factor markets. This so-called neoconservative experiment of the 1970s and 1980s, although originally implemented by a military regime, was deepened and continued during the 1990s, at the same time that a political transition to a standard Western democracy was taking place.

Chile was traditionally characterized by low growth, substantial macroeconomic imbalances, insufficient investment, and a large and inefficient public sector, as well as by protective policies which addressed specific industries and produced a highly distorted allocation of resources. The average per capita annual growth rate in the period 1900–1989 was approximately 1.3 percent (Ferraro and Riveros 1994), while inflation (as measured by annual percentage rise in the consumer price index, or CPI) went from a yearly average of more than 26 percent in the 1960s to a notable hyperinflation process in the early 1970s. The fiscal deficit was normally between 3 and 5 points of the gross domestic product (GDP), while it reached 16 percent of the GDP in 1970–73. During the past eleven years, in contrast, average annual per capita growth has been 5 percent, with yearly inflation rates averaging 15.2 percent and further declining during the 1990s to single-digit levels. The investment rate in the 1990s has reached up to more than 25 percent of the GDP—a level which is substantially above the historical averages of about 15–17 percent of GDP—while the fiscal deficit over the past decade has turned into a surplus averaging 1.8 percent of GDP. Similarly, in the past decade export growth has taken place at an average 14 percent, and despite adverse terms of trade shocks, the balance of payments situation appears quite sustainable thanks to capital inflows.

The labor market has remained one of the most interesting and crucial dimensions of the Chilean economic liberalization. During the 1970s, employment growth suffered a notable stagnation, a situation which turned critical with the financial crash of the early 1980s. Since 1972, real wages substantially declined and unemployment continued at a level equivalent to twice the historical average, in spite of high growth rates seen during 1979–81. Thereafter, unemployment reached up to more than 25 percent of the labor force, as a result of the financial crisis of the 1980s. The continuous high economic growth Chile has experienced since 1986 has resulted in a notable reduction in open unemployment, while real wages have largely recovered from the prolonged collapse which began in 1972. The Chilean unemployment episode is largely related to sectoral productive shifts, while the observed persistence of open unemployment during the expansion of 1979–81 can be reasonably explained by skill mismatch, in combination with a drastic drop in labor demand as a result of stabilization policies. In any case, the Chilean model has been said to have created a critical social situation, or at least one that exacerbated the typical social stance of a Latin American less developed country (LDC), particularly in terms of poverty and income distribution. This issue connects with labor market outcomes and the observed evolution of employment and wages.

ECONOMIC LIBERALIZATION IN CHILE

The Chilean economy underwent significant economic liberalization between 1974 and 1996. In 1974, changes in traditional economic policies started as a response to an economic program of socialist inspiration. This program produced significant macroeconomic disruptions and cumbersome political problems. In 1973, inflation reached more than 600 percent, so the first change that was implemented was a stabilization phase. This stabilization phase (1974–78) included an ample trade liberalization program and fiscal/monetary stringency and produced a notable recession, but enabled the country to reach a manageable inflation rate by the end of the decade. A short-lived recovery was observed in 1979–81, which ended drastically with the world debt crisis of 1982–85. The latter exerted particularly acute effects on the Chilean economy. In 1986–89, the emphasis was on structural adjustment, including public-sector reform, privatization, and export promotion—changes which have continued into the post-1990 period. This significant economic liberalization was carried out by a military regime that took over after overthrowing the Allende administration. The return to political democracy in 1990, however, did not produce contradictory policies with regard to the liberalization implemented in 1973–89. In contrast, the two democratic administrations of the 1990–96 period have reinforced most of the structural adjustment measures and have introduced further progress in the field of macroeconomic stabilization. The crucial emphasis of these two administrations has been on social conditions and on achieving more equitable growth, both major pitfalls of the program carried out by the military regime.

THE SOCIALIST EXPERIMENT, 1971–73

Radical changes were pursued by President Allende to simultaneously attain lower inflation, a better income distribution, a higher GDP growth, and a socialist structure for the economy. Dominant policies included the increase of state intervention in productive affairs and the takeover by the government of several firms and industries considered strategic. This policy approach exacerbated the already visible failures of the import substitution strategy Chile had followed since the 1940s. In order to fulfill the expansionary aim of the socialist program, the fiscal deficit increased from 2.7 to 24.7 percent of the GDP between 1970 and 1973, with an average deficit of 16.1 percent of the GDP, that is, almost five times that of the historical period 1959–70 (Table 6.1). Similarly, the credit issued by the Central Bank increased by about six-hundred times in 1971–73, while on the external front, partly as a result of a sharp drop in world copper prices—Chile's major export at that time—international reserves dramatically dropped from $390 million in 1970 to $161 million in 1971; the trade deficit increased from 1.2 to more than 3.0 percent of the GDP in 1970–73. The policy response was to increase reliance on quantitative restrictions, in addition to the already high tariff rates, averaging more than 100 percent.

The overheating of the economy created serious economic problems, resulting in an average inflation rate for the period of 295.9 percent (Table 6.1). In spite of the obvious need for stabilization policies, maintenance of a progressive and revolutionary reputation was considered more important (Larrain and Meller 1990). Thus, instead of reducing aggregate and public expenditures, the government decided to transfer growing resources to public enterprises. In addition to operating losses, the public sector suffered a dramatic drop in tax collection, as well as

Table 6.1
Economic Indicators

	1959–1970[1]	1971–1973[2]	1974–1978[3]	1979–1981[4]	1982–1985[5]	1986–1989[6]	1990–1996[7]
Real GDP growth	4.0	0.7	1.9	7.2	–1.5	7.2	6.2
Per capita GDP*	(2.0)	(–0.9)	(0.2)	(5.7)	(–3.2)	(5.5)	(4.5)
CPI growth	26.5	295.9	206.4	26.5	23.3	18.3	18.3
Unemployment rate	5.6	3.9	16.5	16.2	24.9	14.1	7.4
Real wages**	73.2	92.1	73.1	103.2	102.4	106.7	121.3
Public deficit***	3.4	16.1	3.6	–2.2	4.1	–0.2	–1.6

Source: Central Bank of Chile.

1. Historical base: Presidents Alessandri (1959–64) and Frei (1965–70).
2. Socialist experiment: President Allende (1971–73).
3. Stabilization phase.
4. Recovery and precrisis.
5. Financial crisis.
6. Deep structural adjustment phase.
7. Democratic governments: Presidents Aylwin and Frei.

*   Yearly rate of growth.
**   Manufacturing index 1970 = 100.
*** Percentage of the GDP.

increasing inefficiencies caused by pricing and management problems, which created additional pressures on fiscal accounts. Yearly inflation skyrocketed to 260.5 and 605.1 percent in 1972 and 1973, respectively, creating economic and political chaos in the midst of widespread black markets and a deteriorating purchasing power of wages. The government intervened heavily in the productive sector. Further, the sector was under the effect of distorted input and output prices and was thereby unable and/or unwilling to provide a supply response to demand-driven policies.

The crisis deepened with the government's decision to strengthen its interventionist policies. The real GDP fell at rates of 1.2 and 5.6 percent in 1972 and 1973, respectively. This decrease was also accompanied by a steady decline in investment from 16 percent of the GDP in 1970 to 8 percent in 1973. Thanks to the high growth of public employment, the open unemployment rate remained at quite low levels, but real wages were rapidly declining as inflation accelerated: in fact, real wages dropped almost 36 percent between 1972 and 1973 (Riveros 1997).[1] The government insisted that economic problems were due to a plot organized by the private sector and by political foreign intervention. Instead of adopting measures aimed at restraining demand growth, it further insisted on seizing private firms and practicing expanding monetary and fiscal policies. Political turbulence was exacerbated due to acute product shortages and hyperinflation. The government faced an active political opposition, which accused Allende of leading the country to disaster and which aimed at a political overtaking along the lines of a Marxist dictatorship. The overthrow of Allende by the Chilean military was the tragic conclusion of the crisis.

THE STABILIZATION PHASE, 1974-78

The post-1973 military government embarked upon a series of intense economic reforms, aimed at improving efficiency in an open economy.[2] The new economic approach after the Allende era was based on stimulating the real sector through a better guidance of relative prices determined through market competition. Hence, after a long period of protectionism and state intervention, the new government made economic liberalization the basic instrument to attain a more efficient resource allocation. As a consequence, price and trade liberalization constituted the primary focus of the economic policies initiated in late 1973. The emphasis of the policies during the post-1973 period was not so much on achieving structural reforms or on achieving higher productive efficiency, but on reducing the high inflation rate to restore the allocative role of prices. The urgent need for reducing inflation required tight fiscal and monetary policies. In addition, the government opened up the external sector, a policy largely inspired by the need to achieve (along the lines of the law of one price) a domestic inflation rate closer to international levels. The loosening of traditional wage and employment controls, both legal and administrative, was another key reform area, as was deregulation of product markets, in order to let markets freely allocate resources.

The Fiscal/Monetary Program

In the early stages, measures were adopted to reform the central government, especially through reducing personnel expenditures and through privatizing public firms. By 1975, however, inflation was still above 300 percent, leading to further fiscal restraints. Hence, a dramatic drop in the fiscal deficit was achieved in one year, accompanied by a tighter monetary policy.[3] As a result, inflation was significantly curbed between 1975 and 1978 from 343 to 37.2 percent per year, and it continued to fall until 1981 (to 9.5 percent) thanks to the implementation of a nominal fixing of the exchange rate.

The attainment of a fiscal surplus in 1977–78 was paramount to the success of the stabilization program. Adopting market-determined prices for public enterprises and implementing an across-the-board reduction in fiscal expenditures were critical in pursuing this target. However, the stabilization effort produced a profound drop in aggregate demand, leading to a real GDP decline of almost 13 percent in 1975 and thereby also involving a high social cost in terms of unemployment and real wages. Also, the real per capita GDP changed very little in levels between 1974 and 1978, while the average inflation for this period was still relatively high (Table 6.1), indicating the need for further efforts to reduce aggregate demand pressures. Nonetheless, the stabilization effort seriously affected long-run growth due to its negative effects on investment and wealth (Edwards 1985).

Trade Liberalization

High trade barriers, allocative inefficiencies, discrimination against agriculture, and a widespread government intervention in economic affairs were major outcomes of the import substitution strategy Chile had followed since the 1940s (Corbo 1985a). Moreover, the effort in achieving an extensive industrial base demanded progressively higher protective barriers, leading to an average tariff rate as high as 105 percent by 1973 (Torres 1982).[4] The post-1973 economic liberalization aimed at a far-reaching opening up, which was expected to bring more investment and employment thanks to the realization of comparative advantages in production. This opening of the economy was chiefly inspired by the need for reducing inflation, and it began to be implemented without a clear final target in terms of tariff levels, the final outcome largely depending upon the observed inflationary path.

Nonetheless, in the period prior to 1980, the new policy failed in developing an export base and in obtaining a quicker recovery of labor-intensive industries. Two drawbacks can be mentioned in explaining this result: (1) the lack of a precise final target with regard to tariff reduction, which led to shifting the policy target repeatedly and created uncertainty for potential investors (Riveros 1986)[5] and (2) the use of the exchange rate as a stabilization device, as the rate was nominally fixed in 1979 while the inflation rate was still around 39 percent per year. This nominal fixing lasted for about three years and produced a notable overvaluation which negatively affected expectations and export industries (Corbo 1985b; Edwards and Edwards 1987). In addition, and amid high domestic interest rates and a growing peso appreciation, the economic authority decided to further open the capital account; in a period of rapidly expanding world credit markets the immediate result was a heavy external indebtedness.[6] In addition to macro imbalances created by the debt problem, this policy allowed large firms to adopt capital-intensive techniques, thereby negatively affecting employment growth in expanding activities and thus fostering unemployment (Edwards and Edwards 1987).

Privatization and Public-Sector Reforms

Paramount in the economic liberalization program were measures aimed at reducing the size of the state in the economy. The share of public firms in the GDP was as high as 39 percent in 1973 (Hachette and Luders 1987), while public employment (i.e., including civil service, local governments and public firms) reached about 14 percent of total employment during that year, equivalent to 36 percent of total formal employment.[7] Due to a public-sector reform, mainly consisting of employment reductions, elimination of the most obvious duplications in the civil service, and privatization of public firms, the share of public employment declined to 7 percent by 1980 and 5 percent in 1988 (Hachette and Luders 1987).

In order to achieve a reduction in the economic size of the state, a major privatization program was implemented after 1973, concurrently with policies aimed at achieving more efficient public services. Firms expropriated during Allende's socialist experiment were immediately privatized: by the end of 1974, 202 out of 259 firms had been returned to their owners (Larrain 1988). Most of these firms were operating at the cost of substantial losses, and a condition for returning them to their original owners was assuming all accumulated debts and waiving any possible damage claim against the government. Assets owned by the state, such as bank shares (US$ 171 million), as well as a significant part of the industrial property (US$ 58 million) were sold by 1975.[8] Since the share of public firms in the GDP decreased from 39 percent in 1973 to only 24 percent in 1981, an additional privatization effort took place at the time of the crisis of the 1980s. By 1981, the state still controlled all of the top ten enterprises in the country (copper, steel, telephones, energy, coal mining, etc.), raising questions about the sustainability of the privatization effort.

Liberalization of Markets

A top priority of the post-1973 reform program was improving the resource allocation through an efficient free-market system. Hence, contrary to the tradition in Chile, price regulation was almost completely eliminated at once.[9] This deregulation included interest rates and the several quantitative constraints existing in the capital markets. The increased market competition forced the private sector to improve its productive efficiency, causing several bankruptcies during the transitional period. Although price liberalization led to an inflationary peak in 1974, it allowed a rearrangement of relative prices and, along with macroeconomic stabilization policies, produced a better investment climate.

Factor markets were also the target of price liberalization. Interest rates were deregulated, instead of being arbitrarily fixed by the authorities. Similarly, the wage determination was left to the prevailing labor market conditions (Edwards and Edwards 1987).

THE ECONOMIC RECOVERY, 1979–81

Between 1979 and 1981 the government shifted the emphasis away from stabilization policies toward structural adjustment. The yearly inflation rate in 1978 and 1979, however, was still around 38 percent, making policy efforts focus on price stabilization. The move toward structural adjustment involved three major components. First, an education and health reform introduced the decentralization of local governments. Second, a social security reform allowed for the replacement of the pay-as-you-go system administered by the government with a new system in which private firms would collect and manage pension funds as simple savings accounts. Third, a new labor law was enacted in order to allow for a more flexible and competitive market; this provided a basic institutional framework in support of the economic liberalization program.

In the recovery period 1979–81, economic growth was high, while inflation returned to historical levels (Table 6.1). Inflation reached 31 and 9.5 percent in 1980 and 1981, respectively, as a result of the fixing of the nominal exchange rate in 1979. Real wages showed an important recovery in this period, while public-sector accounts produced a surplus, after a prolonged period of fiscal mismanagement (Table 6.1). Reforms were, however, incomplete. A large portion of the economic activity was still in public hands, including energy, communications, and social security. Also, export growth was slow, largely a result of a falling real exchange rate and relatively low investment since 1973. In addition, another concern was the presence of relatively high unemployment despite the relatively strong economic recovery in 1979–81 (Table 6.1). This was the result of the elimination of public-sector employment due to privatization and the substantial skill mismatch in the labor market.

The health system was reformed in 1981 to increase the participation of the private sector in insurance and health care industries. At the same time, government social services (public health and education) were decentralized, with the respective cabinet ministries retaining responsibility for policy formulation but not for the direct administration of personnel and the budget. These functions, in education and health care, were transferred to local governments, making them directly responsible for their administrative decisions. Similarly, a program of targeted assistance, in the form of monetary subsidies to the poor, the elderly, and the unemployed, was put into place. These changes were important as they allowed for a better targeting of fiscal social expenditures to the poor.

Also in 1981, social security was transformed from a pay-as-you-go system in which benefits depended only on individual contributions to a privately managed savings account system. This change was vital to allow for a successful privatization program given the significant potential of social security to accumulate savings and mobilize financial resources. In a longer-term perspective, the social security reform can be considered the prime reform in the context of economic liberalization: it allowed management of long term savings by the private sector (an issue which had been traditionally considered a "social" matter) as well as the consolidation of the financial sector and the stock exchange and provided a solid basis for the privatization of the remaining public assets.

The most important criticism of the post-1973 economic liberalization was its social impact, manifested in the deteriorating income distribution and increasing poverty. For instance, the Gini coefficient for the income distribution had reached a value of about 0.47 in the mid-1960s and remained above 0.51 in the period of economic recovery, 1979–81. The income share of the poorest group fell dramatically from almost 13 percent in the 1960s to less than 11 percent in 1980, while the fiscal expenditure plummeted and the efficiency of the social services became wanting (Riveros 1997). It was then clear that a social strategy was needed in order to attain political sustainability for the structural adjustment phase. Also, as the labor market provided a poor response to the need for reallocating labor from contracting to expanding industries, reforms aimed at making its role more dynamic and flexible were of paramount importance in order to attain lower unemployment.

THE FINANCIAL CRISIS, 1982–85

The 1982–85 financial crisis brought a sharp economic decline, amid serious problems in the balance of payments. Domestic economic policies introduced at the end of the 1970s created macroeconomic disequilibria, which, in turn, led to unsustainable high expectations and, ultimately, to a disruption in the economic recovery initiated in 1976. These policies included the nominal fixing of the exchange rate aimed at reducing price inflation, while the full opening of the capital account, under a fixed exchange rate regime, produced large capital inflows and heavy external indebtedness. This combination of policies was burdensome and still more problematic under the binding full indexation of wages to past inflation, which was introduced with the 1979 labor law. All this resulted in increasing production costs for exporters, whereas the production of nontradables was fostered by a rapidly appreciating real exchange rate, and large capital inflows financed an otherwise unsustainable expansion of private consumption and the real estate industry.

After difficult recessionary years and a recovery period in 1979–81, the country was dominated by high expectations and a certain far-fetched optimism, which led to a consumption boom but also to significant external indebtedness. Optimism about future trends was based on the stable growth path experienced since 1976, the balanced public budget, the sustained improvement in real wages seen after 1975, and the successful opening of the economy. However, the consumption boom of 1980–81 was basically financed with foreign credit generously provided through expanding world financial markets, with few resources being allocated to productive investment, particularly in export-oriented activities. The magnitude of the financial crisis Chile underwent in 1982–84 is revealed by the increase in the external debt, from 2.7 times total exports in 1979 to 4.6 times in 1983. As a share of the GDP, the external debt increased from 40 percent to 100 percent between the same years, while yearly interest payments increased from 3 to 10 percent of GDP. At the same time, due to an early policy reaction to the crisis, led by a significant devaluation of the exchange rate in 1982, the value of imports in real terms declined by more than 40 percent in 1982. This triggered a GDP drop of more than 14 percent during this year.

The debt crisis was accompanied by an important external shock, the magnitude of which is reflected in the deterioration in terms of trade, from 119 in 1979 to 88 in 1983, and in the increase in real (LIBOR) interest rates.[10] The sharp curtailment of capital inflows in early 1982 with the Mexican crisis amplified the problem and pushed the economy into a deep recession in 1982–83. The macroeconomic results were generally poor for the 1982–85 period, as the GDP dropped by an average 1.5 percent. The accumulated drop of the GDP in 1982–1983 reached almost 15 percent. Unemployment, for this period, was as high as 25 percent, while real wages dropped and the fiscal deficit increased above the historical reference period (Table 6.1). In addition to these problems, there were important negative consequences of the ongoing crisis in the financial sector and of the loss of credibility of the private banking industry, which was partly in bankruptcy.

The policy approach used to counter the effects of the financial crisis consisted of stimulating aggregate demand to encourage output growth through expanding fiscal outlays and further external indebtedness. As a result, the external debt increased from US$ 17.4 billion to US$ 18.9 billion in 1983–84. Also, in this period, the real exchange rate did not depreciate as fast as it should have, since the real index dropped from 118 to 115 (Table 6.2). Consequently, exports increased by a modest 7 percent (which can be explained by a persistent drop in terms of trade) while imports expanded by 16 percent. Hence, the current account deficit doubled and reserves decreased by about 8 percent between 1984 and 1985 (in addition to the 50 percent already lost in 1980–83). These adverse developments led to repeated use of International Monetary Fund (IMF) credits and to an increase in the fiscal deficit from 4.0 to 6.3 percent of the GDP.[11] Although economic growth was 6.3 percent in 1984,

Table 6.2
Macroeconomic Indicators during Economic Liberalization

	1970	1971	1972	1973	1974	1975	1976	1977	1978	1979	1980	1981	1982
Real exchange rate (index)	41.0	37.6	39.0	60.3	89.1	106.4	97.3	88.8	108.1	112.7	100.0	79.6	86.3
Real exports growth (%)[1]	10.0	−24.3	−18.1	33.5	77.8	−43.9	23.8	−3.4	5.1	43.5	7.4	−26.1	−10.3
Real wage manufacturing (index)	97.1	106.6	101.2	68.4	62.2	58.3	78.6	78.6	87.4	94.2	100.0	115.5	110.7
Real minimum wage (index)	81.0	106.8	101.7	46.2	90.6	105.1	100.1	84.6	97.4	98.3	100.0	111.0	122.2

	1983	1984	1985	1986	1987	1988	1989	1990	1991	1992	1993	1994	1995
Real exchange rate (index)	104.4	107.2	130.9	148.8	152.7	159.5	155.7	161.6	156.6	140.5	139.4	118.9	117.7
Real exports growth (%)[1]	−1.7	−9.2	−1.0	7.5	20.8	30.3	9.6	−1.4	2.3	9.1	−11.1	23.3	34.9
Real wage manufacturing (index)[2]	102.9	99.0	97.1	101.9	103.2	109.8	111.8	116.1	123.8	129.7	133.1	138.0	142.6
Real minimum wage (index)	93.2	82.1	74.3	78.8	66.9	74.2	80.1	87.9	101.0	108.1	119.6	124.1	129.1

Source: Central Bank of Chile.

Percentage and real index 1980 = 100

1. The series was obtained through the average CPI of industrial countries (IMF).
2. For 1994 and 1995, data correspond to the new series of real hourly wages.

the availability of external resources posed a tough constraint to the planned expansion in aggregate expenditures, making the recessionary effect even worse after that year.

THE STRUCTURAL ADJUSTMENT PHASE, 1985–90

Using expansionary policies to deal with the financial crisis was deemed necessary on political grounds. By 1984, the economic situation was extremely harsh, with significant macroeconomic problems as well as adverse conditions in key sectors such as the banking system. The economy needed policies aimed at reversing the real effects of the financial crisis, attaining a more sustainable macroeconomic situation particularly through encouraging export growth, and continuing with the plan of structural reforms initiated in the late 1970s. Thus, by 1985, the government decided to change the approach used in 1983–84 to manage the economic crisis, an experience which shows the failure of the traditional policy approach in terms of balance of payments, debt, and macroeconomic stabilization. The decision was taken in order to continue with the economic liberalization which had started in the 1970s, based upon restrictive fiscal and monetary policies and an increasing role of markets and the private sector in resource allocation. The government also realized that the exchange rate should play a key role with regard to developing a more dynamic export basis and that the need for promoting investment, both domestic and external, required adequate signals to investors on the institutional character of the economy and its expected evolution.

Consequently, with the idea of continuing the broad economic liberalization program initiated in the 1970s, the government pursued the maintenance of a high real exchange rate (Table 6.2), introduced a program to continue the privatization of public firms, persisted in a drastic control of fiscal expenditures, created mechanisms to convert external debt into domestic investment, gave specific incentives to exports, and strengthened a system to target social expenditures to the poor.[12] In doing this, several structural reforms initiated before the crisis, such as those regarding the social security system, the labor law, and the reform of the social sector, were of critical importance.

A policy aimed at introducing a systematic real exchange rate devaluation, accompanied by other standard export promotion policies, was a key element in attaining a strong economic growth. The real exchange rate increased by 23.5 percent between 1985 and 1990 (Table 6.2), while export growth occurred at an average rate of 16.6 percent in this same period. The economic expansion led to an average GDP growth of 7.2 percent in 1986–89, while inflation declined to about 14 percent of the labor force in this same period (Table 6.1). With regard to the macroeconomic context, the fiscal accounts showed an average surplus of 0.2

percent of the GDP, while inflation dropped to an average lower than historical figures. During this period, aggregate investment reached a yearly rate of more than 20 percent of the GDP, a figure which positively contrasted with historical averages of 15–17 percent.

The increase in the relative price of tradables to non-tradables allowed for the nominal devaluation of the exchange rate, in combination with policies aimed at the control of aggregate expenditures, and produced substantial factor mobility toward export and import-substituting industries, producing positive trade balance results. The increasing capital inflow and the expanding domestic investment, jointly with a growing and more efficient financial sector, enabled a highly satisfactory intersectoral capital mobility and a substantial productive expansion. A well-functioning labor market allowed for the labor reallocation needed after the recessionary shock, as suggested by the notable drop in unemployment seen between 1986 and 1990.

The privatization strategy fulfilled a key role during the 1985–89 period. As a result of the debt crisis of 1982–85, the financial system was in a very difficult situation. Largely indebted and characterized by a very low public credibility, it was unable to produce the capital mobility needed to start a meaningful recovery. However, a market solution, which would have implied the bankruptcy of important banks indebted beyond their capital, would have produced a clear negative impact on the credibility and viability of the Chilean economic model as a whole. Therefore, solving the problems of the banking system and of other financial institutions was considered a top policy priority. This gave rise to a policy scheme whereby newly issued shares of banks and other financial institutions were sold to small investors. Thus, the capitalization strategy—literally, a "rescue" operation—instituted large, long-term debts of most beneficiary banks with the Central Bank. The banking sector also provided the credit to purchasers of the new shares. This "popular capitalism" solved the property issue as, in the case of largely indebted banks, it was politically unpalatable to return all of the new banking assets to private interest groups.

By 1985, many large enterprises were still owned by the state. The decision to privatize them was based on the need to reduce their fiscal deficits. More important, however, was the need to improve their productive efficiency and provide adequate signals to foreign creditors about the deep economic liberalization carried out and the indisputable leading role allotted to the private sector in the overall economic strategy. Large public enterprises were sold either through open stock market operations or by means of direct allocation of shares.[13] Energy was one of the sectors privatized through the direct sales of shares to small investors. By the same token, the telephone company, the steel industry, coal mining, and other secondary industries, still in the hands of the state at the beginning of the 1980s, were transferred to the private sector. This privatization process made use of an increasing flow of foreign resources, allowed by debt-equity swap operations. In sum, Chile introduced changes in the areas of state ownership and external debt management and adopted a macro policy framework aimed at encouraging growth and exports and at the same time allowed a more prominent role to the private sector in resource allocation.

THE RETURN TO DEMOCRATIC GOVERNMENTS, 1990–96

After a long period of military dictatorship, a democratic vote decided the return to a normal Western-style type of government. The political support was obtained by the Concertación, a group of political parties which systematically opposed the Pinochet government. Aylwin's election in 1990 was largely an expression of the desire to return to a sustainable political democracy, but it was also a reflection of the social costs of the adjustment in the post financial crisis. In fact, unemployment was still double the historical averages, and real wages had not followed suit with the expansion of exports and the GDP during 1986–89. Although the macroeconomic indicators were promising and revealed the capacity of the country to get out of the financial crisis, the social indicators were wanting.

Contrary to the expectations of many, the democratic governments consolidated the economic liberalization initiated by the military, since its results in terms of growth and stability were considered highly satisfactory. Since then, efforts have continued to lower the inflation rate.[14] In 1995–96, the inflation rate was lowered to single-digit levels as a result of the conservative monetary policies carried out by an independent Central Bank. At the same time, the country has experienced an unprecedented high rate of economic growth, with an average of 6.2 percent in the same period. The export sector and investment have led this growth, the latter reaching an average of 24 percent of the GDP in 1990–96. Unemployment has declined to its natural level, while real wages have grown at a yearly average of almost 5 percent. On the fiscal side, a permanent surplus averaging 1.6 percent of the GDP prevailed.

The Aylwin and Frei administrations not only sheltered the changes carried out by the military administration but also designed further steps to deepen economic liberalization. Average tariff rates, which were increased during the financial crisis from 10 to 17 percent, dropped to an average of 11 percent during the 1990–96 period. The privatization program has continued, although sluggish in certain areas, such as transportation and sanitary services. In the public sector, a system of conceding the public works to the private sector has been put into place, whereas modernization of the entire public sector is still pending.

As a result of the political agreement on a tax reform, fiscal expenditures have grown by more than 90 percent in 1990–96, allowing for a drop in poverty from 40 to 26 percent of the households. The economic growth has apparently provided the necessary conditions to significantly improve the labor market, to increase the efficiency of the public sector, and to introduce better social policies.

LABOR MARKETS AND ECONOMIC LIBERALIZATION

The Prominent Role of Labor Markets in the Liberalization Process

Economic liberalization implies far-reaching key institutional reforms and crucial changes in relative prices. Among these reforms, the opening to international trade, the reduction in the economic size of the state and the deregulation of product and factor markets are prominent. Economic liberalization implies a restructuring of the economic activity across industries, whereby the labor market has a key role in the building up of a supply response. As a result of a structural shift in prices, the liberalization process produces contracting and expanding productive industries, thereby requiring a labor reallocation from industries and sectors in contraction toward those in expansion. Nonetheless, this process requires a correspondent change in relative wages and can be complicated by prevailing rigidities in the labor market, such as constraints on the firing/hiring process, the existence of institutions that render the required change in relative wages difficult, and the presence of skill mismatch. In addition, the likely presence of labor supply pressures, as well as increased union activism and legal constraints, can make the labor mobility industries and sectors much more difficult, thereby lengthening the transition period. In general, however, one can always expect the presence of short-run unemployment, mainly due to the existence of wage rigidities and the presence of skill mismatch in expanding sectors.

The Chilean economic experience fits into this stylized description of the labor market adjustment during liberalization. There were distressing dislocations in the labor market, featured by high and persistent unemployment and a significant drop in real wages. Apparently, however, relative wages did not change as much, relative to the large drop in average real wages derived from macroeconomic policies and the industrial restructuring (Riveros 1994). The employment growth took place slowly, as expectations and economic signals stemming from macroeconomic policies did not always favor the expansion of economic activities with comparative advantages in trade. At the same time, the lack of an appropriate legal framework in the labor market during the period of trade liberalization (1974–79) promoted uncertainty and did not help progress toward greater employment dynamics, and at the same time an important skill mismatch surrounded the reallocation of labor across industries (Sapelli 1990).

The Liberalization of the Labor Market

Like other Latin American countries, Chile was characterized by a significant body of labor regulations. Two broad reasons prevailed for an extensive government regulation of labor markets. The first was the assumption that workers needed to be protected from the machinations of an unfettered market-based economy. Widespread state intervention in the labor market was then founded on a distrust of market outcomes—especially on equity grounds—and on the rejection of the simplistic idea that markets freely set wages and determine employment levels. Clearly, not all markets are competitive, and when conditions are far from ideal, such institutions as collective bargaining, job security provisions, and labor standards, which protect the welfare, safety, and health of workers, can enhance labor productivity. Throughout time, however, these institutional arrangements developed into a drastic constraint on achieving a better resource allocation.

A second reason for enduring interventionist labor market policies is the assumption that the state can do all and do it well and fairly. This belief is rooted in the idea of a paternalistic state that can provide for all needs, redistributing benefits and costs and intervening in all spheres of social and economic activity. This view reflects the classical welfare theory of what the government's role is supposed to be: it is supposed to correct any market failure by funding public goods and by subsidizing goods that generate positive externalities while taxing those that yield negative externalities. This role apparently included the state as employer, allowing the government and large state-owned enterprises to account for a dominant share of employment.

Experience shows that government intervention can indeed benefit labor, for instance, through programs that provide incentives for private enterprises to supplement the education of their workers and through legislation which enables the development of collective bargaining mechanisms and other means for resolving labor disputes and for protecting unorganized workers against monopsonistic practices by employers. Nevertheless, experience also shows that state interventions in the labor market do not always benefit the intended beneficiaries. Political interests may be directed toward interventions that deter investments, prevent appropriate supply responses to economic shocks and lower the demand for labor. Perhaps even more frustrating is that good intentions can fall by the wayside because of an unwieldy and incompetent bureaucracy which fails to deliver.[15]

The Chilean labor market was traditionally regulated with regard to four key aspects. First, substantial severance costs were mandated, making labor mobility unnecessarily expensive and introducing an extreme job security, according to which all dismissals had to be turned into the Ministry of Labor or a labor court, thereby substantially curtailing the right of the firm to manage its inputs. Second, collective bargaining was allowed at an aggregate level, usually at industry level, thereby disturbing the necessary connection between wages and the labor productivity that must exist at the firm level. This approach also prolonged the conflicts since it caused a virtual disconnection between labor and the specific situation at the firm or product level. Third, unionization was mandatory. The law permitted only one union per firm or activity and fostered the organization of labor coalitions at industry and inter-industry levels. Fourth, the government intervened heavily in the labor market, either directly, through wage indexation and minimum wage regulations, or indirectly, through public employment and wage policies.

During the 1960s, the economy was characterized by low unemployment (Table 6.1) and relatively acceptable growth rates of the real wage (Table 6.3). Paradoxically, however, employment growth in manufacturing was negatively affected by the import substitution strategy Chile had followed since the 1940s and labor market segmentation was made deeper due to the need for labor protection and strong unionization (Riveros 1994). Similarly, the real wage path became increasingly unrelated to labor productivity. These trends were exacerbated in 1970–71, when, thanks to government policies, real manufacturing wages and the real minimum wage increased significantly (Table 6.2), and unemployment dropped under its natural level (Table 6.1). Subsequently, of course, the increase in prices significantly eroded real wages—leading to negative growth rates for the period 1971–73 (Table 6.3). Nonetheless, employment significantly expanded in this latter period, at a rate of 3.5 percent per year, thanks to public firms and the central government. Surprisingly, combining the information on GDP and employment growth rates, an empirical employment-output elasticity of 5.0 is calculated for the 1971–73 period, in contrast with the 0.7 for the historical (i.e., pre-1970) period.[16]

The economic liberalization that occurred after 1973 introduced key changes in the labor market. Acute government intervention and union activism were replaced by a wave of deregulation. A partial liberalization in prevailing wage-setting schemes was achieved. Also, the elimination of over-employment in the public sector was declared a top priority by the government. Notwithstanding, post-1973 policy measures aimed at simply dismantling the institutional organization of the labor market rather than attempting to replace the existing regulations by measures providing more flexibility. Hence, collective bargaining and union activities were eliminated simultaneously after 1973, while job security provisions were also removed: massive labor dismissals

Table 6.3
Labor Market Indicators, 1959–96 (growth rates)

	1959–70	1971–73	1974–78	1979–81	1982–85	1986–89	1990–96
1. Employment	2.8	3.5	1.2	5.2	1.5	5.9	4.2
2. Participation rate	-0.3	-1.4	0.5	0.5	0.3	1.2	1.0
3. Real wages	4.1	-9.2	3.8	8.6	-3.7	3.0	4.6
4. Real minimum wages	NA	-9.1	21.6	4.6	-8.8	2.4	5.7

Sources: 1. and 2.: University of Chile, unemployment survey for the greater Santiago area.
3. and 4.: Central Bank of Chile.

The periods correspond to the same classification used in the text.

required only a simple administrative authorization from the government. Moreover, unions were de facto eliminated, their leaders being hand-picked by the government itself. The labor law was "suspended" and the private sector was given full power to implement its preferred employment-wage strategy.

The absence of a legal framework in the labor market during most of the 1970s was, nonetheless, a factor which fed into unfavorable expectations. During the entire 1973–79 period, no new legal rules governed labor relations, including wage bargaining, job security, the right to strike, negotiation of working conditions, and union activities. However, after a long history of labor market intervention, and as private employers may have envisaged a return to an environment characterized by confrontations with the unions, the legal vacuum of 1973–79 did not favor a more labor-intensive production technology. On the other hand, minimum wages and non wage cost regulations were upheld by the military regime, and a wage indexation system was introduced after 1973, although with little real effects, given the lack of appropriate enforcement (Edwards and Edwards 1987; Riveros 1986). These interventions were, however, apparently reason enough to foster segmentation of the labor market, making wage adjustment and the inter-industry labor mobility far more difficult (Paredes and Riveros 1993).

In 1979, the government enacted a new labor law which introduced a drastic change vis-à-vis the traditional institutional organization of the labor market. This new law, largely inspired by U.S. experience, introduced significant changes in three important areas. First, in order to create a closer relationship between the negotiations and the actual conditions of the firm, particularly in connection with wages and productivity, collective bargaining was allowed only at the firm level. The right to strike was curtailed by granting firms the privilege to hire temporaries, while public employees' right to strike was banned. With regard to unionization, the new law introduced the principle of voluntary affiliation, allowing the presence of more than one union at the firm level. Second, labor market flexibility was encouraged by reducing severance payments, from one month per year of service, with no limit, to a similar unitary payment, but with an eight-months' limit. Also, the dismissal procedure was made more flexible, without involving the Ministry of Labor or returning to the system of labor courts that had been in place since the late 1920s. Third, the direct role of the government in the labor market was reduced only to the fixing of the minimum wage, since the wage setting was entirely left to private negotiations.[17] Indeed, the indirect influence of the public sector was also significantly reduced with the downsizing of the state.

Notably, after the economic crisis in 1985–89, a significant employment dynamic prevailed which strongly contrasts with that observed during the recovery that took place after the stabilization period (1979–81). In this latter period, the employment-GDP elasticity was 0.72, while in 1985–89 it reached 1.2. One explanation for this contrast deals with the role played during the first period by negative expectations, concerning the uncertainty about the institutional environment that was planned for the labor market. The second period, in contrast, was characterized by a new labor law, which gave adequate signals to the private sector, thereby fostering employment and investment.

As it has been shown in Paredes and Riveros (1993), the employment-output elasticity structurally increased after the labor market reforms of the early 1980s. These reforms fostered greater inter-industry labor mobility and promoted greater flexibility, since the new job security norms made the hiring and firing processes less expensive, allowing for the effective reentry of the unemployed.[18]

The Unemployment Story

The reforms of the 1970s exerted major effects on the labor market. Open unemployment increased from an average of 6 percent of the labor force in the 1960s to more than 16 percent during 1974–81 (Table 6.1).[19] The average unemployment rates during the stabilization (1974–78) and economic recovery (1979–81) periods are strikingly similar (Table 6.1), despite the difference in average GDP growth rates (1.9 and 7.2 percent, respectively). A major cause of the higher unemployment in 1974–78 was the productive shock resulting from both the stabilization program of 1975 and the opening up of the economy to trade. The reduction in the public-sector employment in this period, and the greater participation by the secondary labor force caused by the higher unemployment itself, were also key factors in explaining the rise in unemployment (Riveros 1986). The government reacted by creating emergency employment programs in 1976, which provided modest monetary subsidies for the urban unemployed, contributing to the reduction of the social impact of open unemployment, but also fostering a higher participation by the secondary labor force.

Even in the presence of a strong economic recovery in 1979–81, open unemployment remained high relative to the historical standard (Table 6.1). To a large extent, the persistence of abnormally high unemployment relates to the substantial shift in production that occurred in the economy as a consequence of the open trade regime. As a substantial skill mismatch prevailed in the labor force and no institutional mechanism was prepared to provide a proactive answer (Riveros 1994), transitional and mismatch unemployment was high.[20] At the same time, substantial change toward capital-intensive techniques was taking place in production, particularly in manufacturing and services, leading to a structurally higher, open unemployment. This latter outcome is derived from the wrong signals emanating from the uncertainty surrounding the labor market following the suspension of the labor laws. The financial and productive crisis of 1982–84 produced additional pressures on the labor market, on top of the already high unemployment existing in 1981; the unemployment rate skyrocketed, reaching as high as 30 percent of the labor force in 1983.[21] This was a demand-driven result, since participation rates did not notably change during the recession. From 1985 onward, and as a result of a strong economic recovery and a more fluid labor market, unemployment sharply dropped, leading to a level close to the natural rate in the early 1990s.

Behavior of Real Wages

An outcome related to the observed persistence in open unemployment was the drop in real wages in the 1970s and early 1980s. A sharp decline of real wages occurred in the period 1971–78, a large portion of which took place in 1972–75 as a result of the stabilization effort. Thereafter, a notable recovery was observed, which averaged more than 8 percent per annum in 1979–81 (Table 6.2). This outcome which took place regardless of the presence of higher unemployment (Table 6.1), again suggests the likely presence of skill mismatch. In this period, the average increase in real wages was greater than the increase in labor productivity, due to the indexation rule introduced in the 1979 labor law and the fact that wages were indexed to past inflation with the inflation rate dropping significantly (Sapelli 1990; Riveros 1986). The rise in real wages was also due to the appreciating real exchange rate (Garcia 1993) and created a significant increase in labor costs, which did not contribute to the generation of employment within the expanding sectors.[22]

Average real wages again declined dramatically between 1982 and 1983, partly as a result of the economic recession and partly because of the presence of the growing unemployment rate. Between 1982 and 1985, real wages further declined along with open unemployment, the real wage index (1980 = 100) reaching a value of 93 in 1985, which compares poorly with the value of 109 seen in 1981.[23] In the period of economic crisis, real wages declined by an average 3.7 percent per year (Table 6.2). This poor behavior of real wages in the 1970s and 1980s can also be attributed to the low and relatively stable labor productivity (Jadresic 1990).

After 1985, average real wages increased slightly, more notably in manufacturing as real wages followed the behavior of labor productivity (Riveros 1997). In 1986–89, GDP grew by 7.2 percent per year (Table 6.1), while the average and the minimum wages increased only by 3.0 and 2.4 percent, respectively (Table 6.3). This may have allowed for the significant drop in unemployment seen in 1985. At the same time, employment was increasing in the expanding sectors, such as construction, in which skill mismatch was not a fundamental problem, given their likely intensity in unskilled labor. With unemployment close to the natural rate, the growth rate of wages has been fairly similar to that of the per capita GDP during the 1990s. It is important to note that during the latter period, real minimum wages have grown at an average 5.7 percent per year, recovering the loss experienced during the financial crash of the 1980s. The actual level of the minimum wage in Chile is about US $120, comparable to that prevailing in most Latin American countries.

Employment Trends during Liberalization

The employment drop in manufacturing was significant during the period of the opening up to trade and during the financial crisis (Table 6.4). Afterwards, manufacturing employment grew at high rates (5.8 percent per year), quite similar to the average growth rate of the GDP. At closer inspection (Table 6.5), it appears that the employment dynamics in the manufacturing industry were largely associated with the behavior of export-oriented industries, such as wood and paper, or food. In contrast, import-substituting industries, such as textile and metallics (including the electronic industry, which collapsed very early in the liberalization process), showed a much steadier employment dynamic throughout time. It is easily seen in Table 6.5 that the employment gain was much larger in export-oriented manufacturing industries.

It is also important to note that the employment increase in nontradable industries was much higher than in the case of manufacturing (Table 6.4). This is probably the result of liberalization policies which disfavored trade protection and promoted market liberalization, which contributed to the expansion of nontradables, such as construction and commerce.

The data in Tables 6.4 and 6.5 are on urban Santiago. Table 6.6 is based on a national survey and provides information on agriculture as well. It is important to note that the employment increase in agriculture has not been as strong as that in the nontradable industries, particularly after the financial crisis. A likely explanation for this is that most export activities in agriculture are less labor-intensive than certain nontradables.

CONCLUSIONS

The economic liberalization in Chile consisted of a comprehensive policy package, which has been systematically applied for more than twenty years. Even though the policy design was always consistent with the basic purposes of liberalization, its application was not exempt from mistakes and certain policy reversals. Overall, however, there has been significant progress in terms of growth, macroeconomic stability, ex-

Table 6.4
Employment Trends in Liberalization

	1974	1979	1981	1985	1989	1996
Mnaufacturing	101.3	92.2	101.6	84.8	139.3	157.9
Nontradable A[1]	93.0	90.3	104.4	108.1	146.2	186.1
Nontradable B[2]	71.0	92.7	100.9	121.8	133.1	180.9

Source: University of Chile, employment survey for the greater Santiago area.

Index 1980 = 100

1. Includes construction, tranportation, communication, and public utilities.
2. Includes commerce and public and private services.

Table 6.5
Employment in Manufacturing during Liberalization

	1974		1979	1981	1985	1989	1996	
Food	89.2	(9.5)	94.5	102.7	97.3	162.2	210.8	(16.8)
Textiles	99.1	(34.1)	87.4	106.7	84.9	121.0	110.9	(28.5)
Wood and paper	43.5	(5.8)	100.0	119.6	82.6	134.8	176.1	(17.5)
Metallics	109.8	(16.2)	113.7	100.0	117.6	164.7	188.2	(20.7)
Chemical	152.4	(9.2)	133.3	119.0	114.3	214.3	266.7	(12.1)

Source: University of Chile, employment survey for the greater Santiago area.

Index 1980 = 100

Figures in parentheses are the corresponding share of each branch in total manufacturing employment.

ports, and domestic investment and in attaining a more efficient economic organization. The reform process cannot be considered concluded, but it has already achieved a mature system characterized by an open trade regime, a subsidiary role of the state, and an ample role for markets in resource allocation. Admittedly, the reforms were initiated and mostly implemented under a military regime; however, the transition to a democratic system in the 1990s has not implied any substantial change with regard to its fundamental aspects. In addition to a greater emphasis on equity issues, democratic governments have furthered progress in attaining macro stability and in opening up the Chilean economy to international trade.

The labor market has played a key role in the process of economic liberalization. This role has been twofold: first, with regard to the inter-industry labor mobility and, second, with regard to the role of wages to adequately reflect the social opportunity cost of labor. To a large

Table 6.6
Employment by Industry at National Level

	1980	1981	1982	1983	1984	1985	1986	1987	1988	1989	1990	1991
Agriculture, fishing, and others	100.0	105.4	108.0	98.6	102.9	108.2	110.2	116.7	124.5	121.8	120.8	125.8
Mining and manufacturing	100.0	100.2	80.0	69.8	82.2	92.6	100.9	106.2	121.0	123.8	132.3	139.7
Construction, transport, communication	100.0	111.5	94.3	80.8	93.7	100.7	110.9	113.3	131.7	140.0	146.3	154.8
Nontradables other	100.0	104.2	102.0	109.8	113.7	121.3	125.2	131.0	127.4	129.8	138.9	141.5

Source: Department of Economics, Universidad de Chile.

Base 1980 = 100

extent, the difficulties of the labor market in attaining a more dynamic response in connection with these issues have been due to prevailing regulations and institutions and the presence of a substantial skill mismatch. In general, however, and after a long period of adjustment, the labor market is characterized by a natural unemployment rate and a rapid growth of real wages, leaving human capital investment and labor productivity as major issues to be focused on in the future.

The Chilean liberalization experience has displayed four key labor market characteristics. The first is the presence of high and persistent unemployment, which has resulted mostly from skill mismatch, inappropriate job security regulations, and the existence of institutional wage rigidities. The second is the importance of the legal framework in affecting employment growth. The Chilean experience suggests that expectations about this framework can be a crucial factor in terms of employment creation. The third feature concerns the crucial role of macroeconomic policies, such as those affecting the real exchange rate, which may have significant effects on labor costs. Finally, the fourth is the social impact of the labor market outcomes, such as unemployment and declining real wages. These call for proactive policies, such as training, employment services and subsidies targeted to the poor.

ACKNOWLEDGMENTS

I appreciate discussions on the subject with my colleagues at the Department of Economics, University of Chile, specially Ricardo Paredes, as well as with Albert Berry and Van Adams, and the research assistance of Carlos Briceno.

NOTES

1. An average unemployment rate for the period 1971–73 of 3.9 percent (Table 6.1) is believed to be under the natural rate of unemployment, which has been calculated at about 6.0 percent (Paredes and Riveros 1993).

2. See Edwards and Edwards (1987), Walton (1985), and Corbo (1985a).

3. The fiscal deficit (measured as a percentage of GDP) declined from 24.7 to 10.5 between 1973 and 1974. A further drop to 2.6 was achieved in only one year, between 1974 and 1975, thanks to a reduction in public expenditures.

4. Ad valorem tariff rates ranged from 0 to 750 percent, while import prohibitions applied to 187 tariff classifications, a ninety-day import deposit requirement was in effect for 2,800 others, and 2,300 categories required special approval from the Central Bank.

5. Initially, tariffs were planned to reach an average of 60 percent by 1977. By 1975, average tariffs had reached 57 percent, while almost all quantitative restrictions were eliminated. In a second stage, a new structure, with tariffs ranging from 10 to 35 percent, was in place during the third quarter of 1977.

Finally, a more radical reform allowed the average nominal tariff rate to reach a uniform 10 percent by late 1977.

6. The total external debt increased from US$ 8.5 billion to 17.1 billion in 1979–82.

7. The share of public firms in GDP had been 14 percent in 1965. The socialist aim of the Allende administration is also shown by the fact that public employment grew 38 percent in 1970–73, although per capita GDP was declining. In 1970, only about 10 percent of the labor force was employed in the public sector.

8. This was a year of unprecedented economic decline (GDP felt by 12.9 percent per year), thereby leading to unprofitable sales. At the same time, firms were sold below their book values, although still above their stock market value (Larrain 1988).

9. After an era in which more than 3,000 prices were set and eventually controlled by the authority, only thirty-three commodities remained under control, most of them utilities.

10. See Corbo and Sturzenegger (1988). Between 1978 and 1984, the real LIBOR increased from a level of 1.1 percent to 6.1 percent.

11. This was the highest deficit observed in the post-1974 period and it led to inflationary pressures, since the CPI growth increased from 20.7 percent in 1982 to 26.4 in 1985. The fiscal deficit was clearly associated with the increase in expenditures rather than with dropping revenues during the period.

12. The latter was based upon debt-equity swap operations managed by the Central Bank, which made use of the prevailing low prices of debt-related instruments in international markets. In fact, Chilean debt bonds were being priced at about 50 percent of their face value.

13. This was, for instance, the case of public employees purchasing shares of the Energy Company (ENDESA) using their severance funds.

14. As a matter of fact, inflation behaved rather erratically after 1985, showing a certain persistence which produced a level still above 27 percent in 1990. This was partly the result of the monetary expansion associated with the presidential elections in 1990. However, a factor underlying the persistence of the inflationary record is the existence of widespread indexation mechanisms, which include all financial obligations and rental prices, creating downward inflexibility in output prices. This explains the concern of both of the most recent democratic governments with inflation.

15. More mature economies are not above this conflict of interest. The *World Development Report* observes: "Political rather than economic considerations explain why the governments of many OECD countries intervene in support of ailing industries or regions. The resurgence of protectionism among OECD countries in the 1980s, the problems encountered in the current round of GATT negotiations, and the slow pace at which some industrial countries addressed their macroeconomic imbalances in the 1970s and 1980s highlight how, even in societies with secure institutions, much-needed economic reforms can be blocked" (International Bank for reconstruction and Development 1991:129).

16. This indicator is the percentage growth rate of the aggregate employment (Table 6.3) as a proportion of the percentage growth of the GDP (Table 6.1).

17. The 1979 labor law included a wage indexation scheme, by which the floor for the wage negotiation was the past period inflation rate. Naturally, this

caused several problems regarding the flexibility needed to attain a productive response on the part of the productive sector. This was more complicated since the wage indexation scheme was created at the time when the nominal exchange rate was frozen as a stabilization policy, thereby creating huge problems in export-oriented activities. The wage indexation rule was eliminated in 1982, in the wake of the world financial recession, when its effect was causing severe damage in the balance of payments.

18. Using cross-country comparisons, Allen et al. (1994) found that the Chilean labor market is relatively more flexible than other countries in the region, particularly with regard to labor dismissals and the process of labor mobility across industries.

19. This average includes unemployed individuals participating in emergency employment programs (EEG). If EEG members are excluded, the average unemployment in 1974–81 reaches about 13 percent of the labor force.

20. Sapelli (1990) shows that unemployment was concentrated among the elderly and more educated workers, arguing that this provides ground to think of the presence of substantial skill mismatch. Also see Riveros (1986).

21. It is important to insist that this rate more than doubled the historical average and that it persisted even after five years when GDP grew at an average per capita rate of more than 5.5 percent per year.

22. Garcia (1993) also indicates that, as expected, the real wage increase in tradables was much larger than in the case of nontradables, further constraining the employment creation in trade-related industries.

23. It is important to note that the 1981 level was still below the one corresponding to 1970.

REFERENCES

Allen, S. G., A. Cassoni, and G. J. Labadie. 1994. Labor market flexibility and unemployment in Chile and Uruguay. *Estudios de Economia* 21:129–45).

Corbo, V. 1985a. Reforms and macroeconomic adjustment in Chile during 1974–1984. In *World Development*. Washington, DC: World Bank.

——. 1985b. *The Role of the Real Exchange Rate in Macroeconomic Adjustment: The Case of Chile 1973–82*. Discussion Paper DRD145. Washington, DC: World Bank.

Corbo V., and F. Sturzenegger. 1988. Stylized facts of the macroeconomic adjustment in the indebted countries. Washington, DC: The World Bank. Mimeographed.

Edwards, S. 1985. Economic policy and the record of economic growth in Chile 1973–1982. In *The National Economic Policies in Chile: Contemporary Studies in Economic and Financial Analysis 51*, edited by G. M. Walton. Greenwich, CT: Jai Press.

Edwards, S., and A. Edwards. 1987. *Monetarism and Liberalization; The Chilean Experiment*. Cambridge, MA: Ballinger Publishing Company.

Ferraro, R., and L. Riveros. 1994. *Historia de Chile: Una Vision Economica*. Santiago: Departmento de Economia, Universidad de Chile.

García, N. 1993. *Ajuste, Reforms y Mercado Laboral. Costa Rica (1980–1990); Chile (1973–1993); México (1981–1991)*. Santiago: PREALC-OIT.

Hachette, D., and R. Luders. 1987. Aspects of the privatization process: The case of Chile, 1974–85. World Bank. Mimeographed.

International Bank of Reconstruction and Development (IBRD). 1991. *World Development Report*. Washington, DC: World Bank.

Jadresic, E. 1990. Salarios en el largo plazo: Chile, 1960-1989. *Coleccion Estudios CIEPLAN* 29:9–34.

Larrain, F. 1988. Public sector behavior in a highly indebted country: The contrasting Chilean experience 1970–1985. Washington, DC: World Bank. Mimeographed.

Larrain, F. and P. Meller. 1990. The socialist-populist Chilean experience: 1970–73. Santiago. Mimeographed.

Paredes, R., and L. Riveros. 1993. El rol de las regulaciones en el mercado laboral: El caso de Chile. *Estudios de Economía* 20(1):41–68.

Riveros, L. 1986. Labor market mal-adjustment in Chile: Economic reforms and friction among sub-markets. *Analisis Economico* 1(1):1–12.

———. 1994. Labor markets in an era of adjustment: Chile. In *Labor Markets in an Era of Adjustment*, edited by S. Horton, R. Kanbur, and D. Mazumdar. Washington, DC: World Bank.

———. 1997. Chile's structural adjustment: Relevant policy lessons for Latin America. In *Adjustment and Equity Impact in Latin America*, edited by A. Berry (Forthcoming).

Sapelli, C. 1990. Ajuste estructural y mercado del trabajo. Una explicacion de la persistencias del desempleo en Chile: 1975–1980. *Estudios de Economía* 17(2):257–77.

Torres, C. 1982. *Evolución de la política arancelaria: Período 1973–1981*. Central Bank Report 16. Santiago: Central Bank of Chile.

Walton, G. M., ed. 1985. *The National Economic Policies in Chile*. Contemporary Studies in Economic and Financial Analysis 51. Greenwich, CT: JAI Press.

7

Argentina: Neoliberal Restructuring and Its Impact on Employment, Income, and Labor Organization

Aldo C. Vacs and Trudi J. Renwick

Due to its relatively small population, a vigorous process of import substitution industrialization (ISI), and populist socioeconomic policies, Argentina's labor market was characterized in the postwar years by several factors: low unemployment rates; a substantial proportion of industrial workers; relatively high wages and fringe benefits; and the presence of strong labor unions. Since the late 1960s, the exhaustion of ISI, population growth, productivity decline, high inflation, and political instability have combined to impair labor's employment rates, income levels, and organizational strength.

By the early 1990s, after multiple authoritarian and democratic governments had failed to reverse these trends by applying developmentalist, populist, and orthodox liberal strategies, the Menem administration (1989–95/1995–99) succeeded in implementing a neoliberal program for economic stabilization and structural adjustment. This market-oriented strategy included measures such as trade and financial liberalization, fiscal discipline, privatization of state enterprises, deregulation of economic activities, and the pegging of the local currency to the dollar. This program was able to eliminate inflation, eradicate fiscal deficits, foster the growth of export-oriented activities, and promote the rise of a free-market economy. These same policies, however, also had a strong negative impact on labor, as they became associated with high rates of open unemployment and underemployment, and important declines in real wages and social coverage. They also lead to further reduction in the number of industrial workers, a substantial increase in the proportion of self-employed and service workers, and a substantial decrease in the labor organizations' strength in terms of membership, mobilization capacity, bargaining ability, and political influence.

This chapter explores the contents of the economic liberalization programs implemented in Argentina since the mid-1970s and their impact on labor. Due to their structural consequences, it examines more in depth the features of the neoliberal economic policies advocated and implemented by the Menem administration (1989–95/1995–99), attempting to clarify the political and socioeconomic reasons why this restructuring attempt succeeded in establishing a free-market economy while contributing to the generation of an unprecedented increase in unemployment and the parallel decline in the role of organized labor.

THE POLITICAL ECONOMY OF DECLINE: IMPORT SUBSTITUTION EXHAUSTION, SOCIOECONOMIC TENSIONS, AND NEOLIBERAL ATTEMPTS IN ARGENTINA

The consolidation of economic neoliberalism in Argentina was the culmination of a process that resulted from the exhaustion of the ISI model and the inability of civilian administrations and military governments to reverse this negative trend. Finally, in the 1970s, the growing political and social tensions associated with the decline of the industrializing and redistributionist experience led to the rise of an authoritarian military regime committed to implementing a drastic neoliberal restructuring program.

The decline of Argentina's ISI started in the 1950s, when economic stagnation and the saturation of the domestic market by locally produced light manufactures indicated the need to promote the production of consumer durable, intermediate and capital goods. The required changes in economic strategies included adjustment programs aimed at reducing the growing balance-of-payments deficits, incentives for foreign investment in order to attract new capital and technology, and stabilization plans aimed at reducing inflation. The stabilization plans, nevertheless, affected the nationalistic and redistributionist premises of populism and led first to the weakening and collapse of the Peronist regime and afterward, throughout the late 1960s and early 1970s, to a succession of failed attempts by developmentalist military and civilian governments to restructure the Argentine political economy (Di Tella and Dornbusch 1989; García-Vázquez 1995; Peralta-Ramos 1992; Smith 1989).

Notwithstanding their different origins and ruling styles, the administrations established during this period maintained state intervention in the economy while trying to shift the country's industrialization strategy. This shift was in a direction which combined relative protection and support for local producers with incentives for foreign investment and the inflow of financial capital in an attempt to promote exports (especially of manufactures), in order to foster international competitiveness and modernize the economy.

These attempts failed as a result of adverse international and domestic economic trends and situations such as the relative scarcity of foreign investment and global recessions. Unfavorable trade and financial environments, infrastructural deficiencies, inflationary pressures, hard-currency shortages, and state mismanagement also contributed to this failure. Moreover, the struggle among well-organized socioeconomic sectors for preserving or augmenting their respective shares of a dwindling economic pie was focused on the state. The state was used as an instrument for the attainment of their sectoral goals. This ultimately led to inflation, social conflict, and a progressive state paralysis that intensified the economic crisis and heightened political instability (Portantiero 1987).

Throughout this period, labor scarcity diminished as the economically active population grew and job opportunities declined, because industrialization faltered and agricultural activities became more capital intensive (Lo Vuolo 1994). Unemployment remained relatively low, for these adverse developments were countered by three factors: the growing absorption of workers by the service sector (particularly commerce and construction); the decline in foreign immigration and rural-urban migration to the established industrial areas (domestic migrants looked for job opportunities in the public and private service sectors of the provincial capitals); and the "withdrawal effect" caused by the decline in real wages that might have made it fall below the reservation wage of some labor market participants (Riveros and Sánchez 1990). In the public sector, the number of federal workers remained high during these years and, at the same time, there was also a sustained increase in the number of employees hired by the provincial administrations. A consequence of this was a trade-off between productivity, income, and employment. As the less productive and lowest-paid occupations became the main generators of employment, the more dynamic ones (modern industry and agriculture) registered very low or negative rates of job creation (Lo Vuolo 1994).

Institutionally, the General Confederation of Labor (CGT, Confederación General del Trabajo), its provincial affiliates, and many individual labor unions remained sufficiently strong as to be able to prevent dismissals in the private and public sectors. They did this through the promulgation and enforcement of labor laws and collective bargaining regulations favorable to the workers (stability in the job, high severance payments, etc.), as well as by the use of strikes, demonstrations, and other forms of direct action. Finally, the political strength of labor made it very difficult for any administration to risk implementing policies that could result in rising unemployment rates, as witnessed by the collapse of the elected Frondizi. The Illia and Perón administrations were facilitated by growing union opposition and by the inability of the 1960s military governments to remain in power when faced with widespread labor protests. Thus, both civilian and military regimes tried to accommodate labor demands, particularly those related to full employment and social benefits, although this was often done at the cost of accepting declining productivity and real wages.

During 1976–83, authoritarian rulers believed that this economic impasse resulted from the incapacity of previous administrations to escape from the populist and corporatist mold. The military and its civilian supporters believed that the loosening of the free-market forces—up to then fettered by the existence of an interventionist state and a semiclosed economy typical of the import substitution industrialization strategy—would not only create the conditions for renewed economic growth but would also discipline the social actors' behavior, destroying the socioeconomic and political basis for the emergence of populist and corporatist experiments (Canitrot 1979). The socioeconomic groups would perceive the futility of trying to influence public policies in their favor because the market, and not the state, would assume the role of allocating resources and distributing income. As a result of these actions, high levels of mobilization affected governability and led to the implementation of state-led and protectionist economic strategies.

The restrictions imposed by the armed forces on the economic team's ability to reduce military budgets and privatize state enterprises, and the application of misguided economic policies (especially the strategy of "foreign exchange rate lag" that led to the overvaluation of the peso), made it difficult, in practice, to implement this approach. The regime collapsed, amid growing economic problems, foreign debt crisis, political turmoil, and the Falklands-Malvinas conflict. Some other factors include the persistent refusal of the economic agents to modify their expectations and behavior in the anticipated direction, adverse international conditions after 1979, and the eruption of the debt crisis in 1982 (Schvarzer 1981, 1983; Sourrouille and Lucangell 1983; Vacs 1986).

During this period, the military government's labor policies, although aiming to destroy the power of the unions through repression of labor leaders and the takeover and weakening of their organizations, were not intended to promote economic adjustment through massive dismissals in the private or public sector. Thus, to prevent socioeconomic and political tensions, they tried to maintain high levels of employment. They did this by refusing to impose drastic cuts in public employment, while easing the transition of wage and salaried workers to self-employment by offering high severance payments. Their policies, however, succeeded in changing Argentina's socioeconomic structure by generating deindustrialization, reducing the power of organized labor, and dividing the middle sectors. Some other changes include creating conditions for the growth of new leading capital sectors (made up of large horizontally diversified and vertically integrated domestic economic groups and foreign corporations linked to the local and export markets); eliminating the declining ones (which specialized in a single activity and produced for one specific market); and reducing the state commitment to social and economic policies favorable to domestic-oriented producers and low-income groups (Aspiazu, Basualdo, and Khavisse 1986; Filgueira 1984; Nun 1987; Villareal 1987).

DEMOCRATIZATION AND THE TURN TOWARD NEOLIBERALISM, 1983–89

After the reestablishment of democracy, the trend toward neoliberal restructuring was resumed in a hesitant manner by the Radical administration of Raúl Alfonsín (1983–89). Alfonsín's electoral promise to shift course, abandoning the liberal economic model favored by the authoritarian regime was replaced, after some initial heterodox attempts, by a growing inclination to foster free-market policies.

Initially the Alfonsín administration tried to fulfill its electoral promises by implementing an economic program with Keynesian components (Machinea 1990; Smith 1990; Vacs 1986). This program was expected to facilitate economic growth and stability and a moderate redistribution of income through a general agreement on wages and prices accompanied by state intervention to promote investment and exports and a negotiated reduction of payments on the foreign debt. The attempt collapsed after a few months amid growing inflation, capital flight, stagnation, and socioeconomic conflict fostered by the refusal of domestic labor and capital sectors, as well as foreign banks and international institutions (such as the International Monetary Fund, or IMF) to support it. The weakened state, inherited from the military, lacked the capacity to control key economic variables and to impose or promote any pact among the socioeconomic sectors that dominated the market (financial speculative institutions and large economic groups) or preferred to fight for their economic shares in a traditional way (labor, middle sectors, small and medium farmers and industrialists).

In June 1985, the original Keynesian economic program was discarded and replaced by the "heterodox" Austral Plan. This program combined several orthodox stabilization measures: increases in public tariffs and taxes; decreases in public expenditures; privatization of state enterprises; monetary stringency and a commitment not to print more money to finance the public sector; substantial devaluation; and introduction of a new currency, the austral, pegged to the dollar. Some unorthodox measures were also included: wage and price freezes; scheduled deindexation of debts; and fixed real interest rates. Initially, the plan succeeded in stabilizing the economy and improving the government's popularity: the monthly rate of inflation fell from around 30 percent to less than 3 percent, the exchange rate remained stable, and the international reserves increased.

After a few months, however, the distributive struggle and the sectoral pressures on the administration intensified as inflation began to rise. The consumer price index (CPI) grew around 7 percent monthly after July 1986, mainly because of the failure to reduce the fiscal deficit. Developments in the external sector contributed to worsen the economic situation: the relative prices of major Argentine agricultural export products declined in 1986, and the value of Argentine exports fell by more than 16 percent. Also, in 1987, Argentina's foreign debt reached US$ 56 billion with interest payments of US$ 3.9 billion (Vacs 1990).

In this context, labor demanded increases to compensate for the decline in real wages. Industrialists asked for lower interest rates and taxes, lifting of price controls, and new subsidies for industrial promotion. Agricultural producers demanded the elimination of export taxes for their products, lifting of price controls, reduction of government expenditures, and an end to the governmental transfer of resources from the agricultural to the industrial sector. The commercial associations requested the lifting of price controls and the establishment of a free-market environment, while the financial groups called for free interest rates and greater participation by the private banks in the renegotiation of the foreign debt. The governmental attempts to satisfy some of these demands led to contradictory and ineffective policies, including wage increases and the lifting of price controls.

Meanwhile, fulfilling an agreement between government and labor sponsored by the International Labor Organization, a congress was held to reorganize the CGT. Peronist labor leaders won a majority and formulated a populist program that called for a moratorium on foreign debt interest payments, wage and pension increases, full employment, credits for the industrial sector, and adequate prices for agricultural products.

The new CGT leadership reflected some of the changes in the composition of the Argentine working class that had taken place during the 1976–86 period, showing an increase in the number of moderate service- and public-sector union leaders and a decline in the number of industrial delegates. Some of these leaders negotiated an agreement with the government, and one of their members, Carlos Alderete, was appointed minister of labor. During Alderete's tenure as minister, between April and late September 1987, the labor movement was able to make some gains (Gaudio and Thompson 1990). The administration sent to Congress a package of labor legislation which satisfied some demands of the union leaders. These bills included those regulating collective bargaining, social services provided by the unions, and the organization and rights of trade unions. The latter was particularly opposed by the entrepreneurs, because it allowed large numbers of union delegates in the workplace, offered these delegates job security and protection against dismissal without judicial authorization and guaranteed the right to strike and "adopt other direct action measures." The entrepreneurs also rejected the collective bargaining mechanism, which they considered too favorable to labor, and the increase in employers' contributions to social service funds administered by the unions. As promulgated, these laws consolidated the political, economic, and social power of organized labor and established the basis for the recomposition of the corporatist role played by the CGT and unions in Argentine society.

However, the CGT's attempts to force the government to decree general, real-wage raises were met by a refusal to promote massive wage increases that could result in inflation, entrepreneurial discontent, and loss of external support. By mid-1987, facing a new inflationary upsurge and an intensification of the distributive struggle, the government concluded that the "heterodox" economic programs had failed. The minister of economy, Juan V. Sourrouille, denounced the populist and facile model as being closed, centralized, and statist and announced a neoliberal economic package aimed at opening and deregulating the economy, privatizing public enterprises, reducing the size of the state, and cutting public expenditures (Vacs 1990). Inflation, however, continued to climb (174.8 percent in the CPI in 1987), the gross national product (GNP) grew less than 2 percent, the fiscal deficit remained around 9 percent of the GNP, and real interest rates remained high. In August 1988, the government reacted by implementing a new economic program labeled the "Spring Plan," which included some measures tried before and a few novelties (Machinea 1990). The plan relied on the signing of voluntary agreements between the government and industrialists and retailers to stabilize prices. These groups accepted a temporary freeze on prices in exchange for the administration's commitment to reduce public expenditures and the money supply, and to freeze public services, tariffs, and import duties. A multiple-tier exchange market was created, with a lower rate of exchange for agricultural exports in an attempt to control the expansion of the money supply and with higher rates for nontraditional exports to promote diversification and economic modernization.

Initially these measures resulted in a reduction of the inflation rate, in part because the private and public sectors had raised their prices and tariffs in anticipation of the freeze, creating a temporary buffer. The continuous opposition, however, of the agricultural exporters to the exchange policy, the inability of the government to significantly reduce the fiscal deficit, and the growing reluctance of producers and retailers to respect the price agreements led to renewed inflationary strains by early 1989.

The Radical defeat in the September 1987 elections showed that the political gambit of incorporating Peronist labor leaders into the administration was no longer effective. The government was not able to rely on this tactic to increase its popularity, nor could the labor leaders perceive any advantage in remaining in the cabinet. The temporary alliance collapsed and the traditional lines of battle between labor and government were once again clearly drawn. As the economic situation worsened, real wages declined, social services deteriorated, delays in salary payments multiplied, and unemployment grew, creating fertile conditions for labor conflicts.

In September 1988, the CGT organized a general strike accompanied by street demonstrations to oppose the Spring Plan. The level of absenteeism was high, but a demonstration in front of the presidential palace led to violent confrontations with the police. A call for a second strike to protest the repression was not supported by some important labor leaders and Peronist politicians who feared new violent incidents. The Peronist leadership was especially concerned with the impact that this violence could have on the undecided voters and tried to disassociate itself from it. As a result, the new strike failed, and afterward, heeding Menem's wishes, the CGT changed tactics and avoided new calls for general strikes. Localized conflicts in different sectors continued, yet without leading to open violence. Organized labor opted for bargaining with the government and was able to secure some moderate increases in wages. In December 1988, Congress passed a bill that reestablished union control over the *obras sociales*, the institutions which provide health and vacation services to workers and which are financed with obligatory contributions from employers and employees. In exchange, the administration gained congressional approval for a national health insurance system. The year ended with the CGT strengthening its corporate power while playing again the traditional role of organizing and mobilizing support for a Peronist presidential ticket. The Radical administration had been unable to change this pattern, though at least the climate of confrontation with labor subsided and the electoral campaign proceeded in a peaceful manner (Vacs 1990).

Nevertheless, a military revolt in December 1988 and a leftist attack on a military garrison in January 1989 created political uncertainty leading to pressures on the exchange market, increasing prices and fostering shortages. The run on the exchange market upset the administration's capacity to maintain an overvalued exchange rate. In February 1989, with the Central Bank reserves practically depleted and interest rates rising to 20 percent monthly, the government was forced to admit the collapse of the Spring Plan and to announce a new set of short-term policies (Majul 1990). The Central Bank announced the suspension of its sales of hard currency except for essential imports and allowed the exchange rate to rise freely (around 50 percent in one week).

At the same time, it was announced that public-sector tariffs and wages would rise 6 percent monthly and that a similar rate of price increases would be authorized in the private sector.

The resentment of the economic actors who had trusted the government's repeated promises of refraining from a devaluation and the loss of credibility associated with the surprise announcements made it impossible for the administration to renew the agreement with the private sector for the maintenance of controls on price increases. In the following two months, the economic situation deteriorated rapidly. The dollar rose around 175 percent, although interest rates climbed to 24 percent monthly. The CPI grew 9.6 percent in February and 17 percent in March. In late March, the pressure of socioeconomic groups combined with political developments (the rise of Menem in the electoral polls and public calls for changes in the economic cabinet made by the Radical candidates) led to the resignation of the economic cabinet.

The new economic authorities, however, were unable to reverse the economic trend. After a brief decline, the dollar continued to rise (100 percent in April), commercial banks' interest rates rose to 60 percent monthly, and the CPI grew 33 percent. Successive attempts to control the situation by creating a free exchange market, reintroducing price controls, and diminishing the money supply by issuing new government obligations failed. Uncertainty was aggravated by the imminence of the presidential elections, as each sector tried to protect itself by using different means: a rise in prices and interest rates, a run on the dollar, strikes for higher wages, the refusal to supply goods and services, and lockouts. In the week prior to the election, the dollar rose 24 percent, interest rates skyrocketed to around 100 percent monthly, and prices grew more than 50 percent (Vacs 1996).

The Peronist victory in the general election was predictable, and Carlos Saul Menem secured 51.7 percent of the presidential votes. Following the election, the progressive paralysis of the Alfonsín administration, combined with the misgivings concerning Menem's vague economic and social promises, worsened the crisis. In less than one week, the dollar leaped 65 percent in value, short-term loan rates fluctuated between 180 percent and 300 percent monthly, and prices and tariffs went up another 50 percent. Frantic attempts made by the administration to reach an agreement with the Peronists to manage an orderly transition, anticipate the transfer of power, and obtain support for some economic stabilization measures failed. A one-week bank and exchange holiday was decreed in late May and was followed by a growth of close to 100 percent in the dollar exchange rate and a jump of interest rates to around 150 percent monthly. The enormous increase in prices was not accompanied by a similar raise in wages, igniting a social explosion that resulted in violent demonstrations and looting of super-markets and food stores. In June, the CPI rose 123 percent, the dollar rose 170 percent, and the monthly rate for commercial bank loans reached 195 percent. At the same time, it was estimated that industrial production had declined 25 percent since June 1988 and that the purchasing power of wages had fallen 60 percent in the same period. Finally, on June 12, Alfonsín addressed the nation and announced that he and the vice-president, Victor Martinez, considering the critical juncture and the impossibility of reaching an agreement with the elected authorities, had taken the unilateral step of resigning their offices as of June 30 to facilitate Menem's early inauguration (Garfunkel 1990).

THE MENEM ADMINISTRATION AND THE COMPLETION OF NEOLIBERAL RESTRUCTURING, 1989–97

After his inauguration, Menem surprised many of his followers and adversaries alike by embracing the neoliberal economic policies he had denounced during the presidential campaign. The promises of huge wage increases and of a "productive revolution," based on the revival of the domestic market during the electoral campaign, were replaced by a neoliberal economic program to be executed by some of the most representative figures of Argentina's conservative elites and orthodox economic thinking. The initial measures conformed to a severe program for economic stabilization and structural adjustment, aiming primarily to contain hyperinflation and involving a devaluation and the elimination of subsidies, the lifting of restrictions on foreign investment, reduction of public expenditures to attain a balanced fiscal budget, privatization of state enterprises including the phone, airline, and railroad companies, and tax reform (Acuña 1994; República Argentina, Ministerio de Economía 1989). They also, however, included a freeze on wages and salaries and on prices in exchange for a state commitment to maintain stable public tariffs, and interest and exchange rates.

Meanwhile, Congress passed the state reform and economic emergency laws to facilitate the creation of a free-market economic system (Garfunkel 1990). The state reform law authorized the administration to privatize a large number of state enterprises and services including the phone, airline, railroad, shipping, coal mining, and highway companies, the postal, and insurance services, the public television and radio stations, and several petrochemical companies. The economic emergency law reduced the industrial and mining promotion subsidies and the preferential purchase regime for local manufactures, suspended hirings and authorized dismissals in the public sector, and canceled some special salary systems for state employees.

Most labor organizations, which were under Peronist control and had participated in the electoral campaign, supported Menem, but some labor leaders refused to forgo the possibility of strikes under a Peronist administration. After the inauguration, Menem loyalists among union leaders were appointed to important positions in the administration and unconditionally backed the administration policies (El Bimestre 1989a, 1989b). Organized labor split into two rival organizations, weakening its traditional ability to influence policies. The loyalist sector fully supported the economic plan, including its adjustment and privatization components. The opposition group stated its support for Menem but announced that it would continue to fight for higher wages and against dismissals in the private and public sectors.

Meanwhile, the exporters' opposition to the exchange policies resulted in a growing reluctance to exchange their export earnings in the Central Bank, forcing the administration to announce substantial reductions in the export taxes applied to agricultural and industrial products. After a brief truce, business groups, dissatisfied with the inability of the administration to reduce the fiscal deficit and contain the growth of the money supply, started to raise prices. External support (from the IMF, World Bank, and developed countries' governments) also faltered due to these problems, as well as the governmental incapacity to accelerate the pace of the privatization process.

Faced with this growing opposition, Menem replaced the minister of economy but reaffirmed his decision to continue with the application of the neoliberal program, including state reform, privatization and deregulation, and opening of the economy, until the final establishment of a "popular free-market economy." The preservation of some corporatist mechanisms (such as the voluntary price truce and the negotiations with the unions), the maintenance of state controls over the exchange market, protectionist tariffs and industrial subsidies and the reluctance by different sectors to abandon the model of state-led growth in a semiclosed economy were seen as the main obstacles for the completion of this task.

The new economic measures implemented in late 1989 reflected the governmental decision of quickening the pace of economic liberalization. These decisions included the establishment of a completely free exchange market, removal of all price controls, elimination of the increase on export taxes, the conversion of public debt obligations into dollar denominated bonds, and a small wage increase (*Clarín* 1989). Subsequently, when a new inflationary surge occured, other emergency policies eliminated the commercial bank short-time deposits and forced their conversion into ten-year dollar denominated bonds, froze public utility rates, and emphasized the government's determination to halt the expansion of the money supply by reducing the fiscal expenditures (*Clarín* 1990a).

This resulted in an abrupt decrease in liquidity, accompanied by a decline in the exchange rate and a rapid rise in interest rates. The gross domestic product (GDP) declined 2.7 percent in the first quarter of 1990, with the manufacturing output falling 14 percent and construction plummeting 34 percent. In these recessionary conditions, high interest rates and a persistent demand for money rekindled the inflationary pressures. Prices climbed fast. The CPI rose 79 percent, 62 percent, and 95 percent in the first three months of 1990, with interest and exchange rates following suit while real wages plunged. In March 1990, average industrial real wages were 24 percent lower than in December 1989.

The economic team tried to check the hyperinflationary spiral by implementing another emergency package. This fiscal adjustment plan included a moderate increase in export and capital gains taxes, the application of a value-added tax to most transactions, daily indexation of all taxes, and suspension of payments to state suppliers and contractors for public works. Some other adjustments included the elimination of more than one-hundred state secretariats and undersecretariats, closing of state banks, termination of Treasury financing of public deficits, early retirement of civil servants, suspension of the collective bargaining contracts for public employees, and renewed commitment to privatize most state enterprises (*Clarín* 1990b). This tough adjustment package restored some degree of public confidence in the government's economic strategy, and inflationary pressures subsided but did not disappear. In early September, worried about the possibility of a new inflationary surge, the government announced tighter controls on the expenditures of the central administration and state enterprises, dismissals of public employees, increases in the prices of fuels and public tariffs, elimination of remaining tax exemptions and indexation of tax payments, acceleration of the process of privatization of state-owned companies and consolidation of the domestic public debt into ten-year adjustable bonds (*Clarín* 1990b). As a result of these measures, the rate of inflation began to decline, with the CPI increasing 4.7 percent in December 1990.

The stringent monetary and fiscal policies, the growing trade surpluses, the increase in the Central Bank's reserves, and its repeated interventions in the exchange market contributed to stabilizing the exchange rate. The cuts in public spending affected the quality and availability of public services (particularly health, education, and justice) but generated operational surpluses for the Treasury, reducing the quasi-fiscal deficit and contributing to curbing the expansion of the monetary base. The trade surplus rose to unprecedented levels, around 7.8 billion dollars by the end of 1990, helped by an increase in exports and a decline in imports attributed, in part, to the recession (*Clarín* 1991b). The level of reserves increased, giving the Central Bank the opportunity to regulate the exchange rate through commercial operations in the exchange market. The disparity between a relatively high rate of inflation and a declining real exchange rate, however, led to a sharp revaluation and a corresponding rise in real prices, especially those of food, clothing, and public services.

An important consequence of these stabilization and adjustment policies was the continuation of the downturn in the real sector of the economy. The gross domestic product declined by around 3.0 percent in 1990, while the industrial GDP was 4 percent less than in 1989 (*Clarín* 1991c). Total investment comprised less than 50 percent of the capital necessary to replace obsolete equipment. Average real wages declined by 3.5 percent in 1990. Unemployment decreased only slightly in the second half of the year, reaching 6 percent in October, while the combined rate of unemployment and underemployment remained around 14 percent. In early 1991, it was estimated that the average wage of unskilled and skilled industrial workers was sufficient to purchase only 72 percent and 79 percent, respectively, of a minimal basket of essential goods and services (Aronskind 1990; *Clarín* 1991a). It was estimated that, in 1990, more than ten million people lived under the poverty line, making it impossible for them and their families to meet their basic needs. The transfer of income from the low- and middle-income groups to the high-income groups consolidated a new category of poor, the "pauperized" (former working- and middle-class individuals and families that, as a result of the crisis, experienced an acute downward mobility until they became members of the poor sector of the population), and generated a growing concentration of income among the most affluent sectors of the population (Instituto Nacional de Estadísticas y Censos 1989; Lauro 1990a, 1990b; Minujín 1992; Minujín and Kessler 1995). The growing inequality in the distribution of personal income was accompanied by a crisis of the regional economies, especially in the poorer provinces that were the most affected by the federal budget cuts. The elimination of federal subsidies, the suspension of payments for the exploitation of natural resources, the cancellation of the systems of industrial promotion, and the transfer to the states of health, educational, and financial responsibilities imposed new burdens on the provincial governments which, in some cases, led to economic and political collapses.

Meanwhile, the privatization program began to be implemented at a firmer pace (Manzetti 1992; Menem and Dromi 1990; Verbitsky 1991). The national phone and airline companies, the railroad services in the main grain-producing areas, sections of the federal highway system, and the exploration and production activities of the national petroleum company were rapidly sold. The minister of economics was put in charge of all the state enterprises with a presidential mandate to control spending, reduce the number of employees and speed up the process of privatization. The haste with which the plan was devised and the lack of adequate regulatory provisions resulted in improvisations, allegations of improprieties and corruption, and inadequate valuations of the assets owned by the state companies.

In early 1991, a number of adverse developments, which included charges of widespread corruption (particularly the accusations of bribery against high officials made by the U.S. ambassador), renewed inflationary pressures, fiscal revenues that were less than expected, and the rise of the dollar, signaled to Menem that the time had come to replace the minister of economics and, thereby, to reinforce the neoliberal program. The new minister, Domingo Cavallo, was a former Central Bank president during the military government and had advocated market liberalization and an outward-oriented strategy of growth instead of the traditional Peronist approach based on state intervention and the expansion of the domestic market (Cavallo 1982; Cavallo, Domenech, and Mundlak 1989).

Cavallo's economic package, called the "Convertibility Plan," completed the neoliberal turn. From this plan, a new currency was created, the peso, freely convertible in dollars at a parity rate of 1 for 1. More rapid privatization of public enterprises and a debt-for-equity plan were announced, as well as massive dismissals in the public sector. The Brady Plan was accepted as the means to reduce foreign debt; taxation reform and further opening of the economy were promised (Gerchunoff and Torre 1996; Minsburg and Valle 1995; World Bank 1993). Later in 1991, a comprehensive executive decree deregulated most of the economy and established a free-market environment, lifting regulations concerning transportation, professional and commercial activities, import and export trade, financial transactions, collective bargaining, and social security arrangements while most official regulatory agencies were abolished.

Cavallo's economic policies succeeded in accomplishing some impressive results: inflation was contained (the CPI rate of growth declined from 84 percent in 1991 to 3.9 percent in 1994), the GNP grew at an annual rate of 7.7 percent in the period 1991–94, consumption increased 40 percent, the fiscal deficit was eliminated, the rate of exchange remained unchanged, privatizations moved forward, and capital inflows increased spectacularly (Gerchunoff and Torre 1996). Convertibility, however, meant that the economic authorities lost the ability to control the monetary and exchange variables, fostering a growing vulnerability to external shocks, particularly those related to short-term capital flows (Valle and del Pont 1995). At the same time, the program reinforced the trends toward regressive income distribution, concentration of wealth, and oligopolization of the economy; facilitated import growth and hindered exports, leading to a growing trade deficit; and failed to reduce unemployment (Minsburg and Valle 1995). Although wage earners were favored by the price stability (particularly in terms of food consumption and purchase of durable goods on credit), those working in sectors open to external competition suffered a decline in their real wages (10 percent in industry between 1991 and 1994) as well as in the levels of employment (Gerchunoff and Torre 1996). The middle sectors, in turn, were affected by the higher cost of private services, especially education and health, and of the newly privatized public services.

Meanwhile, by 1993, unemployment rates had begun to rise steadily, increasing from 6.9 percent in 1992 to 10.8 percent in 1994, and under-employment rates rose from 8.3 percent to 10.4 percent in the same period (Jabbaz 1995). At the same time, since 1993, labor demand fell below the rate of growth of the economically active population, with a larger number of workers moving into the informal sector. This lack of adequate employment growth, at a time when the economy was expand-ing rapidly (in the period 1991–94, the economy grew 34 percent, but employment increased only 5 percent), has been attributed to one of several factors. One is the rigidities created by labor legislation. The second is a continuous growth in productivity in the more modern firms, accompanied by the closing or reduction in size of the less competitive ones, as the administration's critics believed (Barbeito and Rodríguez 1995; Lozano and Feletti 1995; Monza 1995). It was also argued that the job cuts resulting from the reductions in public employment and privatization contributed to the decline in family incomes and forced new groups (especially older and younger people and women) to search for jobs, increasing the numbers of those actively seeking employment. It was also asserted that the reduction in import tariffs and the relative overvaluation of the local currency favored the importation of capital goods and inputs, reducing the cost of capital relative to labor and facilitating the use of capital-intensive technology and imported inputs over labor-intensive activities and locally produced materials.

In this context, the strongest opposition to the neoliberal program emerged among public-sector employees who were threatened by dis-missals, and it led to strikes and demonstrations. In the private sector, trade unions were reluctant to engage in a direct confrontation with the government and employers as long as unemployment rates remained high. Perceiving these divisions and the generalized weakness of the labor movement, the administration refused to budge and reacted forcefully against its opponents, dismissing state workers, imposing obligatory conciliation in conflicts in the private sector, and recognizing the pro-government branch of the labor confederation as the only legal representative of the workers (*Clarín* 1990a). A bill limiting the right to strike of public and private workers employed in health services, public utilities, telecommunications, public transportation, education, and jus-tice administration was sent to Congress. After a majority refused to pass it, the measure was enacted by presidential decree in October 1990 (*Clarín* 1990c). Afterward, new measures were promulgated that fur-ther weakened labor's capacity to challenge the neoliberal policies: new rules for collective bargaining decentralized the negotiation process and eliminated state intervention; labor contract laws were modified, mak-ing it possible for employers to change the conditions of work, fringe benefits, and wages; wage and salary increases were tied to increases in productivity; and new legislation limited the capacity of the trade unions to control the social coverage institutions (*obras sociales*) that provide health and recreation services for workers who had traditionally been the main source of funds for organized labor (FBIS 1992a, 1993).

Nevertheless, political support for the stabilization features of the program remained high, as the Peronist victory in the 1991 congressional elections demonstrated. Meanwhile, the neoliberal policies were generating structural, market-oriented transformations that seemed irreversible: the interventionist state and the distributive socioeconomic coalitions that had been the basis of the populist and developmentalist experiences of the past were no longer viable as the processes of deregulation, opening, and privatization unfolded. Thus, in November 1992, a general strike organized by some labor leaders—but disowned by the pro-Menem groups—to demand higher wages and full employment failed. Menem denounced it as an attempt by labor leaders who lived in the past "to play some role in the leadership of the state," adding that "they can hold one or 20,000 strikes, but they can alter neither our path, nor the economic model, nor the proposals we are submitting to the parliament to make the labor legislation more modern and flexible" (FBIS 1992b).

The preeminence of Peronism was confirmed in the congressional elections of September 1993, in which it obtained 43 percent of the votes (against 30 percent for the Radicals) and was able to win nine extra seats in the lower chamber. Interpreting these results as a confirmation of his popularity, Menem called for a constitutional reform convention that, in 1994, authorized presidential reelection (FBIS 1994). In the May 1995 elections, most of the electorate showed its preference for the political and economic stability associated with the existing administration, and Menem was reelected to a four-year term with close to 50 percent of the votes, while his supporters gained an absolute majority in Congress (*Clarín* 1995).

As Menem started his second presidential period in July 1995, the economic situation began to deteriorate. The Mexican crisis of December 1994, with its massive devaluation, dramatic capital flight, and recession, had a devastating effect on Argentina, whose economic program was seen as a replica of the Mexican one and, consequently, as being prone to similar problems. The so-called tequila effect sowed fears that the Argentine government might also announce a massive devaluation. As a result, financial capital flew (an eight-billion dollar flight), interest rates skyrocketed and an economic crisis characterized by illiquidity, a fall in investment and consumption, and general recession began to develop (Bouzas 1996). By 1995, the positive economic trends were reversed. GNP declined by 4.4 percent, consumption faltered, the fiscal deficit rose as tax revenues diminished, and a financial crisis emerged.

At the same time, negative economic effects worsened with declining employment, regressive income distribution, and external vulnerability.

Throughout 1995 and 1996, the continuous rise in unemployment, the decline in workers' income, and the growing political and social discontent generated by these developments became critical political and economic problems for the administration. Amid the 1995 recession, unemployment reached a record 20 percent in May before diminishing to 17.5 percent in October. Economic recovery in 1996 did not result in a significant improvement in the situation. On the contrary, in May, the unemployment rate was 17.1 percent while, in October, it reached 17.3 percent, even though the economy was expected to grow 3 percent by the end of the year (*Clarín* 1996a, 1996c). Compounding the problem was the fact that underemployment also increased steadily during this period, reaching 13.6 percent in October 1996 (*Clarín* 1996b). As a result, it was estimated that more than 30 percent of the economically active population had been affected by employment problems. At the same time, after 1994, real wages declined between 15 percent (including fringe benefits) and 10 percent (excluding fringe benefits), although labor costs, according to the administration and several analysts, remained high in relative terms (Bour 1995; Lozano and Feletti 1995).

Faced with the political and social repercussions of this situation, which included an electoral defeat in the special elections for the Federal capital administration and strikes organized by increasingly disgruntled unions and the CGT, the government blamed workers' tax exemptions and the high cost of labor for the growing fiscal deficit, recession, and employment problems. Consequently, in early 1996, it attempted to reduce the overall family benefit component of wages and to tax food benefits as part of the workers' income. At the same time, it tried to decrease the labor costs by eliminating some employers' contributions, cutting fringe benefits, and altering the conditions and outcomes of collective bargaining. The strong opposition to these measures, however, combined with the growing political and economic dissension between the minister of the economy and the rest of the administration, led, in July 1996, to the resignation of Cavallo, who was then replaced by Roque Fernández, the president of the Central Bank. Fernández, a specialist in money and banking with a Ph.D. in economics from the University of Chicago, was more orthodox than Cavallo, but he promised to maintain the neoliberal program and, especially, to preserve its convertibility component while trying to overcome the fiscal and labor problems. The first measures announced by the minister were aimed at reducing the fiscal deficit, extending the value-added tax to services (transportation, education, health, and entertainment), increasing fuel taxes, and reducing transfers of federal revenues to the provinces (*Clarín* 1996a). At the same time, the administration began to promote a labor reform intended to promote more "flexible" work regulations and conditions. The proposed reform was intended to decentralize collective bargaining, transferring it to the firm level, and enabling the firms or the government to modify the existing rules and regulations through new collective agreements; to abrogate special labor statutes; to transfer the cost of severance payments and unemployment insurance from the employers to the workers by creating a fund financed by employees' contributions; and, in general, to facilitate modifications in the workers' job descriptions, work hours, vacations, and amount of wages and fringe benefits (*Clarín* 1996b, 1996c, 1996d). The response of the CGT to these proposals was to call for a general strike and street demonstrations, which were successfully held in September 1996, and to try to negotiate an agreement with the administration to protect most labor rights (*Clarín* 1996b). By the end of the year, as unemployment remained high and the labor-government negotiations stalled, the administration suspended talks, introduced, by decree, new rules that weakened the collective bargaining regime, and announced its intention to do the same with the severance payment regulations (*Clarín* 1996c). Organized labor's response was to call for a new general strike and demonstrations to be held by the end of the year. As 1996 came to an end, the labor-government confrontation was becoming more acute while employment, real wages, and labor strength continued to decline.

CONCLUSIONS

In Argentina, the exhaustion of the import substitution industrialization model and the parallel decline of the populist and redistributionist experiences marked the beginning of a series of political economic experiments aimed at reestablishing conditions for economic growth, social peace, and political stability. Subsequent attempts made by democratic or authoritarian governments to modify the political economic model by eliminating some of its re-distributionist and nationalistic features, while favoring a developmentalist state-led strategy of development, failed due to adverse international trends and the effective opposition mounted by the socioeconomic and political actors whose fortunes were linked to the subsistence of the populist state. The authoritarian military regime attempted to solve this problem by combining the use of military repression with the implementation of neoliberal programs aimed at atomizing and weakening these socioeconomic and political groups. The use of military repression and free-markets to generate the conditions for the rise of a liberal export-oriented economy succeeded in changing Argentina's socioeconomic structure and processes but failed to attain its ultimate goal. The authoritarian regime implemented some neoliberal policies but, for political and social reasons, could not complete the application of a neoliberal program, nor guarantee its maintenance in the long run. The continuity and deepening of the neoliberal restructuring appeared to require the existence of critical economic conditions, as well as the establishment of a political regime able to legitimize the economic model and facilitate its survival during periods of economic and social strain. The Argentine authoritarian regime failed to meet this political condition and was finally forced to transfer power to a civilian elected government, jeopardizing the continuation of the neoliberal program of structural transformation.

Although initially reluctant to embrace a neoliberal program, the elected democratic government rapidly found that attempts to implement Keynesian or heterodox economic policies faced strong domestic and foreign opposition and led to critical situations. Thus, the Alfonsín administration followed a hesitant path toward increasingly orthodox economic policies but was unable to satisfy the powerful internal and external actors that demanded a complete neoliberal restructuring, advocating fiscal discipline, elimination of subsidies, moderate taxation, market-determined interest and exchange rates, trade and foreign investment liberalization, privatization of state enterprises, deregulation, and respect for private property rights. The vacillations of the Radical administration vis-à-vis these demands, its attempts to follow a moderate redistributionist approach and to negotiate corporatist socioeconomic agreements with labor and capital, and its inability to overcome the opposition to the privatization, deregulation, and opening of the economy contributed to an economic crisis characterized by stagnation and hyperinflation.

The catastrophic failure of the Alfonsín government contributed to the creation of some of the necessary preconditions for the formulation and successful implementation of a radical neoliberal program in Argentina. Popular fear of the repetition of the 1989 hyperinflation generated strong support for any program potentially able to promote economic stability even if it was done at a high cost in terms of income, consumption, and employment. Moreover, as a democratically elected government with adequate control over Congress and the provincial administrations, the Peronists were better prepared than their military and civilian predecessors to effectively apply neoliberal policies, which reduced public expenditures (particularly the military budget), promoted trade liberalization that favored consumers over specific groups of producers, obtained support for privatization and deregulation decisions, and reduced uncertainty concerning the respect for property rights by underscoring the rule of law. Economic neoliberalism was presented as the only viable strategy to ensure development given not only the collapse of the state-led model of import substitution industrialization, but also the simultaneous crumbling of socialist and populist experiences in other parts of the world and the trend toward the development of a global market political economy in which the role of the states has been severely limited. At the same time, the critical socioeconomic situation in which Menem assumed power encouraged the concentration of power in the executive branch, especially in the techno-bureaucratic economic teams, offering it the opportunity and resources necessary to impose its will on Congress, parties, and socio-economic organizations. Moreover, the Peronist tradition of personalistic leadership facilitated this concentration of power in the hands of a charismatic president who reinforced the exclusion of other political or socioeconomic actors from the decision-making process by denouncing their propensity to favor the implementation of policies that could unleash, according to the administration, a new inflationary surge. Finally, the success of the neoliberal policies in creating economic stability and their temporary capacity to generate some economic growth gave the government the time and popular support necessary to complete most structural transformations before the shortcomings in terms of employment, income, and growth began to emerge.

The impact of these neoliberal policies on employment, income distribution, and labor's organizational strength has been substantial. The pattern of maintaining a relatively high level of employment and a relatively low number of underemployed workers—characteristic of Argentina since the 1940s—has been shattered and replaced by the emergence and consolidation of a high level of structural unemployment and a significant number of underemployed. Since 1989, with the implementation of the Convertibility Plan, there has been a continuous increase in the size of the economically active population, accompanied by a very low or negative growth in the number of jobs. At the same time, there has been a decline in the real salaries and wages, which has paradoxically been accompanied—in conditions of fixed exchange parity and economic opening—by strong indications of a rise in labor costs. This situation has led to attempts by the administration to "flexibilize" labor legislation and rules in the belief that it is the rigidity of these rules—particularly in terms of compensation, work hours, severance payments, and fringe benefits—that leads to growing unemployment and economic stagnation. This interpretation has been disputed by other analysts, who point out that the unemployment problem might have resulted from a combination of growing labor productivity, privatization and shrinking of the state, indiscriminate trade liberalization, and overvaluation of the local currency that reduced the demand for labor, cut state jobs, and generated the closing of less competitive firms. The impact of these developments on employment remained less noticeable during the expansive 1990–94 period but became evident as soon as the repercussions of the Mexican crisis hit the Argentine economy in 1995.

Institutionally, the impact of the neoliberal policies applied by the Menem administration has been to significantly weaken the capacity of organized labor to promote its traditional redistributionist and full-employment goals, as well as its ability to exercise political influence. The socioeconomic changes fostered by these policies, including the decline in the numbers of industrial and public workers, the rise in self-employed, and the growing "unemployed reserve army," have contracted organized labor's traditional basis of support while raising fears in those workers that remain employed. Moreover, the fact that these policies were implemented by a Peronist administration created a dilemma for organized labor, which since the 1940s had been considered the backbone of the Peronist movement. Most labor leaders had supported Menem, and many of them refused to oppose him openly. Those who did were isolated by the administration, which did not have any reservations about splitting the CGT and denouncing any labor opposition as inept and corrupt. The consequence of this was that organized labor became completely ineffective in resisting the application of the neoliberal program, and by 1996, when rising unemployment and a decline in real wages led to workers' growing discontent, the lack of labor organization, leadership, and strength made it impossible to promote any realistic alternative to the neoliberal policies.

In fact, Argentina's neoliberal restructuring seems to have reached the point of no return, narrowing the range of options faced by supporters and opponents of the present administration alike. The structural transformations already completed in Argentina—with the consequent decline in labor's strength, the breakdown of the redistributionist, industrialist, and state-led model that favored full employment, and the current inability to find an alternative to the neoliberal policies—indicate that there is a high probability that, in the future, even if there are variations in the intensity of the neoliberal drive or of some of its contents, the current free-market model characterized by high unemployment, regressive income distribution, and the frailty of organized labor will remain unaltered.

REFERENCES

Acuña, C. H. 1994. Politics and economics in the Argentina of the nineties (Or, why the future no longer is what it used to be). In *Democracy, Markets, and Structural Reform in Latin America: Argentina, Bolivia, Brazil, Chile, and Mexico*, edited by W. C. Smith, C. H. Acuña and E. Gamarra, 31–73. New Brunswick, NJ: North-South Center/Transaction Publishers.

Aronskind, R. 1990. El salario dolarizado: Un mínimo que se hunde. *El Bimestre Político y Económico* 49(April):9–11.

Aspiazu, D., E. Basualdo, and M. Khavisse. 1986. *El Nuevo Poder Económico en la Argentina de los Años Ochenta*. Buenos Aires: Legasa.

Barbeito, A. and C. Rodríguez. 1995. Empleo, remuneración del trabajo, y distribución del ingreso. In *Argentina Hoy: Crisis Del Modelo*, edited by N. Minsburg and H. W. Valle, 283–310. Buenos Aires: Ediciones Letra Buena.

Bour, J. L. 1995. Los costos laborales en la Argentina. In *Libro Blanco Sobre el Empleo en la Argentina*, edited by Ministerio de Trabajo y Seguridad Social, 179–98. Buenos Aires: Ministerio de Trabajo y Seguridad Social.

Bouzas, R. 1996. *The Mexican Peso Crisis and Argentina's Convertibility Plan: Monetary Virtue or Monetary Impotence?* Buenos Aires: FLACSO/ CONICET.

Canitrot, A. 1979. La disciplina como objetivo de la política económica: Un ensayo sobre el programa económico del gobierno Argentino desde 1976. *Estudios Cedes* 2(6).

Cavallo, D. 1982. *Volver a Crecer.* Buenos Aires: Sudamericana-Planeta.

Cavallo, D., R. Domenech, and Y. Mundlak. 1989. *La Argentina Que Pudo Ser: Los Costos de la Represión Económica.* Buenos Aires: Fundacion Mediterránea/Manantial.

Clarín. 1989. 19 December.

———. 1990a. 2 January.

———. 1990b. 5 March.

———. 1995. 16, 17 May.

Clarín—edicion internacional. 1990a. 20–26 August.

———. 1990b. 27 August–2 September.

———. 1990c. 15–21 October.

———. 1996a. 13–19 August.

———. 1996b. 24–30 September.

———. 1996c. 10–16 December.

———. 1996d. 17–23 December.

Clarín—suplemento economico. 1991a. 6 January.

———. 1991b. 3 February.

———. 1991c. 3 March.

———. 1996a. 28 July.

———. 1996b. 18 August.

———. 1996c. 5 September.

———. 1996d. 29 September.

Di Tella, G., and R. Dornbusch, eds. 1989. *The Political Economy of Argentina, 1946–1983.* Pittsburgh, PA: University of Pittsburgh Press.

El Bimestre Político y Económico. 1989a. 46(October):37, 41–42, 46, 53–54.

———. 1989b. 47(December):19, 22, 27, 33, 41–42, 43–44.

Filgueira, C. 1984. El estado y las clases: Tendencias en Argentina, Brasil y Uruguay. *Pensamiento Iberoamericano* 6(July–December):35–61.

Foreign Broadcast Information Service (FBIS)—Latin America. 1992a. 29, 15 July.

———. 1992b. 20, 3 December.

———. 1993. 25–26, 5 March.

———. 1994. *Constitution of the Argentine Nation—1994.* 14 October.

García-Vázquez, E. 1995. *La Política Económica Argentina en los Últimos Cincuenta Años.* Buenos Aires: Ediciones Macchi.

Garfunkel, J. 1990. *59 Semanas y Media Que Conmovieron a la Argentina.* Buenos Aires: EMECE.

Gaudio, R., and A. Thompson. 1990. *Sindicalismo Peronista / Gobierno Radical: Los Años de Alfonsín.* Buenos Aires: Fundación Friedrich Ebert—Folios.

Gerchunoff, P., and J. C. Torre. 1996. *Argentina: La Política de Liberalización Económica Bajo un Gobierno de Base Popular.* Buenos Aires: Instituto Torcuato Di Tella.

Instituto Nacional de Estadísticas y Censos (INDEC). 1989. *La Pobreza en el Conurbano Bonaerense.* Buenos Aires: Estudios INDEC 13.

Jabbaz, M. 1995. El debate sobre la flexibilidad y la precarización del trabajo en la Argentina. In *Argentina Hoy: Crisis del Modelo,* edited by N. Minsburg and H. W. Valle, 311–34. Buenos Aires: Ediciones Letra Buena.

Lauro, A. 1990a. Extinción de la clase media Argentina. *Clarín—Edición Internacional* 10, 27 August–2 September.

———. 1990b. Los rostros de las dos Argentinas. *Clarín—Edición Internacional* 9, 26 November–2 December.

Lo Vuolo, R. 1994. *Análisis de la Actual Situación del Mercado de Trabajo y Su Probable Proyección Futura.* Buenos Aires: PRONATASS—Ministerio de Trabajo y Seguridad Social/Secretaría de Seguridad Social.

Lozano, C., and R. Feletti. 1995. Convertibilidad y desempleo: Crisis ocupacional en la Argentina. *Cuadernos del Sur* 11(20):25–45.

Machinea, J. L. 1990. *Stabilization Under Alfonsín's Government: A Frustrated Attempt.* Buenos Aires: Documentos CEDES 42.

Majul, L. 1990. *Por Que Cayó Alfonsín: El Nuevo Terrorismo Económico.* Buenos Aires: Sudamericana.

Manzetti, L. 1992. *The Political Economy of Privatization through Divestiture in Lesser Developed Economies: The Case of Argentina.* Miami, FL: North-South Center.

Menem, C., and R. Dromi. 1990. *Reforma del Estado y Transformación Nacional.* Buenos Aires: Ciencias de la Administración.

Minsburg, N., and H. W. Valle, eds. 1995. *Argentina Hoy: Crisis del Modelo.* Buenos Aires: Ediciones Letra Buena.

Minujín, A., ed. 1992. *Cuesta Abajo: Los Nuevos Pobres.* Buenos Aires: UNICEF/Losada.

Minujín, A., and G. Kessler. 1995. *La Nueva Pobreza en la Argentina.* Buenos Aires: Planeta Argentina.

Monza, A. 1995. Situación actual y perspectivas del mercado de trabajo en la Argentina. In *Libro Blanco Sobre el Empleo·en la Argentina,* edited by Ministerio de Trabajo y Seguridad Social, 137–62. Buenos Aires: Ministerio de Trabajo y Seguridad Social.

Nun, J. 1987. Cambios en la estructura social de la Argentina. In *Ensayos Sobre la Transición Democrática en la Argentina,* edited by J. C. Portantiero and J. Nun, 117–37. Buenos Aires: Puntosur.

Peralta-Ramos, M. 1992. *The Political Economy of Argentina: Power and Class since 1930.* Boulder, CO: Westview Press.

Portantiero, J. C. 1987. La crisis de un régimen: una mirada retrospectiva. In *Ensayos Sobre la Transición Democrática en la Argentina,* edited by J. C. Portantiero and J. Nun, 57–80. Buenos Aires: Puntosur.

República Argentina, Ministerio de Economía. 1989. Discurso del Ministro de Economía, 07/9/89 and Principales medidas económicas del 07/9/89. Press release 2/89. Buenos Aires: Ministerio de Economía.

Riveros, L., and C. E. Sánchez. 1990. *Argentina's Labor Markets in an Era of Adjustment*. Policy, Research and External Affairs Working Paper 386. Washington, DC: World Bank.

Schvarzer, J. 1981. *Expansión Económica del Estado Subsidiario, 1976–1981*. Buenos Aires: CISEA.

———. 1983. *Martínez de Hoz: La Lógica Política de la Política Económica*. Buenos Aires: CISEA.

Smith, W. C. 1989. *Authoritarianism and the Crisis of the Argentine Political Economy*. Stanford, CA: Stanford University Press.

———. 1990. Democracy, Distributional Conflict, and Macroeconomic Policymaking in Argentina (1983–1989). *Journal of Interamerican Studies and World Affairs* 32(Summer):1–42.

Sourrouille, J. V., and J. Lucangell. 1983. *Política Económica y Procesos De Desarrollo: La Experiencia Argentina Entre 1976 y 1981*. Santiago, Chile: CEPAL.

Vacs, A. C. 1986. The politics of foreign debt: Argentina, Brazil and the international debt crisis. Ph.D. Diss., University of Pittsburgh.

———. 1990. Argentina. In *Latin American and Caribbean Contemporary Record 7:1987–1988*, edited by J. Malloy and E. Gamarra, B3–B9. New York: Holmes and Meier.

———. 1996. Argentina: The melancholy of liberal democracy. In *Establishing Democracies*, edited by M. E. Fischer, 149–77. Boulder, CO: Westview Press.

Valle, H., and M. M. del Pont. 1995. Dolarización, convertibilidad, y soberanía económica. In *Argentina Hoy: Crisis del Modelo*, edited by N. Minsburg and H. W. Valle, 59–84. Buenos Aires: Ediciones Letra Buena.

Verbitsky, H. 1991. *Robo Para la Corona*. Buenos Aires: Planeta.

Villareal, J. M. 1987. Changes in Argentine society: The heritage of the dictatorship. In *From Military Rule to Democracy in Argentina*, edited by M. Peralta-Ramos and C. H. Waisman, 69–89. Boulder, CO: Westview Press.

World Bank. 1993. *Argentina: From Insolvency to Growth*. Washington, DC: World Bank.

8
Liberalization
and Mexican Labor Markets

Tim Koechlin

Mexico's recent experience with liberalization has been discouraging at best. More than three years after the implementation of the North American Free Trade Agreement (NAFTA) and more than a decade after liberalization became the guiding principle of Mexican economic policy, the Mexican economy is a mess. Real gross domestic product (GDP), real GDP per capita, real wages, and domestic investment have all declined since NAFTA became law on January 1, 1994, according to the Organization for Economic Co-operation and Development, or OECD (1977). Unemployment rates have nearly doubled, and social programs have been cut dramatically. And worse still, the pain associated with this crisis has been felt most intensely by those at the bottom of the income distribution—unskilled workers, peasants, and small landholders.

The evidence from the U.S. side of the border is less daunting but far from encouraging. The U.S. trade balance with Mexico has deteriorated significantly, and U.S. direct foreign investment (DFI) in Mexico has grown substantially, bearing out the predictions of NAFTA's critics. A strong prima facie case can be made that NAFTA has hurt the typical citizen on each side of the border.

And yet many of NAFTA's defenders claim that the agreement has been a success. NAFTA, they point out, has led to a large increase in trade flows between the U.S. and Mexico, and the considerable benefits from this trade have been temporarily swamped by the fallout from the peso crisis of 1994–95 (Hinojosa et al., 1996). The Clinton administration has begun taking steps toward expanding NAFTA to Chile and, ultimately, to the rest of Latin America.

What does Mexico's recent experience teach us about the likely consequences of trade liberalization? And, in particular, what does

Mexico tell us about the ways in which trade liberalization might affect labor market outcomes? This chapter is an attempt to address these questions. I argue in this chapter that Mexico's decade-long commitment to liberalization has had mixed results, but the typical Mexican worker clearly has been hurt by rising unemployment and declining real wages. I argue, further, that this did not have to happen. A different model of economic integration could make things better.

This chapter argues that an assessment of free trade and liberalization depends fundamentally on the model one employs and, in particular, the assumptions one makes about labor and capital markets. Mainstream models of NAFTA—those rooted in the classical theory of trade—pay too little attention to the agreement's effects on capital flows and, more generally, these analyses are based on a set of restrictive and unreasonable assumptions. The result is an overly optimistic assessment of the likely (and actual) effects of liberalization. A less restrictive set of assumptions leads to a more ambiguous set of conclusions and a more reasonable basis for assessing Mexico's experience with liberalization. I then discuss the performance of the Mexican economy since the middle of the 1980s, when the Mexican government committed itself to liberalization. Next I focus on the effects of liberalization on unemployment and real wages in Mexico. Finally I offer some conclusions and policy implications.

ASSUMPTIONS AND ASSESSMENT: COMPETING MODELS OF LIBERALIZATION

Attempts to assess NAFTA and trade liberalization more generally can be divided into two major categories: those rooted in classical trade theory and those which view the classical theory of trade with considerable skepticism.[1] Contrasting these two approaches provides considerable insight into the terms of the debate over NAFTA before its adoption and the assessment of its effects four years later.

The classical theory of trade contends that trade liberalization will compel a country to specialize in the production of the goods and services in which it has a comparative advantage. This specialization promotes a more efficient allocation of resources, real income growth, and an improvement in aggregate welfare for every country. From this perspective—one held by most economists—more liberalization is almost always better. Paul Krugman writes: "If there were an Economist's Creed it would include the affirmations 'I understand the Principle of Comparative Advantage' and 'I advocate Free Trade'" (1987:131).

These basic premises of classical trade theory are at the core of many empirical studies of NAFTA, including most computable general equilibrium (CGE) models of North American integration.[2] These studies employ a complicated and impressive modeling technique which allows their authors to make detailed projections about NAFTA's effects. But this elaborate mathematical structure is ultimately just a very detailed elaboration of the simple, familiar model of trade presented in the previous paragraph. For NAFTA analysts working in this tradition, the question has not been whether NAFTA will benefit Canada, Mexico, and/or the U.S. The issue, rather, has been to predict the extent and distribution of NAFTA's inevitable benefits.

The reassuring conclusions of classical trade theory, and the "mainstream" studies of NAFTA cited above, depend fundamentally on a few dubious assumptions, which all but ensure the conclusion that trade liberalization will benefit every country. I discuss three particularly important assumptions in this section.[3]

Classical trade theory assumes that labor markets clear, both before and after liberalization. This assumption limits the array of conclusions we might reach about liberalization in at least two important ways. First, the full employment assumption helps to ensure the conclusion that liberalization will increase real output. As labor shifts from low- to high-productivity industries, a fully employed labor force will produce more—hence, there are gains from trade. Second, this assumption dismisses a priori the possibility that liberalization might create aggregate unemployment. Thus, the issue to which this volume is dedicated is ruled out by assumption. This assumption also has implications for the wage effects of liberalization. The threat of import competition, capital flight, and plant closings is less daunting in a fully employed economy, because the absence of long-term, involuntary unemployment means that workers will not trade off wages and benefits for job security. The assumption of full employment renders irrelevant the potentially important connections among capital flight, unemployment, bargaining power, and wages.

The classical theory of trade assumes further that capital is immobile internationally, and it provides little insight into the relationships among trade, capital flows, and domestic economic outcomes. It provides, rather, a framework for understanding the trade effects of liberalization and a limited one at that. This is a problem, as capital flows may overwhelm or supplement the gains from trade. It is especially problematic in the case of NAFTA because (1) NAFTA liberalizes capital flows as well as trade; (2) international capital flows have played a crucial role in Mexico's stormy economic history; and (3) the Mexican government has clearly hoped that NAFTA will encourage foreign investment in Mexico.

One need not reject the classical theory of trade because of the assumption of immobile capital. A more complete assessment of the effects of liberalization could easily combine a serious consideration of capital flows with the insights of trade theory. But mainstream models of NAFTA, many of which modeled trade with incredible subtlety, either ignored capital flows or treated them in an ad hoc manner. Some simply assumed that NAFTA would not motivate direct foreign investment (DFI) flows into Mexico, making the projected trade effects of NAFTA— which were inevitably positive—the entire story. Others estimated the effects of a one-time increase in Mexico's capital stock of essentially arbitrary magnitude. "Investment," Sidney Weintraub comments in his review of the NAFTA literature, "drops in like manna from heaven" (1992:113). No mainstream model allowed the possibility that DFI flows to Mexico might be at the expense of investment in the U.S. or elsewhere, and thus DFI can only supplement the traditional gains from trade.[4]

Like all moves toward free trade, NAFTA was expected to increase income and aggregate welfare for all participating countries. But this is not necessarily true for all individuals. Mainstream trade theory predicts that owners of a country's scarce factor of production will see their incomes decline with liberalization, while owners of the abundant factor will enjoy income gains. The United States International Trade Commission, or US ITC (1991), for example, predicted that NAFTA would mean small losses for "unskilled workers." Leamer concludes that, for unskilled U.S. workers, "earning reductions on the order of $1000 per year seem very plausible" (1993:57). Beyond losses of this type, some members of each country will have to endure adjustment costs as resources are reallocated. This does not contradict the essential conclusion that liberalization enhances welfare. The gains of the winners will exceed the losses of the losers, and in this sense, the nation as a whole gains.

Several studies include model features which suggest that the benefits from NAFTA will be even greater than classical trade theory might lead us to expect. The traditional gains from trade (rooted in specialization) may be supplemented by gains associated with economies of scale (Brown, Deardorf, and Stern 1992), technology transfer and "dynamic gains from trade" (Kehoe 1992), and a growing capital stock (Brown et al., 1992; US ITC 1992). These additional considerations allow several studies to conclude that NAFTA will raise the income of capital owners and workers on both sides of the border (US ITC 1992).

Two major concerns about NAFTA—that it might motivate a relocation of productive investment from the U.S. to Mexico and destroy jobs in the U.S.—are assumed away by virtually every mainstream NAFTA study. A third concern—that NAFTA will erode wages in the U.S.—is assumed away by most of them.

Mainstream trade theory clearly captures an important truth about trade. But its restrictive assumptions provide an unnecessarily narrow basis for assessing the full effects of liberalization. The conclusion that NAFTA will benefit workers in the U.S. and Mexico ultimately reflects more about the conventional assumptions of trade theory than it does about the reality of North American integration.

Economists working in the "political economy" (PE) tradition have assessed NAFTA quite differently from their mainstream counterparts.[5] While the approaches of these economists are, in many cases, quite diverse, their work on liberalization has a few important elements in common. First, economists in this tradition assume that unemployment is a regular feature of a capitalist economy and that liberalization, through its impact on productivity growth, aggregate demand and/or the industrial structure of the economy, may create or destroy jobs in the aggregate. Second, PE focuses considerable attention on the determinants and consequences of capital mobility and capital flight. Third, PE economists contend that the distribution of income and the content of state policy are, in large part, the result of struggle among domestic capital, international capital, workers, and other interested political economic actors. They are, therefore, interested in the ways in which liberalization (or any important change in the political economic landscape) might affect the bargaining power of mobile corporations, workers, and others.

The story about NAFTA that emerges from this literature is quite different from the mainstream story, especially with regard to NAFTA's effects in the U.S. PE studies have generally argued that NAFTA would motivate a surge of U.S. DFI in Mexico and, as a consequence, U.S. workers would be hurt by job loss and wage erosion (Blecker 1996a; Stanford 1993; Koechlin and Larudee 1992).

NAFTA is likely to increase the appeal of DFI in Mexico for a few reasons. First, NAFTA explicitly limits the ability of the Mexican government to regulate U.S. corporations, thus locking in Mexico's commitment to grant these corporations "national treatment." David Ranney (1993) has described NAFTA as a "corporate bill of rights." Second, the reduction of trade barriers allows U.S. companies to take advantage of low Mexican wages without sacrificing access to the lucrative U.S. market, enhancing Mexico's appeal as an "export platform."

These projected DFI flows (the most dramatic estimates represented less than one percent of annual U.S. domestic investment) would hurt some U.S. workers quite directly by destroying their jobs. Several PE studies argued that NAFTA would hurt employed U.S. workers as well by undermining their bargaining power relative to that of footloose corporations.

This literature has had less to say about NAFTA's effects on Mexican workers. My study with Larudee argued that U.S. DFI would create new jobs, especially in manufacturing, but that these employment gains were likely to be overwhelmed by rising unemployment in the countryside (Koechlin and Larudee 1992). Others have argued that NAFTA represents a lost opportunity to craft a deal that would improve the lot of Mexican workers. Whatever NAFTA's benefits for Mexican workers, a better trade deal was possible (Blecker 1996a; Koechlin and Larudee 1992; Faux and Lee 1992).

Does all of this imply that trade liberalization inevitably hurts workers? Absolutely not.[6] Trade is likely to generate gains of the sort described by mainstream theory. Depending on institutional, historical, and macroeconomic circumstances, trade may well increase labor demand, and wages and reduce income inequality as well.[7] But it might not. The PE literature differs from the mainstream literature in that it seriously considers the possibility that liberalization might be associated with unemployment, capital flight, wage erosion, and/or environmental degradation.

Members of these two camps also tend to evaluate the effects of liberalization by different criteria. In particular, economists in the PE tradition are generally more concerned about the distribution of the costs and benefits of liberalization than are their mainstream counterparts. Mainstream trade theory concludes that free trade is beneficial because it increases total output, thereby easing the collective budget constraint of each country. Some individuals and/or categories of individuals win, others lose, but aggregate welfare is improved in the sense that the winners could compensate the losers and still have some left over. But notice that by this standard, a policy which leads to an increase in corporate profits and a (smaller) decrease in wages would represent an improvement in social welfare. "I am prepared to bet big money," Larudee (1996:7) writes, "that labor and environmental activists would be virtually unanimous in their rejection of this concept of social welfare and would have a good portion of the public on their side."

THE LIBERALIZATION AND THE MEXICAN ECONOMY

Mexico began actively pursuing a policy of economic liberalization in the mid-1980s. This policy shift was a dramatic departure from more than three decades of import substitution industrialization (ISI), during which time Mexico's economic relations with the rest of the world were heavily regulated. Mexico joined the General Agreement on Tariffs and Trade (GATT) in 1986 and unilaterally reduced its tariffs and other import barriers significantly during the latter half of the decade. Between 1985 and 1989, Mexico's average trade-weighted tariff fell from 25 percent to 10 percent (US ITC 1991). By the early 1990s, over a third of the U.S. exports to Mexico were duty-free (Larudee 1996). Restrictions on DFI, which had been quite elaborate and extensive, were reduced considerably, and the attraction of DFI became a major policy objective. Debt relief agreements with the International Monetary Fund (IMF) and the U.S. government required the Mexican government to privatize many state-owned enterprises, eliminate or reduce a wide array of government subsidies, and reduce its budget deficit. Mexico became "a very open economy in less than four years" (OECD 1997:81).

The alleged failure of ISI notwithstanding, Mexico enjoyed an impressive average growth rate of 6.5 percent between 1965 and 1980. The debt crisis of 1982 and the painful adjustment period that followed erased years of economic progress. GDP stagnated and real wages fell by nearly half between 1980 and 1986 (OECD 1997).

The economy improved under the new policy regime, although its performance was far from stellar. From 1987 to 1993, real GDP grew at an average annual rate of 2.5 percent. The official unemployment rate rose slightly between 1987 and 1993. Investment and real wages rebounded to some extent, although, in 1993, the median real wage was just 60 percent of its 1981 level (OECD 1997). Mexico's debt burden remained enormous, even though it was more manageable, than it had been in the early 1980s.

Mexico's integration with the rest of the world, especially the U.S., increased substantially during this period. Mexico's exports more than doubled, while imports grew by a factor of four. DFI flows averaged $4.7 billion a year between 1991 and 1993, more than seven times the 1985 level. Portfolio investment was negligible during the first few years of liberalization, but it began to take off in 1991, peaking at $28 billion in 1993 (International Monetary Fund 1994). This was seen by many as a sign of success. Mexico appeared to have regained the confidence of foreign investors and was attracting the capital it so desperately needed.

NAFTA eliminates many of the remaining barriers to U.S.-Mexico trade. Its more important effect has been to reduce barriers to capital flows between and among Mexico, Canada, and the U.S. "The central motivation of the Mexican government in proposing NAFTA," writes Blecker (1996a:137), "was not to lower US trade barriers but rather to attract more foreign investment—especially direct foreign investment in productive enterprises." NAFTA is also important because it formalizes Mexico's commitment to liberalization and, more specifically, to friendly treatment of foreign investors. NAFTA is particularly important for Mexico, because the U.S. accounts for the overwhelming share of Mexico's exports, imports, and capital flows. This connection to the United States and Mexico's economic size (Mexico's GDP is about 3 percent of U.S. GDP) make Mexico much more sensitive to NAFTA's effects.

Trade between the U.S. and Mexico grew by more than 23 percent in NAFTA's first year, while DFI in Mexico increased from $5 billion to $8 billion (OECD 1997). But late in 1994, the roof fell in on Mexico's economy. The long-overdue devaluation of the peso sparked a financial crisis and ultimately a depression, from which Mexico has only begun to emerge. GDP, employment, investment, and real wages all plummeted. What happened? And what, if anything, does this crisis imply about the hazards of liberalization?

The peso appreciated by more than 75 percent between 1987 and 1993. A few observers commented during the NAFTA debate that the peso was overvalued and that a devaluation was all but inevitable (Blecker 1996a; Faux and Lee 1992).[8] The Salinas government chose to prop up the peso by spending down its foreign reserves, at least, in part, out of concern that a devaluation of the peso would worsen the U.S. trade balance with Mexico and thus damage NAFTA's prospects in the U.S. Congress. The Mexican government continued to support the peso throughout 1994, apparently hoping to delay a devaluation until after the December presidential election. The government also felt considerable pressure from U.S. investment banks to support the peso. In April 1994, a group of investment banks, called the Weston Forum, offered to channel US\$ 17 billion into Mexico if its policy suggestions regarding the peso were adopted (Larudee 1996). The government managed to postpone the devaluation of the peso by attracting foreign capital through the sale of *tesobonos*, short-term, dollar-denominated securities which protected foreign investors from exchange rate risk. When the government finally took steps to devalue the peso in December 1994, a panic set in. The peso lost 50 percent of its value in a matter of days. The Mexican stock market crashed and billions of dollars of short-term capital fled the country. Mexican interest rates skyrocketed. The U.S. Treasury engineered a US\$ 50 billion loan which allowed the Mexican government to pay off its *tesobonos* and prevent the collapse of Mexico's banking system.

The real effects of this financial crisis have been disastrous. In 1995, GDP fell by 7 percent, domestic investment fell by 30 percent, and the unemployment rate nearly doubled. Real wages fell by 22 percent in 1995 and by another 15 percent in the first half of 1996 (OECD 1997). Social programs were cut by 12 percent in 1995. Public investment fell by 17 percent (OECD 1997).

The typical Mexican is clearly much worse off than he or she was three years ago, and many of the threatening predictions of NAFTA's critics have come to pass. The U.S. trade balance with Mexico has swung from a \$5 billion surplus in 1993 to a \$16 billion deficit in 1996, and U.S. DFI in Mexico, especially in its export-oriented *maquiladoras*, has increased considerably and destroyed hundreds of thousands of U.S. jobs.[9]

Is it reasonable to pin the unraveling of the Mexican economy on NAFTA or on Mexico's broader efforts at liberalization? The answer is yes and no. Financial panics and depressions are clearly not inevitable consequences of trade and investment liberalization, and even the shrillest of NAFTA's critics did not predict a disaster of this sort or of this magnitude. But it is unreasonable to treat this crisis as an exogenous shock. The crisis is linked to Mexico's liberalization efforts in a number of ways. First, the ongoing overvaluation of the peso was not simply a policy error. It was, rather, a calculated response to the political realities surrounding the NAFTA debate. Devaluing the peso in 1993 may well have led to NAFTA's defeat. Second, the liberalization of

Mexico's financial markets facilitated the massive inflow of short-term capital into Mexico in the early 1990s. And this financial boom, along with the sometimes euphoric expectations associated with NAFTA, helps to explain the misassessment of risk by foreign investors and the Mexican government. Third, Mexico's formal and ideological commitment to liberalization, along with its dependence on the U.S. government, the IMF, and foreign investors, severely limited the ways in which it might have prevented or responded to this crisis. If a government chooses to rely on international capital markets, it risks being burned by them.

A recent NAFTA study by Hinojosa et al., (1997:14) is one of several which attempt to separate the effects of NAFTA from the effects of the peso crisis. Hinojosa et al. conclude that "NAFTA related institutions and policies represent a net plus." My argument here implies that this is a meaningless exercise because the peso crisis is, in part, a consequence of these institutions and policies.

LIBERALIZATION AND LABOR MARKETS

Mexico's short but eventful experience with liberalization can be divided into three phases: unilateral liberalization; NAFTA; and the peso crisis and its aftermath. I argue in this section that although liberalization has improved the performance of the Mexican economy in a variety of ways, the lot of the Mexican worker deteriorated during each of these three phases.

Official Mexican unemployment rates have historically been very low. Between 1987 and 1994, Mexico's unemployment rate did not exceed 5 percent. OECD (1997) and others are partly correct when they note that Mexican wages are relatively flexible, and that unemployment rates are less responsive to demand shocks than they might otherwise be. But the implication that Mexico does not have a serious unemployment problem is quite wrong.

Mexico's low unemployment rates are partly explained by the way in which the Mexican government calculates them. A person of age twelve or older is considered employed if, during the previous week, she or he (1) was self-employed or worked at least one hour for barter or money; (2) did some work as an unpaid family or nonfamily worker; (3) expected to start a job in the next four weeks; or (4) was temporarily absent from work. These criteria are much less restrictive than those used by most OECD countries and, consequently, Mexico's official unemployment rate is deceptively low.

Like many poor countries, Mexico has a large informal sector which includes large numbers of underemployed workers doing what they can to get by in the absence of reasonable alternatives. Many of these workers are counted as employed; others are considered out of the labor force. An alternative estimate by OECD (1997) (accounting for involuntary part-time and discouraged workers) puts unemployment at about 10 percent in the middle of 1996. The Mexican National Institute of Statistics estimates that 23.3 percent of Mexican workers are either unemployed or underemployed, while the Mexican Association of Industrial Relations Executives estimate about 30 percent (Resource Center of the Americas 1997). Paul Rich (1997:40) asserts that fewer than half of Mexico's economically active population of twenty-five million have paying jobs: "The rest survive with part-time employment." Blecker is surely correct when he notes that "the traditional assumption of full employment does not hold in Mexico" (1996a:161).

Liberalization clearly has not eliminated Mexico's unemployment problem. Indeed, it appears that it has not improved demand conditions in Mexico's chronically slack labor market at all. As I have noted above, mainstream trade theory predicts that Mexican workers—the owners of Mexico's abundant factor of production—should be among NAFTA's winners, and this is what most NAFTA studies predicted. In particular, liberalization should lead to an increase in labor demand and real wages. It appears, to the contrary, that liberalization has been associated with a reduction in labor demand, an ongoing unemployment problem, and declining real wages.

Before NAFTA and the peso crisis, the effect of liberalization on unemployment in the aggregate appears to have been small. The rate of unemployment, as measured variously by the OECD (1997), fell during the years immediately following liberalization, but by 1994 the unemployment rate was slightly higher than it had been in 1987. Still, a number of factors associated with liberalization have tended to reduce the demand for labor.

The changing and diminishing role of the state in the economy has tended to reduce labor demand. Most directly, budget cuts have led to a reduction in government employment, especially in state-run enterprises (OECD 1997). Blecker (1996a) argues that between 1986 and 1994, restrictive macroeconomic policy—budget cuts, high interest rates, and an overvalued peso—stifled employment growth unnecessarily.

Surprisingly, employment in manufacturing—which accounts for more than three-quarters of Mexico's exports—declined by 126,000 between 1985 and 1993, despite substantial increases in exports and output (Padilla 1995). Modernization and rationalization have meant that productivity in manufacturing has grown faster than output; therefore, labor demand has fallen (OECD 1997). Marquez Padilla (1995) estimates that the output elasticity of employment in Mexican manufacturing declined considerably after 1985. Some of this productivity growth is explained by the growing presence of foreign firms in Mexican manufacturing. Several studies indicate that U.S. firms operating in Mexico tend to use techniques similar to those employed in their U.S.

plants, rather than choosing a significantly more labor-intensive technology (Shaiken 1990; Alcorte 1995).

Higher productivity and higher demand for manufacturing exports have not been associated with rising real wages either. The real wage in manufacturing was lower in 1995 than in 1990, despite annual productivity growth in manufacturing of nearly 6 percent (OECD 1997). The growth of manufacturing exports has been associated with rapid growth of the *maquiladora* sector, where, since 1965, (mostly foreign) firms have produced for export. Output, exports, and employment have all grown dramatically in the *maquiladora* sector during the 1980s and 1990s, but real wages declined by 45 percent between 1977 and 1992 (Gambrill 1995). The peso devaluation has further accelerated the growth of the *maquiladoras*, as the demand for cheap Mexican manufactures has grown. But real wages in the *maquiladoras* have continued to decline during this period (OECD 1997). The fact that productivity growth has not been translated into higher wages is troubling to anyone interested in seeing the living standards of poor Mexicans rise. But it is also important because it raises questions about the ability of mainstream trade theory to predict the consequences of liberalization. In the world described by classical trade theory, liberalization should improve the lot of Mexican workers, as productivity gains and rising labor demand lead to higher wages. But the critical assumption of full employment does not hold in the case of Mexico, where workers have not been in a position to demand the spoils of productivity increases. Productivity gains have, rather, been absorbed by debt payments to foreign banks, profits, and higher salaries for white-color workers (Gambrill 1995; OECD 1997).

Liberalization has also had a substantial impact on the Mexican countryside. The share of agriculture in total employment declined by about half between 1960 and 1979, and it has continued to shrink since, albeit at a much slower rate (OECD 1997:82). Nearly a quarter of Mexico's work force is in agriculture. Agricultural price supports, subsidies, and protection from foreign competition have been crucial in keeping many poor rural families afloat economically. Levy and van Wijnbergen (1994) comment that these agricultural subsidies are Mexico's de facto antipoverty program. Fiscal pressures and a commitment to liberalization have led to serious cuts in government support of agriculture. NAFTA compels Mexico to eliminate tariffs on most agricultural imports over the next ten to fifteen years. This will surely have a devastating effect on the millions of Mexican families who make their livelihoods producing corn, often very inefficiently. Robinson et al. (1992) and Levy and van Wijnbergen (1994) argue that the liberalization of trade in corn will compel hundreds of thousands of Mexicans to migrate from the countryside to the city, putting downward pressure on wages there. The causes of peasant uprisings in Chiapas and other poor, rural

Mexican states are complex, but "the rebels have made the North American Free Trade Agreement the focus of their fury" (Rich 1997:72) because of the widespread sense—and compelling evidence—that liberalization has made life more difficult for the typical Mexican peasant.

While liberalization's impact on aggregate employment appears to have been small from 1986–94, it clearly disrupted the economic lives of millions of Mexicans. Government layoffs, declining and shifting labor demand in the manufacturing sector, dislocation in the countryside and privatization of public enterprises have forced Mexican workers to bear considerable costs of adjustment. They have not, generally speaking, enjoyed the benefits of liberalization.

Cuts in social programs and subsidies have made the plight of Mexican workers more difficult. The U.S. government, the IMF, and Wall Street have applauded Mexico's "fiscal discipline," but this discipline has come at the expense of many poor Mexicans. Even if a future government were to make the lot of workers its top priority, NAFTA and Mexico's external indebtedness would severely constrain its ability to pursue policies that might increase the demand for labor and/or improve the distribution of income.

If we look at Mexico's record over the past two years and acknowledge that the peso crisis and its consequences are at least partly related to liberalization, then this assessment of Mexico's experience with liberalization becomes considerably more discouraging. Unemployment has grown by at least half, real wages have fallen by more than half, investment has collapsed, and Mexico's external debt has ballooned to $165 billion (Resource Center of the Americas 1997). The rapid growth of the *maquiladora* sector reflects the irony of liberalization's "successes." Mexico is currently running a large trade surplus with the U.S. and DFI; employment and output in the *maquiladoras* have boomed since early 1995. But this growth is based on low and declining wages and the inability of Mexico's workers to command a share of productivity gains. In fact, despite a 9.6 percent increase in *maquiladora* employment between September 1994 and September 1995, the real value of the wage bill fell by 9 percent (Larudee 1996).

CONCLUSIONS

It is, of course, inappropriate to reach sweeping conclusions about liberalization based on one country's experience. But the Mexican case does suggest a few conclusions about the theory and practice of economic liberalization.

First, Mexico's experience supports the contention that the restrictive assumptions of mainstream trade theory limit its ability to predict and assess the consequences of liberalization. The liberalization of the Mexican economy appears to have promoted productivity gains of the sort that mainstream theory highlights. But mainstream studies of NAFTA assumed away two important consequences of NAFTA: unemployment and the relocation of productive investment from the U.S. to Mexico. In part because of the assumption of full employment, these models also misassessed the impact of liberalization on wages. In contrast, Mexico's experience makes sense from the PE perspective. The less restrictive set of assumptions adopted by economists in this camp provide a more useful framework for evaluating the consequences of liberalization. A more realistic assessment of liberalization might provide the basis for a trade agreement that serves the interests of the typical North American better than NAFTA has.

On the other hand, economists critical of NAFTA and suspicious of liberalization have tended to downplay the potential gains from trade. Debates over the wisdom of liberalization would be more fruitful if they were less polarized.

Second, Mexico's experience highlights the need to qualify the central claim of mainstream trade theory, that is, that freer trade generates efficiency gains. If the productivity gains from liberalization are not matched by increases in labor demand, workers may not share in the gains from trade.

What can be done about this? A North American trade and investment agreement should include provisions designed to distribute the costs and gains associated with liberalization fairly because the market is not likely to. The wages of government employees and the minimum wage (which has fallen by half since 1985) could be indexed to productivity growth.[10] The U.S. government should require that its corporations pay a wage that is well above Mexico's minimum wage. Multinational corporations from other countries should be taxed if they do not do the same. A tax on exports, imports, corporate profits, and/or foreign creditors could be used to finance tax relief and/or cash payments to poor Mexican families. Those bearing substantial adjustment costs should be compensated for their losses through more generous and widely available systems of unemployment insurance and trade adjustment assistance.

There is a danger, of course, that all of this will scare off some investors. The evidence suggests, however, that DFI flows are quite unresponsive to profit rate differentials (Koechlin 1992; Epstein 1995). Small increases in Mexican wages will not, in most cases, overwhelm the appeal of producing in Mexico for export to the enormous U.S. market. Still, policies of this sort will be more effective if they are embodied in a continent wide agreement, because this would send the message to investors that these are among the costs of doing business in North America. These policies—or other policies reflecting the same objectives—would be dramatically more effective if they were embodied in the GATT and/or other multilateral trade agreements. Policies designed to promote a progressive redistribution of income are less likely to scare off investors if these investors face similar policies elsewhere. The U.S., as the world's largest and most important economy, should take the lead on this matter.

This is not free trade as traditionally defined. But a trade deal which included provisions of this sort would be better than NAFTA and better than the GATT, because it would distribute the gains from trade more equitably. A trade agreement that does not improve the economic prospects for citizens of below-average means should not be considered a success.

Third, the liberalization of Mexico's capital markets increased the volatility of capital flows. The hypermobility of short-term capital turned the peso devaluation into an economic disaster. Capital controls and/or a tax on international capital movements would make Mexico—and its rich northern neighbors—less vulnerable to the whims of international investors.

Fourth, the fate of the Mexican economy does not hinge on trade policy alone. Debt relief would arguably do more to improve Mexican living standards than even the most cleverly crafted trade deal. Mexico's external debt is approaching US$ 170 billion, and annual debt service is nearly US$ 15 billion (Resource Center for the Americas 1997). If the IMF and the U.S. government are interested in promoting growth in Mexico, they should use their considerable influence to reduce Mexico's enormous debt burden. Mexico's meager growth has come at great cost to Mexican workers. Growth at the (very minor) expense of Western banks is considerably more appealing and equitable than the status quo.

If the goal of Mexican economic policy is to raise the living standard of the typical Mexican—as it should be—then Mexico and North America need a set of policies designed to improve the distributional effects of liberalization. Liberalization as we know it is not the only option. I recognize that this would require a significant shift in the ways that economists and policymakers think about trade, and a trade deal of the sort I have suggested would not be viewed favorably by financial markets and most multinational firms. But if something like this does not happen, then liberalization will continue to undermine the living standards of Mexican workers and many other workers around the world. Unfortunately, this is a very likely outcome.

NOTES

1. This categorization is clearly an oversimplification, but it is useful in this context. "Mainstream trade theory" includes models that accept the basic assumptions and conclusions of the classical theory of trade. In particular, economists in this category believe that comparative advantage is the key principle upon which an analysis of trade should be based and that trade

liberalization enhances welfare. Economists in the political economy tradition view many of the tenets of the mainstream approach with skepticism and are less sanguine about the consequences of liberalization. For a more detailed discussion, see Koechlin (1997).

2. See Brown (1992) for a review of CGE models of NAFTA and Stanford (1993) for a terrific critical assessment of this methodology. US ITC (1992) presents several of the most influential CGE models.

3. These are three of several assumptions underlying mainstream trade theory. See Stanford (1993) and Skott and Larudee (1997) for more elaborate discussion of this issue.

4. See Koechlin (1993) for a critical assessment of the treatment of DFI in mainstream studies of NAFTA.

5. I have used the label "heterodox" to describe this crowd elsewhere (Koechlin 1997). This is a diverse group, ranging from liberal institutionalists to Marxists. The approach I have in mind here is, however, along the lines of Koechlin and Larudee (1992); Stanford (1993); Faux and Spriggs (1991); Skott and Larudee (1997) and the papers presented in Blecker (1996b) and Baker et al. (1997).

6. Having said this, one must acknowledge that some writers in this tradition tend to emphasize the threatening possibilities associated with globalization while ignoring the potential benefits of trade. See Anderson et al. (1996) and Ranney (1993), for example.

7. This was surely the case for the U.S. during the twenty-five or so years following World War II.

8. In contrast, Hufbauer and Schott's widely cited claim that NAFTA would create 170,000 U.S. jobs hinged on the assumption that the U.S. trade surplus with Mexico would grow to $9 billion and remain there through the end of the century (Hufbauer and Schott 1993).

9. If one assumes that $1 billion in exports corresponds to 14,000 jobs, then the worsening trade balance with Mexico has cost the U.S. about 300,000 jobs. See Bolle (1996) for a discussion of this formula.

10. See Larudee (1996) for a more careful discussion of this idea.

REFERENCES

Alcorte, L. 1995. The impact of new technologies on industrial structure: Case studies from Brazil, Mexico and Venezuela. Paper presented at the Latin American Studies Association Meetings, September 28–30, Washington, DC.

Anderson, S., J. Cavanaugh, and D. Ranney, eds. 1996. NAFTA's first two years: Myths and realities. Washington, DC: Institute for Policy Studies. Mimeographed.

Baker, D., G. Epstein, and R. Pollin, eds. 1997. *Globalization and Progressive Economic Policy*. Ann Arbor: University of Michigan Press.

Blecker, R. A. 1996a. The political economy of the North American Free Trade Agreement. In *U.S. Trade Policy and Global Growth*, edited by R. Blecker, 136–76. Armonk, NY: M. E. Sharpe.

——, ed. 1996b. *U.S. Trade Policy and Global Growth*. Armonk, NY: M. E. Sharpe.

Bolle, M. J. 1996. *NAFTA: Estimates of Job Effects and Industry Trade Trends after Two Years*. Washington, DC: Congressional Research Service, Economics Division.

Brown, D. K. 1992. The impact of a North American free trade area: Applied general equilibrium models. In *North American Free Trade: Assessing the Impact*, edited by N. Lustig, B. Bosworth, and R. Lawrence, 26–68. Washington, DC: Brookings Institution.

Brown, D. K., A. Deardorf, and R. M. Stern. 1992. A North American free trade agreement: Analytical issues and a computational assessment. *World Economy* 15(1):11–30.

Epstein, G. A. 1995. International profit rate equalization and foreign direct investment: A study of integration, instability and enforcement. In *Macroeconomics after the Conservative Era*, edited by G. A. Epstein and H. Gintis, 308–33. Cambridge, MA: Cambridge University Press.

Faux, J., and T. M. Lee. 1992. *The Effect of George Bush's NAFTA on American Workers. Ladder Up or Ladder Down?* Washington, DC: Economic Policy Institute.

Gambrill, M. 1995. La politica salarial de las maquiladoras: Mejoras posibles bajo el TLC. *Comercio Exterior* 45(7):543–49.

Hinojosa, R., et al. 1996. North American integration three years after NAFTA. University of California, Los Angeles. Mimeographed.

Hufbauer, G. C., and J. Schott. 1993. *NAFTA: An Assessment*. Washington, DC: Institute for International Economics.

International Monetary Fund (IMF). 1994. *International Financial Statistics*. Washington, DC: IMF.

Kehoe, T. J. 1992. *Modeling the Dynamic Impact of North American Free Trade*. Working Paper 491. Minneapolis, MN: Federal Reserve Bank of Minneapolis.

Koechlin, T. 1992. The responsiveness of domestic investment to foreign economic conditions. *Journal of Post Keynesian Economics* 15(1):63–83.

——. 1993. NAFTA and the location of North American investment: A critique of mainstream analysis. *Review of Radical Political Economics* 25(4):59–71.

——. 1997. The limits of globalization. In *Political Economy of Globalization*, edited by D. Gupta, 59–79. Boston, MA: Kluwer Academic Publishers.

Koechlin, T., and M. Larudee. 1992. The high cost of NAFTA. *Challenge* 35(5): 19–26.

Krugman, P. 1987. Is free trade passe? *Journal of Economic Perspectives* 1(2):131–43.

Larudee, M. 1996. Integration and income distribution under the North American Free Trade Agreement (NAFTA). Paper Presented at Conference on Globalization and Progressive Economic Policy, sponsored by the Economic Policy Institute, June 21–23, Washington, DC.

Leamer, E. 1993. Wage effects of a US-Mexico free trade agreement. In *The Mexico-US Trade Agreement*, edited by P. Garber, 57–125. Cambridge, MA: MIT Press.

Levy, S., and S. van Wijnbergen. 1994. Agriculture in the Mexico-US free trade agreement: A general equilibrium analysis. In *Modeling Trade Policy*, edited by J. Francois and C. Sheills, 151–94. New York: Cambridge University Press.

Marquez Padilla, C. 1995. El sector manufacturero, politicas comercial y cambriaria y la cuestion ocupacional, 1980–1992. *Economia Mexicana, Nueva Epoca* 4(1):151–70.

Organization for Economic Co-operation and Development (OECD). 1997. *OECD Economic Surveys: Mexico, 1997*. Paris: OECD.

Ranney, D. 1993. NAFTA and the transnational corporate agenda. *Review of Radical Political Economics* 25(4):1–9.

Resource Center of the Americas. 1997. *Labor Report on the Americas*. Minneapolis, MN.

Rich, P. NAFTA and Chiapas. 1997. *Annals of the American Academy of Political and Social Science* 551:72–84.

Robinson, S., M. E. Burfisher, R. Hinojosa-Ojeda, and K. E. Thierfelder. 1992. Agricultural policies and migration in a US-Mexico free trade area: A computable general equilibrium analysis. In *Economy-Wide Modeling of the Implications of a FTA with Mexico and NAFTA with Canada and Mexico*, edited by US ITC, 455–507. Washington, DC: US ITC.

Shaiken, H. 1990. *Mexico in the global economy*. Monograph Series 33. University of California, San Diego Center for U.S.-Mexico Studies.

Skott, P., and M. Larudee. 1997. Uneven development and the liberalization of trade and capital flows: The case of Mexico. *Cambridge Journal of Economics*. (Forthcoming).

Stanford, J. 1993. Continental integration: The impact on labor. *Annals of the American Academy of Political and Social Science*.

United States International Trade Commission (US ITC). 1991. *The Likely Impact on the United States of a Free Trade Agreement with Mexico*. Washington, DC: US ITC.

——. 1992. *Economy-Wide Modeling of the Implications of a FTA with Mexico and NAFTA with Canada and Mexico*. Washington, DC: US ITC.

Weintraub, S. 1992. Modeling the industrial effects of NAFTA. In *North American Free Trade: Assessing the Impact*, edited by N. Lustig, B. Bosworth, and R. Lawrence, 109–43. Washington, DC: Brookings Institution.

9
Labor Market Adjustment in an Oil-Based Economy: The Experience of Trinidad and Tobago

Anston Rambarran

For many Third World nations, the 1980s was a decade of adjustment as the debt crisis and international recession exposed their fundamental structural fragilities. In the oil-based economy of Trinidad and Tobago, the experience was no different. Economic difficulties dominated the policy agenda, and reforms were instituted on all fronts. At the onset of the 1980s, however, socioeconomic conditions were quite favorable, and the country was enjoying a standard of living ranked among the highest outside of the mature industrialized economies. Economic rents generated by the oil shocks of the 1970s had yielded considerable benefits in the form of higher foreign exchange earnings and government revenue that were channeled into improving the social and economic infrastructure.

However, as the economy became increasingly dependent on oil revenues, its vulnerability to adverse external shocks was exacerbated. A precipitous decline in international petroleum prices, compounded by the domestic trend of a depletion in oil reserves, invoked the economic crisis in the mid-1980s. The country thereafter experienced substantial fiscal and balance-of-payments deficits, significant currency devaluation, rising inflationary pressures and soaring unemployment levels, and eight consecutive years of negative growth. Against this backdrop, a medium-term adjustment program envisaging radical policy reforms was initiated in the late 1980s.

The program entailed tax reform through the consolidation and reduction of personal and corporate income tax levels, as well as the implementation of a 15 percent value-added tax (VAT); reduction of the fiscal deficit through tighter control of public expenditures; restructuring and divestment of state enterprises; rescheduling of the public-sector external debt; liberalization of the trade, exchange, and investment regimes; a gradual withdrawal of the state and greater participation of the private sector in the economy; and amelioration of the social impact of adjustment. The adjustment program was also supported by two standby arrangements with the International Monetary Fund (IMF) and a number of policy-based loans from the World Bank and Inter-American Development Bank (IADB).

Within the context of economic reform, the labor market is fundamental to ensuring the success of stabilization and adjustment policies and to mediating the impact of these policies on the living standards of the population, particularly the poor. In the case of the stabilization policy, the labor market must ensure that the programmed reduction in expenditure levels does not induce a substantial contraction in national output through persistently high unemployment. With respect to structural adjustment, it is the labor market that facilitates changes in the sectoral allocation of labor, especially to markets that serve the production of tradables. Moreover, the degree of gender segmentation in the labor market and its response to macroeconomic instruments determine the prevailing distribution of income in the economy.

This study examines the varied aspects of the rich interaction between the labor market and the adjustment process in Trinidad and Tobago and seeks to draw out general conclusions, policy lessons, and areas for further research. The chapter is organized as follows. First there is an overview of the adjustment process, that is, the nature of the shock, the policy responses, and the macroeconomic outcomes. The next section addresses the performance of the labor market during adjustment, focusing on unemployment and real wages, sectoral employment shifts, distributive conflict, and the role of labor market institutions. An evaluation of the impact of adjustment, as mediated by the labor market, on income distribution and poverty, the evolution of public social expenditures and the role of women is then conducted.

Finally, the chapter concludes by considering labor market adjustment issues for the future.

THE PROCESS OF ADJUSTMENT, 1983–95

Although the structure of the economy is gradually being transformed, it is still the case that any description of the process of adjustment to falling oil revenues in an open petroleum economy needs to start with the stance of fiscal policy and its impact on fiscal operations. This is because the state is the principal economic agent that monetizes oil incomes (earned in foreign exchange), through the transmission of government expenditure to the non-oil economy. From the mid-1980s, fiscal adjustment has been pursued with the objective of restraining the fiscal deficit, particularly that on current account. Many of the fiscal reforms were initiated during 1989–90, under a formal IMF adjustment program, and sought to reduce the government's net domestic budget deficit by contracting expenditure, expanding revenue intake, and restricting financing options.

The expenditure-reducing measures included a 10 percent cut in wages and salaries of public servants and a temporary suspension of their cost of living allowances (COLA) and merit payments; reductions in transfers and subsidies to statutory authorities and public utilities; and divestment or, in some cases, closure of state enterprises. On the revenue side, the petroleum tax legislation was modified to stimulate production and exploration activity by oil companies, and the tax system was streamlined to emphasize indirect taxation through the introduction of a value added tax at a rate of 15 percent. Other policy actions with implications for fiscal performance arose from the loan conditionalities of the multilateral agencies, including trade and exchange rate liberalization.

In the first years of the economic crisis, declining revenues and a rigidity in recurrent expenditures contributed to the generation of overall public-sector deficits but, as the adjustment process intensified, the rate of deterioration of the fiscal accounts slowed largely on the basis of tighter containment of expenditures and enhanced revenue administration. The conservative stance of fiscal policy resulted in the overall deficit on fiscal operations falling from an average of 5.4 percent of gross domestic product (GDP) at current market prices between 1986 and 1990 to an average of 0.9 percent of GDP in the last five years. Table 9.1 shows that a fiscal current account deficit equivalent to 2.3 percent of GDP emerged in 1986. Deficits persisted until 1990, when a surplus of 0.4 percent of GDP was realized, and since then, the fiscal balance has shown a surplus equivalent to 1.8 per cent of GDP in four of the last five years.

This situation diminished the ability of government to fund public-sector projects out of current revenue, and the significant reduction in the quantum of resources allocated to capital expenditure became a critical feature of the process of fiscal adjustment. The proportion of government revenue allocated to capital expenditure fell from around 48 percent in 1983 to less than 10 percent in 1995. A substantial portion of such capital spending in the late 1980s consisted of transfers and net lending to state enterprises and statutory authorities to meet operating costs and, arguably, that portion was not conducive to capital formation. Both falling oil production and prices adversely affected revenue collections from the petroleum sector, with the share of oil earnings declining sharply from almost 50 percent of total revenue in 1982 to 25 percent in 1995. Among major categories of non-oil government revenue, tax collections from companies, individuals, and international trade fell steadily, but income from taxation on goods and services displayed significant

Table 9.1
Selected Economic Indicators, 1982–95

Indicator	1982	1983	1984	1985	1986	1987	1988	1989	1990	1991	1992	1993	1994	1995
Real GDP at factor cost (growth rate, %)	4.0	–10.2	–5.9	–5.6	–4.3	–5.2	–3.9	–0.7	–0.1	2.7	–1.7	–1.6	4.2	3.5
Fiscal surplus (+) deficit (–) on current a/c (% of GDP)	4.2	1.0	1.3	1.5	–2.3	–2.3	–3.5	–1.2	–0.1	3.1	–1.2	1.4	1.4	1.4
BOP surplus (+) deficit (–) on current a/c (% of GDP)	–8.5	–13.1	–7.1	–1.5	–13.2	–5.1	–2.6	–1.5	8.5	–0.4	2.3	1.4	7.6	0.9
Bank deposits (growth rate %)	32.6	9.1	5.4	1.1	–4.4	3.0	0.5	4.0	3.8	7.3	0.4	–4.3	2.3	5.6
Domestic credit[1] (growth rate, %)	19.7	16.4	7.0	–3.8	1.2	3.1	0.0	1.2	1.0	9.7	3.0	3.7	–2.0	7.4
Excess liquidity[2] (% of deposit liabilities)	7.5	2.2	–0.4	2.8	–0.1	–0.1	0.2	0.9	1.3	18.4	18.4	19.1	26.6	27.7
Stock of public-sector external debt[3] (US$ Mn)	561.7	1306.2	1398.2	1643.4	2064.8	2292.8	2402.6	2400.7	2520.5	2438.1	2215.0	2102.1	2063.5	1905.2
Ext. debt service ratio (% of exports of goods and nonfactor services)	2.4	6.8	5.5	6.3	11.3	15.8	22.3	19.8	19.1	21.1	28.9	32.9	27.4	19.7
Inflation rate (%)	11.4	16.7	13.3	7.7	7.7	10.8	7.8	11.4	11.1	3.8	6.6	10.8	8.8	6.5
Unemployment rate (%)	9.9	11.1	13.3	15.7	17.2	22.3	22.0	22.0	20.0	18.5	19.6	19.8	18.5	17.5
West Texas intermediate spot price[4] (US$/bbl)	33.11	30.42	29.38	27.96	14.87	19.14	15.95	19.58	24.12	21.62	20.57	18.45	17.19	18.44

Source: Central Bank of Trinidad and Tobago, *Annual Economic Survey* (various issues).
1. Comprises total loans, securities of local government and statutory boards, and investments in the private sector, excluding credit to nonresidents and the central government.
2. Effective January 2, 1991, the secondary reserve requirement was removed. The statutory cash reserve requirement of 16 percent was raised to 18 percent on April 13, 1994, and to 20 percent on July 6, 1994. The Central Bank subsequently introduced a new measure of liquidity, which is reflected in the data from 1991.
3. Comprises central government, state enterprises, and Central Bank external debt.
4. Annual average of published quotations and not necessarily realized prices.

growth through the emphasis on indirect taxes and a widening of the tax base. By 1995, indirect taxation accounted for about 32 percent of total tax revenue, compared with a little over 8 percent in 1983.

From 1986, the fiscal deficits were largely financed by the domestic capital market, unlike previous years when external funds were the major source of financing. Moreover, as principal repayments on external loans exceeded inflows in the main, the need to fund a net external transfer resulted in an even greater demand for local financing. The source composition of this financing revealed an increased reliance on medium- and long-term bonds absorbed by nondepository financial institutions and the Central Bank. Net bond financing rose from a little over 1 percent of GDP at current market prices in 1986 to a peak of 3.4 percent of GDP in 1991 before falling to levels attained in the mid-1980s. Although these net proceeds were later supplemented by the divestment of state equity in various enterprises, the swift buildup of central government debt led to a dramatic rise in interest costs, from an average of 1 percent of GDP in the early 1980s to over 5 percent of GDP in the mid-1990s.

Over much of the adjustment period, monetary policy was conducted both formally and informally within the context of the IMF standby arrangements, which aimed at restoring external balance by restricting domestic demand. Monetary targets were established, including limits on commercial bank lending to state enterprises and statutory authorities and on Central Bank lending to the central government. Although the Central Bank made active use of the traditional tools of monetary management, such as the reserve requirement and the rediscount rate, in recent times it has moved to more indirect instruments of monetary control. The lower fiscal stimulus provided by a shrinking net domestic budget deficit, as well as increased outflows of foreign exchange, generally reduced the flow of new resources to the domestic banking system. Net resource creation as measured by the growth rate of commercial banks' deposits was moderate. Table 9.1 indicates that total deposits of the commercial banks grew on average by a little over 2 percent between 1991 and 1995. Further, the distribution of deposit liabilities reveals a shift in liquidity preferences, particularly toward demand deposits at the expense of the traditionally dominant time deposits.

Movements in the monetary sector also highlighted the continued reduction in the level of public-sector borrowings from the domestic financial system, as credit extended to the central government and public sector remained a special target of monetary policy until 1994. Despite the relatively austere stance of the monetary authorities, total credit outstanding grew faster than deposits and resulted in fluctuating liquidity conditions in the banking system. Excess liquidity, measured as a percentage of deposit liabilities, averaged 2.2 percent in 1983 and deteriorated to −0.1 percent in 1987 before rebounding to 1.3 percent in

1990 (Table 9.1). However, after the liberalization of the foreign exchange market, commercial banks began to experience large inflows of foreign currency, thereby substantially enhancing their levels of liquidity and credit-granting capacity. For instance, commercial banks' liquid assets averaged just under 28 percent of deposit liabilities in 1995 compared with a statutory reserve requirement of 20 percent.

Commercial banks experienced deficiencies with respect to their reserve requirements for the major part of the adjustment period, with the progressively higher cost of access to liquidity support from the Central Bank reflected in rising interest rates. The increased cost of funds also had an adverse impact on the level of real-sector activity. As the business environment deteriorated, commercial banks increased their provisions for losses to take account of nonperforming loans and advances. It should be noted, however, that some analysts contend that the large profits realized by banks in the 1970s and early 1980s resulted from wide interest rate spreads which disguised their gross operational inefficiencies. The worsening economic conditions, coupled with a lack of formal regulations, also exposed the weaknesses of several nonbank financial institutions. Although stronger controls were later instituted, these materialized only after depositors' confidence in the nonbank financial intermediaries had weakened considerably.

In light of fiscal restraint, devaluation of the currency, and tightened exchange controls, the current account deficit of the balance of payments narrowed from 13.2 percent of GDP in 1986 to 1.5 percent in 1989. Movements in the capital account of the balance of payments paralleled the current account and reflected a cumulative outflow of resources through the rapid depletion of foreign exchange reserves and an acceleration in the rate of growth of external debt service. From a healthy reserves position of approximately US$ 2,985 million in 1982, total reserves fell to around US$ 80 million in 1987 and were just under US$ –6 million by the end of 1988. The debt service ratio, measured as a percentage of exports of goods and nonfactor services, rose from 2.4 percent in 1982 to a little over 22 percent in 1988 (see Table 9.1).

As the need for additional balance-of-payments support became evident, the government accessed the Compensatory Financing Facility (CFF) of the IMF in November 1988 and entered into a fourteen-month standby arrangement in January 1989. This program was generally successful, and all performance criteria and targets were met. In furtherance of its adjustment efforts, the government then entered into a twelve-month standby arrangement and signed for a US $40 million structural adjustment loan (SAL) with the World Bank in 1990. These arrangements facilitated agreement with the country's major international creditor groups on a wide-ranging package of debt relief and enabled the deferral of some US$ 740 million in payments due between September 1988 and August 1992. Although the overall external payments deficit widened to 3.7 percent of GDP in 1990, due principally to an increase in external debt servicing, the country achieved its highest-ever surplus on the current account, amounting to 8.5 percent of GDP, resulting from a "spike" in oil prices consequent on the Gulf crisis.

In 1991, the return to economic growth exposed the continuing existence of structural weaknesses, as evidenced by the reemergence of a current external deficit equivalent to 0.4 percent of GDP. Nevertheless, in 1992, stabilization and structural adjustment measures achieved some success in restoring the country's external balance with the realization of a current account surplus and a narrowing of the overall balance-of-payments deficit. During 1993–94, the economy recorded an overall external surplus, although there was a slight reduction of the surplus on the current account. Moreover, movements in the capital account suggested that the signals sent by the country's efforts at financial liberalization had been positively interpreted abroad. By 1995, the positive balance of payments outturn was consolidated, as was evident by substantial increases in net official reserves and commercial banks' holdings of foreign assets. Consequently, the evidence from both the internal and external sectors of the economy suggested that, by the mid-1990s, the long-term negative imbalance between aggregate demand and supply had been decisively corrected.

THE PERFORMANCE OF THE LABOR MARKET DURING THE PROCESS OF ADJUSTMENT

Unemployment and Real Wages

Trinidad and Tobago has consistently experienced relatively high rates of open unemployment due to the heavy reliance on the capital-intensive energy sector and the need for an improved efficiency in resource allocation. Indeed, the rate of unemployment averaged about 15 percent of the labor force during the oil boom and did not fall substantially below 10 percent. This situation was compounded in the economic recession of the 1980s, when shrinking job opportunities in the face of an expanding labor force resulted in slow growth of formal-sector employment and rising unemployment levels. As a consequence, the unemployment rate[1] peaked at a little over 22 percent of the labor force in 1987, stabilized at that level for the next two years, and thereafter remained at around 20 percent in the early 1990s. Following the resumption of economic growth, the rate declined to about 17.5 percent by 1995.

Unemployment has to a greater extent affected the youth, females, and the unskilled. High rates of youth unemployment exist for both genders, as these new labor-force entrants often lack the necessary marketable skills to acquire jobs in the highly competitive labor market (see Table 9.2). The unemployment rate among fifteen- to ninteen-year-

Table 9.2
Unemployment Rates for Population Subgroups, 1987–95
(percentages)

	1987	1988	1989	1990	1991	1992	1993	1994	1995
Total	**22.2**	**22.0**	**22.0**	**20.0**	**18.5**	**19.6**	**19.8**	**18.4**	**17.2**
Age-Sex									
M 15–19	44.7	40.9	42.3	39.3	35.9	38.2	36.0	33.7	33.5
20–24	34.2	35.6	34.3	29.3	25.8	28.1	25.9	26.3	25.5
25–34	20.2	22.1	22.7	17.9	16.2	17.6	19.1	16.7	14.7
35–44	12.6	13.3	12.4	11.7	10.3	11.3	12.9	10.9	10.2
45–54	8.9	10.4	9.8	8.7	7.6	9.0	10.5	9.1	9.5
55–64	10.9	9.3	11.3	7.5	8.8	9.2	9.2	10.4	10.0
65+	9.4	9.8	4.0	8.1	2.8	5.0	5.2	4.6	4.7
All Males	**20.7**	**21.1**	**20.8**	**17.8**	**15.7**	**17.0**	**17.6**	**20.0**	**15.1**
F 15–19	58.8	59.6	53.8	58.9	56.6	52.2	59.7	47.5	44.7
20–24	39.3	37.6	43.1	34.7	35.7	34.8	32.5	34.8	31.4
25–34	22.2	23.2	22.8	25.1	22.4	25.9	24.1	23.6	22.8
35–44	17.1	13.5	16.2	16.3	16.0	17.1	16.8	14.6	18.8
45–54	13.0	11.4	12.8	9.8	12.8	13.3	14.0	13.7	10.2
55–64	11.8	15.2	12.1	7.1	9.5	9.4	10.1	11.4	8.5
65+	6.6	8.2	0.0	4.3	3.3	4.5	3.1	4.7	7.9
All Females	**25.2**	**23.7**	**25.5**	**24.2**	**23.4**	**23.9**	**23.4**	**22.3**	**20.6**

Source: Central Statistical Office (CSO), *Labour Force Report* (various issues).

olds grew from around 29 percent in 1983 to a little under 40 percent in 1995, whereas that of the 20 to 24 age group increased from about 18 percent to 28 percent over the same period. For males, relatively high rates of unemployment persist until the age of thirty-five, while for women the unemployment rate remains above 20 percent up to the 25 to 34 age group. Furthermore, it is estimated that over 45 percent of the unemployed have previously held positions classified as elementary.

The unemployment situation is better viewed as a rationing problem rather than a voluntary job search. Under conditions of excess labor supply, job seekers with distinct occupational preferences are more slowly absorbed into employment, but the data suggest that the duration of unemployment for the majority of workers has been relatively short. For instance, the latest published data indicate that, in 1993, a little more than 60 percent of active job seekers with a history of previous employment held a job within the previous six months and less than 30 percent held a job more than a year before. Much of this temporary unemployment would include workers engaged in job searches, moving across sectors or to different jobs within their original sector. Nonetheless, it is evident from Table 9.3 that the persistence in the mean duration of unemployment implies that long-term unemployment is a serious problem, particularly among women. In 1993, over 50 percent of women and 32 percent of men were unemployed for more than one year, with a significant proportion experiencing unemployment spells in excess of two years.

Table 9.4 shows the results of a probit analysis for the determinants of unemployment between males and females based on the 1992 Survey of Living Conditions (SLC).[2] The individual's unemployment status is used as the dependent binary variable controlling for household characteristics, individual characteristics, and local labor market conditions. The analysis clearly highlights that, holding age and other factors constant, experience is negatively related to the rate of unemployment, but there is an important difference between males and females. For males, the rate of unemployment declines monotonically with experience in the labor force. By contrast, the female unemployment experience profile is U-shaped in that unemployment first declines with experience, but as the worker grows older, unemployment rates rise. Indeed, it appears that the experience-unemployment link is stronger and quantitatively much more significant for females.

An important result is that household size or the number of working adults in the household has no effect on the probability of unemployment for either sex. Spouses of household heads are less likely to be unemployed and that finding is equally consistent with the high correlation of male and female participation rates. Another interesting result is that, contrary to the Harris-Todaro type of hypothesis, the incidence of unemployment is not higher in the high-income region. Further, the region of residence does not significantly affect the male unemployment rate, but women in urban areas are more likely to be unemployed than those in rural areas.

Weak labor demand did not result only in unemployment. The data suggest a relatively high prevalence of underemployment,[3] although this is hard to measure. During the last three years, over 14 percent of employed males and 16 percent of women worked less than thirty-three hours per week, while 10 percent of males and 12 percent of females worked less than twenty-four hours per week. Using the convention that two underemployed persons are equivalent to one unemployed person and adding these "converted" unemployed to open unemployment suggests that around 20 percent of the labor force is currently seeking employment.

Table 9.3
Unemployment by Duration, 1987–93

Year	Unemployment Rate	Duration of Unemployment				Mean Steady State Duration (months)	Share of Long-Term Unemployed
		0-3 Months	4-6 Months	7-11 Months	12 or More Months		
1987	22.2	9.3	2.7	2.7	7.5	7.1	33.6
1988	22.0	9.1	3.1	2.3	7.4	6.3	33.8
1989	22.0	8.3	3.2	1.4	9.0	6.8	40.9
1990	20.0	7.5	2.8	1.9	7.8	6.8	39.1
1991	18.5	8.2	2.4	1.6	6.2	6.1	32.9
1992	19.6	8.8	2.9	1.9	5.9	5.9	30.1
1993	19.8	8.9	2.9	1.9	5.8	5.9	29.7

Source: Calculated from Central Statistical Office (CSO), *Labour Force Report* (various issues).

Percentages except where otherwise indicated.

Table 9.4
The Determinants of Unemployment

Dependent Variable	Coefficient Males	Standard Error	Coefficient Females	Standard Error
Household size	0.034*	0.020	−0.032	0.030
Number of working adults in household	−0.192*	0.047	0.0	0.058
Experience	−0.0179*	0.012	−0.040*	0.013
Experience squared	0.000	0.000	0.001*	0.000
Spouse of household head working	−0.948*	0.188	−1.471*	0.176
Urban	−0.237	0.150	0.357*	0.214
Years of education	−0.068*	0.014	−0.050	0.016
Head of household	−0.556*	0.124	−0.429*	0.150
Local unemployment rates	0.799	1.392	0.611	1.938
Local wages	0.672*	0.303	−1.109*	0.611
Household nonlabor income (1000*)	0.007	0.005	0.005	0.004
Number of observations	1544		864	

Source: Calculated from Republic of Trinidad and Tobago, Survey of Living Conditions (SLC), 1992.

* Significantly different from zero at 95 percent confidence level.

A final form of quantity adjustment involved the shift from formal- to informal-sector employment.[4] Even though no reliable estimates exist, casual observations reveal a rise in informal-sector activity triggered by the imbalances in the labor market. As employees lost their jobs or as income became insufficient to cover household expenses, one option in the absence of a system of unemployment compensation was self-employment. As a result, employment and, thus, output often shifted from large, formal-sector firms to smaller, informal-sector ones. The informal sector now constitutes the most significant locus of indigenous entrepreneurial activity, representing a low-income survival strategy for vertically integrated, petty, commercial operations. The most common forms of informal enterprises are street retail vending, small-scale trading, craft and clothing manufacturing, and taxi and domestic services.

Although an accurate assessment of the size of informal activity is critical to the measurement of economic activity and the formulation of policy, by its very nature, this measurement is problematic. Taking into account workers, excluding legislators, professionals, and technicians, as representative of the informal sector, then informal workers currently represent about 12 percent of the labor force and almost 15 percent of the employed. If those classified as unpaid workers, learners, apprentices, and "not stated" are included, then over 20 percent of all workers comprise the informal sector. It can be argued, therefore, that informalization has been an important method of labor market adjustment.

The evidence on wage behavior certainly does not favor the view that real wages were rigid and therefore led to unemployment. By the end of the 1980s, the deepening economic crisis began to be reflected in the evolution of wages in the public sector. In 1987, public servants' merit increases and COLA were suspended, and a 10 percent wage cut was introduced in 1989 but restored in 1991. A 2 percent general wage increase was granted in 1992 and COLA reinstated, even though the issue of arrears, estimated at 5 percent of 1995 GDP at current market prices, is yet to be fully settled. In 1995, a number of public-sector unions agreed to a settlement of the COLA arrears at a discount, the resumption of payment of salary increments in 1996, and the liquidation of arrears through the issue of tax-free, interest-free bonds. Within the private sector, the situation paralleled that of the public service. Many firms were unable to match falling revenue to high operating costs and instituted pay cuts, reduced fringe benefits, and generally "downsized" staffing levels. Furthermore, over the last few years, the almost universal COLA in collective bargaining agreements has given way to the substitution of a fixed-cash supplement in return for its buyout.

Inevitably, the general restraint on wage increases implied a sharp contraction of real wages throughout the industrial sector. Table 9.5 shows that between 1983 and 1995, industrial workers experienced an annual decline in both real minimum wages and average earnings of 9.7 percent and 11 percent, respectively. The fall in minimum wages was both widespread and significant, especially for production and ancillary workers in the textile, garments, and footwear industry and in central and local government. An examination of industrial agreements registered with the Industrial Court reinforced the notion of a declining level of wage settlements, although these agreements cover no more than 20 percent of the labor force and may not accurately reflect market conditions. With respect to the twenty-one agreements analyzed in 1985 for successive triennia from 1983 to 1990, wage increases ranged between 12 and 19.5 percent, with a median of 15.8 percent. By 1991, of the seventy agreements analyzed for a three-year period commencing between 1987 and 1991, the wage increases ranged between 1 and 4 percent and the median wage increase had progressively fallen to 2 percent.

Table 9.5
Real Minimum Wages and Average Weekly Earnings by Sector,
1983–95 (percentage change per annum)

Sector	Minimum Wages	Average Weekly Earnings
Manufacture of food, drink, tobacco	–7.2	–7.4
Manufacture of textiles, garments, footwear	–15.2	–15.9
Other manufacturing industries	–10.4	–11.7[1]
Assembly-type and related industries	–13.9	–14.3
Electricity, water, and sewerage	–5.9	–8.1[2]
Building and construction	–9.9	NA
Distribution	–10.3	NA
Services	–11.8	NA
Transport, communication, and storage	–12.7	NA
Central and local government	–13.6	NA
Petroleum industries	–1.5	–5.3
Sugar	–5.0	–7.9
All industry index	–9.7	–11.0

Source: Calculated from Central Statistical Office (CSO), *Economic Indicators Report* (various issues).

1. Weighted average of printing, publishing, and paper converters, wood and related products, chemicals and nonmetallic products, and miscellaneous manufacturing.
2. Represents electricity only.

At the rural level, the terms of trade moved in favor of agriculture, particularly in the food crop arena, due to the impact of a depreciating real exchange rate and the influx of labor from declining sectors. Small-scale landowners producing a marketable surplus may have been able to protect their real incomes and sustain food consumption levels, but rural workers experienced significant falls in earnings. Although the wage paid to an agricultural laborer varies from farm to farm, the standard is set by the rates existing in the sugar industry. By 1995, real average wages in the sugar industry were more than half the 1983 level, and real minimum wages were lower by more than one-third. Large-scale producers using hired labor probably benefited from this scenario through decreasing wage costs and rising crop prices.

Sectoral Employment Shifts

During the mid-1970s to the early 1980s, the observed sectoral employment shifts were not associated with economic development but were manifestations of the Dutch Disease syndrome (Hilaire 1989; Rambarran 1992). Employment in nontradables expanded more rapidly than in tradables and was mainly explained by the signals from an appreciating real exchange rate. Construction emerged as the major source of employment creation during the oil boom, accounting for about 54 percent of the new jobs created and reflecting the expanded government investment in energy and physical infrastructure. Public- sector employment also grew substantially over this period, while the contribution of manufacturing was modest. Agriculture experienced an outflow of workers owing to its inability to successfully compete for labor with other expanding sectors.

This situation, however, was reversed with the deepening of the economic recession. Construction began to heavily shed labor due to the contraction of public expenditure and the reduction in the number of private-sector projects. The increase in the relative price of urban tradables in response to the devaluation measures enhanced the competitiveness of the agricultural sector but hardly improved that of manufacturing. Simultaneously, the forces that eliminated jobs for the relatively more skilled in the formal industrial sector created them at a lower level of technological sophistication and productivity in the informal sector. Consequently, Table 9.6 shows that between 1983 and 1989, construction lost over 42,000 jobs, manufacturing saw a decline of about 12,000 jobs and the public sector contracted by 4,500 employees. However, around 31,000 jobs were created in the services sector and about 6,000 in agriculture. More recently, the resumption of economic growth has been translated into renewed employment opportunities, particularly in construction.

Labor Market Institutions

The Trinidad and Tobago economy has traditionally been characterized by politically strong, oligopolistic firms producing for the domestic market and an equally powerful and aggressive trade union movement concentrated in the energy-related, capital-intensive manufacturing and public sectors. Labor legislation is defined through collective bargaining and administrative interventions, especially in the form of the Industrial Relations Act (IRA), the Retrenchment and Severance Payments Act, and the Minimum Wages Act.

The IRA can be regarded as a corporatist instrument, in that it restricts the right of workers to strike and obliges trade unions to comply with registration and certification procedures. The act also allows work-

Table 9.6
Sectoral Distribution of Employment, 1983–95 (1,000)

Year	Agriculture[1]	Petroleum[2]	Manufacturing	Construction	Other Services[3]	Total
1983	39.3	16.9	48.0	72.0	206.3	399.4
1985	46.8	13.0	45.4	61.8	232.3	399.6
1987	43.4	15.5	35.5	48.1	229.7	372.2
1989	45.2	16.8	36.5	30.0	237.2	365.7
1991	47.0	18.2	43.3	47.2	248.4	404.1
1993	45.8	15.1	40.3	44.7	258.6	404.5
1995	45.9	16.6	44.2	42.7	282.2	431.6

Source: Central Statistical Office (CSO), *Labour Force Report* (various issues).

1. Includes sugar cultivation and manufacture; forestry; and hunting and fishing.
2. Includes production, refining, and service contractors, and other mining and quarrying.
3. Includes electricity and water; wholesale and retail trade; restaurants and hotels; transport, storage, and communications; financing, insurance, real estate, and business services; and community, social, and personal services.

ers to freely organize in unions, but unions must have the majority of membership in the area of activity to obtain the legal right to bargain with employers. Even though the law protects workers' rights to join or not join a union, the terms of the labor contract agreed to by the representative union and employer are binding on all workers in the activity. Although unions may join federations and confederations, wages and working conditions are not negotiated at an aggregate level; rather, this process remains decentralized.

The Retrenchment and Severance Payments Act states that, in the case of dismissal due to redundancy, severance payments are to be granted as a function of the length of uninterrupted service.[5] Many employers perceive this act as restrictive, in that it tends to limit the degree of flexibility in adjusting employment levels to changing conditions in the product market. As the movement toward a more open economy is furthered, this becomes particularly relevant in terms of the speed of adjustment of the work force to fluctuations in global demand. Reduced job security has also been attributed to the act, since it provides the incentive to shift to contract and temporary workers who are not eligible for severance payments. Furthermore, there are several ambiguities in the wording of the act, as well as its failure to provide a time frame for resolution of appeals.

Under the Minimum Wages Act, minimum wages are set by industry and according to job titles for catering workers, household assistants, gas station attendants, and shop assistants. Adjustments are made after considering the prevailing level of wages established by trade unions, the incidence of poverty, and other relevant factors, such as the current state of the economy. Mandated minimum wages exert important effects on the labor market. First, they set a limit for severance payments, thus affecting the normal rate of job turnover. Second, minimum wages affect prevailing equilibrium wages by shifting the entire wage spectrum upward. Third, given the positive effect of minimum wage changes on average wage changes, the former are also related to existing inflationary pressures. Finally, evidence suggests that high minimum wages positively affect the formal-informal wage gap and negatively affect formal-sector employment.

Clearly, institutional forces play a prominent role in the determination of wages, employment practices, and industrial relations in the organized formal sector. Through the collective bargaining process, trade unions received substantial improvements in the terms and conditions of employment for their membership during the late 1970s and early 1980s. Moreover, because terms of employment are fixed in advance for three years, wage increases have not necessarily reflected the changing economic realities except with a substantial lag.

Distributive Conflict

The availability of enough evidence to suggest that, during the period of adjustment, the labor market seems to have been relatively flexible in terms of real wage declines, sectoral shifts, and relative wage changes does not imply that distributive conflicts have not been major issues. Over the last five years, changes in the management-labor power structure have occurred as the economy began to shift to an export-oriented, private-sector-led status. The general decline in wages and substantial manpower reductions in much of the private and public sector sharply reduced the organizational size and bargaining power of the labor movement. Indeed, during this period, the industrial relations climate has been characterized by a relatively high degree of open conflict with periods of prolonged unrest.

Protest action has tended to be concentrated in the state sector, with the labor movement vociferously demonstrating against the government's deepening of the structural adjustment program, in particular the divestment of state enterprises and public utilities. At times, protest action crossed the conventional boundaries of collective bargaining and descended into overt and veiled threats against management and employees, attacks on property and equipment, and other intimidating tactics. The solidarity of the trade union movement has also been tested over this period, in light of alleged attempts for leadership and control of the confederation body. More recently, the partial reconciliation on the issue of pay arrears to public-sector employees has, to some extent, weakened trade union solidarity. Labor analysts argue that since the contentious nature of industrial relations has been curbed while the prerogatives of management have been strengthened, an environment has been created in which radical changes to working practices can be implemented.

THE CONSEQUENCES OF LABOR MARKET ADJUSTMENT

Income Distribution and Poverty

Conventional adjustment programs are considered to have little human face, as many observers claim that the poor disproportionately bear the transitional costs of adjustment (Jolly and Cornia 1984; Cornia, Jolly, and Stewart 1987; Stewart 1991). In many cases, either the lack or poor quality of data on social and human development indicators hampers the analysis of the link between adjustment policies and poverty alleviation. Even when reliable data exist, the outcomes associated with adjustment need to be compared with a counterfactual situation. One such important outcome relates to earnings (and incomes), the distribution of which is likely to be affected by rapid adjustment in the labor market.

Estimates of the Gini coefficient[6] suggest some worsening of income distribution in Trinidad and Tobago during the adjustment period. The Gini coefficient, based on household income distribution, widened slightly from 0.45 in 1981–82 to 0.47 in 1988 (Henry and Melville 1989; Teekens 1989). A Gini coefficient that was based on per capita consumption, and that was therefore not comparable with previous estimates, was calculated at 0.42 in 1992, substantially lower than the regional average of 0.5 for Latin America and the Caribbean. The sharp drop of real wages in the formal and public sectors during the crisis would be expected to sharply lower labor income for the deciles toward the bottom and the middle of the distribution. Further, the capital share would have risen over this time, implying an increasing concentration of wealth that would go unrecognized in data that either do not include at all or seriously understate capital incomes.

Despite the nonexistence of an official poverty line, all studies that measured poverty trends during the crisis indicate a sharp rise. Henry and Melville (1989) derived a poverty line of TT$ 535 for a family of four in 1988 and, on this basis, estimated that about 18.5 percent of the population were living in poverty. However, as these computations were based on reported income rather than expenditures, they are likely to overstate the extent of poverty. Teekens (1989), using expenditure data, found that absolute poverty increased dramatically from 3.5 percent of households in 1981–82 to 15 percent in 1988. Although relative poverty also increased, the extent was less severe. Moreover, the analysis indicated that heads of households who were unemployed represented 24 percent of the total poor and that, when more than one person in a household became unemployed, the situation worsened. In addition, the incidence of poverty was greater in areas of high unemployment.

The SLC data show that in 1992 the head-count index, the proportion of the population with a standard of living below the poverty line,[7] stood at about 21 percent, while 11 percent of the population could be classified as extremely poor. On average, the incidence of poverty is higher in households where the head is either unemployed or has never worked, in households where the head has less than secondary-school education, and in female-headed households. Other characteristics relating to the nature of poverty, such as geographical location and ethnicity, reveal that the incidence of poverty is slightly higher in urban areas and in households headed by persons of mixed race.[8] Of those in poor households who are employed, about half work in the private formal sector, 30 percent in the informal sector, and the remainder in the public sector.

Traditionally, poverty has been associated with specific groups unable to participate in the labor market, namely, the old, the disabled, and female heads of households. As a result, the social safety net has focused on the national insurance system, old-age pensions, and public assistance programs. Within the last decade, a new group of poor has emerged, comprised of persons unable to find gainful employment to support themselves and their families. Many are ineligible for assistance under the traditional programs due to their demographic characteristics. The government's response to the growing needs of the new poor has entailed rehabilitative assistance for reentry into the labor force through an expansion of the existing public-works scheme and initiation of supplementary feeding- and income-assistance programs. In this regard, the public-works program remains the principal measure and provides temporary employment on infrastructure and community-based projects for two to four fortnights a year for each participant. The school feeding program, which was significantly restructured in 1989, provides nutrition assistance targeted to children and currently reaches one-third of the primary-school population. Presently, it is being extended to preprimary and secondary schools. The SHARE program provides food baskets to about 6,500 individuals and has a rehabilitative component through referral to nongovernmental organizations (NGOs) and other organizations.

In view of the prevailing high level of unemployment among the youth, a number of job-training schemes have been introduced since the early 1990s. Among these are YTEPP, a part-time program of four to nine months' duration for provision of training, supervised work experience, and promotion of self-employment; the National Apprenticeship

Program (NAP), which provides apprenticeship opportunities to ease the transition to the job market; and the Civilian Conservation Corps (CCC), which provides group-based activities for community improvement projects. Recently, the government has begun to provide retraining support to displaced workers and to promote the development of microenterprises. These labor market policies in the main embody the work principle, the aim of which is to accomplish a smooth and rapid transfer of laid-off workers to new employment rather than provide welfare.

Over the past decade, public spending on active labor market policy has never exceeded 4 percent of GDP, with one-third of the total expenditures directly targeted to meet the subsistence and retraining needs of displaced workers. The crucial constraint affecting the efficiency of these programs is the absence of an overall policy framework and of an agency to provide direction in terms of a poverty alleviation strategy. Other factors impacting on the performance of the system include duplication in service delivery, informal targeting mechanisms, and the lack of adequate program monitoring. As a result, the social safety net system has tended to respond slowly to the needs of the displaced, especially with respect to reemployment probabilities.

Public Expenditure on Education, Health, and Other Social Services

As stated earlier, a major austerity measure of the adjustment process involved substantial reductions in the fiscal deficit with the emphasis placed on expenditure restraint rather than revenue enhancement. The reduction in overall public spending induced a significant decrease in expenditure on most social programs, both in absolute terms and as a percentage of GDP. In particular, capital investment in the social sector was mainly affected by these fiscal measures, and by the early 1990s, capital outlays in education and health were about 60 percent below the respective levels of the mid-1980s. This fall in social spending is likely to be detrimental to the poor in the short run by reducing their consumption benefits and, over the long run, can delay any improvement in the human capital stock of the labor force.

Although unit costs of education fell, it was not due to any realization of economies of scale but to a deterioration of schools, reduced commitment and motivation of the teaching force, and lower resource intensity. The financial realities dictated that educational spending focus on the modification and improvement of existing physical facilities, even though some new primary and secondary schools were constructed. Cursory maintenance work was conducted on schools that were either in a dire state of disrepair or needed replacement, and where schools were seriously overcrowded, attempts were made at additional accommodation. Against this backdrop, enrollment at all educational levels continued unabated, and consequently, real public educational expenditure per school-aged child contracted sharply at an annual average rate of 6.5 percent over the adjustment period.

Teachers, as part of the public-sector work force, faced the 10 percent cut in salaries and, as an integral part of the country's educated manpower, may have experienced some disincentives to effective performance. A reduction in subventions to the university not only created additional costs to matriculating students, but also acted as a signal barrier to entry for prospective students. An examination of capital costs revealed that about 60 percent of development expenditure was allocated to the tertiary sector. Even though the interpretation of rates of return to education is still controversial, it appears that the disparity in resource allocation between primary and tertiary education may translate into low private and social rates of return in the long run. Indeed, the education system as a major instrument of social reform has been placed under strain. A greater lack of discipline among staff and students, a rising incidence of absenteeism and lack of punctuality, and unsatisfactory levels of functional literacy and numeracy are emerging signs of a distressed educational system.

Although the impact of the economic crisis on health care will only become obvious in the longer run, there are signs of some deterioration in overall health standards. Spending on health declined from its 1981 high and was reflected in the overcrowding of hospital wards, lack of basic materials and equipment for routine procedures and operations, and inadequate and inconsistent supplies of very essential and necessary (VEN) drugs. The unavailability of medical personnel often resulted in longer waiting periods in emergency situations, delays in obtaining appointments for clinical visits, and a heightened frustration at the lack of basic health services.

Of all the targets identified within the World Health Organization's (WHO) philosophy of "Health for All by the Year 2000," only the infant mortality rate, a particularly sensitive indicator of health stress during adjustment periods, displayed a declining trend. A gradual worsening of nutritional conditions was also evidenced by the rising number of cases associated with nutritional marasmus, anemia, and other forms of protein-calorie malnutrition. Falling nutritional standards have long-run effects on productivity and output, resulting in greater absenteeism due to disease or care of the sick, an unsustainable work capacity, increased health care costs, and shortened life expectancy.

In addition to the services in the education and health sectors, government provides other social services in the areas of old-age pensions, sport and culture, family life, school guidance, and prison welfare. However, the fall in expenditures for these services was moderate when compared to that of education and health.

Gender Aspects and the Role of Women

In order to assess the distribution of the employment, income, and consumption effects associated with adjustment in the labor market, one needs to consider the individual's ability to respond and to reallocate resources. Since societal norms ascribe different socioeconomic roles for men and women, then gender is the basis for the fundamental division of labor between productive and reproductive activities. In most societies, women have borne the major responsibility for carrying out reproductive activities, as well as contributing to income-generating activities. As a result, feminist economists argue that macroeconomic policies are gender-blind rather than gender-neutral, because these roles impose additional constraints on women's abilities to respond to changes initiated by macroeconomic policy.[9]

The evidence from historical experience shows that the long-term relationship between the female share of the labor force and the level of economic development is characterized by a U-shaped pattern. During initial stages of development, the female labor-force-participation rate falls and then begins to rise after the economy reaches a particular level of industrialization and urbanization. However, structural adjustment has the potential to alter this relationship. Standing (1989) argues that adjustment has given rise to a global feminization of the labor force through the substitution of women workers for men, since women tend to have a lower reservation wage. Cagatay and Ozler (1995) demonstrate that structural adjustment policies have a positive impact on feminization of the labor force through changes in income distribution and shifts in the outward orientation of the economy. Stabilization policies worsen the distribution of income, thereby drawing women into the labor force to supplement family income, while trade policies have the effect of absorbing women into the labor force as employers seek cheap labor to compete in global markets.

Survey data indicate that although female participation rates tend to be lower than those for men, male participation rates have declined since the early 1980s, while those of women have increased, an apparent reflection of the global trend of the rising female labor supply. This would suggest that the added worker effect predominated for females during the crisis; that is, the income effect of lower earnings during a recession induced the household to supply additional labor. Female unemployment and underemployment rates also tend to be higher than those of men, but over time the differential has narrowed. Further, the percentage of women who are salaried has risen during the economic crisis, narrowing the relative earnings differential. In general, women dominate employment levels in the service sector, especially in education, health, administration, and domestic service. There is little evidence that adjustment has had particularly adverse effects on women in the labor force in Trinidad and Tobago. However, this view must be juxtaposed against women's roles in the unrecognized economy, that is, as producers, home managers, mothers, and community organizers.

Although no evidence in the form of detailed statistics by gender or time allocation studies exists in Trinidad and Tobago, some generalizations can be made about the indirect impact of the adjustment process on these roles of women. As producers, women contribute to the generation of household income and to national output and national welfare. The effects of falling employment, declining incomes, and deteriorating work conditions can constrain the productive capacity of women, particularly in areas where they are substantially involved, such as small-scale agriculture and the informal sector. In their role as home managers, women are mainly responsible for household maintenance and budgeting, especially in meeting basic needs. Sharply rising prices because of price deregulation, elimination of food subsidies, and devaluation have accentuated the role of women as strategic planners in family survival. According to Haddad et al. (1995), this may be manifested in traveling longer hours to obtain lower prices, the production of more household goods, and the purchase of less prepared, more time-intensive foods.

As mothers, women are primarily responsible for the welfare of children and often care for old or sick relatives. Declining government expenditure on education and health, falling household income, and increased time spent on seeking additional income have all added to the already heavy burden placed on women. Finally, as community organizers, women have constantly displayed the art of bonding themselves into a network of community relationships to solve economic difficulties and to provide social services. But, simultaneously, their time burdens have grown, making it even more difficult to fulfill this role.

LABOR MARKET ADJUSTMENT ISSUES FOR THE FUTURE

In response to declining international oil prices during the 1980s, Trinidad and Tobago initiated a comprehensive adjustment effort that focused on reduction of the fiscal deficit, tax reform, restructuring and divestment of state enterprises, liberalization of the trade, exchange, and investment regimes, and rescheduling of debt repayments. The country has moved forward in its economic adjustment program, even though economic growth has been tempered by the continued vulnerability to movements in world oil prices. This chapter has examined the experience of Trinidad and Tobago with respect to two important issues related to labor markets and adjustment; (1) how well have labor markets functioned in terms of assisting or impeding macro adjustment efforts and (2) what have been the effects of some of these adjustments on the labor market.

The evidence casts considerable doubt on the theoretical concerns that aggregate real wage rigidity and labor market inflexibility were impediments to adjustment. Real wage declines have been dramatic and often far greater than the fall in real value-added. Indeed, it is possible that aggregate demand feedbacks from the excessively large declines in real wages may have inhibited economic recovery in the early 1990s. Generally, sectoral employment shifts have not been in the desired direction, that is, toward tradables. Agricultural employment has increased, but that of manufacturing has declined with shifts into informal services and commerce. Nonetheless, sectoral wage changes have been largely in the appropriate direction. The fall in government wages is one factor that caused relative wages in nontradables to decline.

In turning to the second broad topic, the outcomes of labor market adjustment, one must recognize the difficulties in distinguishing between the effects of policies instituted before the adjustment process and those specifically adopted as elements of an economic reform program. In this regard, an attempt is made at examining the relevant outcomes without too much concern for the issue of attribution. In addition, the presence of an informal sector may obscure the transmission of policies to various socioeconomic groups. Estimates of the Gini coefficient indicate some worsening of income distribution, while poverty studies show a higher incidence of absolute poverty. Although relative poverty increased, the extent was less severe. On the intertemporal aspect, the evidence is a little more mixed. The fall in social spending is likely to be detrimental to the poor in the short run by reducing their consumption benefits and, in the long run, can delay any improvement in their human capital stock. As a major instrument of social reform, the education system has been placed under some strain, while there have been signs of some deterioration in health standards. There is little evidence from survey data that adjustment has had particularly adverse effects on women in the labor force, but this view must be juxtaposed against women's roles in the unrecognized economy, that is, as producers, home managers, mothers, and community organizers.

Although implementing and sustaining a program of structural adjustment involve severe difficulties, change is inevitable in Trinidad and Tobago. Even if no external shocks had occurred, the country would still have had to shift the structure of production in appropriate directions. The policy focus should now be to sustain the pace of economic growth while generating a critical mass of investments in human capital sufficient to reduce poverty. To achieve this goal, the government needs to tackle several human resource and labor market problems in line with expected changes in the production structure.

The first problem relates to maintaining the thrust of economic diversification away from oil and gas. Such an effort is fundamental to the maintenance of labor-intensive economic growth, because this sector's contribution to direct job creation is minimal, and its preferential status in the past has attenuated the potential of more labor-intensive sectors. In this regard, the government must ensure the competitiveness of the non-oil sectors through the maintenance of an appropriate real exchange rate, continued revision of the investment regime, and improvement of infrastructural services. Boltho and Glyn (1995) point out that, contrary to the pronouncements of jobless growth, the link between growth and employment has not weakened once the period is extended to include the early 1990s. The authors state that for every 1 percent improvement in a country's growth rate over the last decade, there has been a corresponding improvement in the employment record.

The second problem concerns complete access to quality education, health and nutrition services, which is critical to reducing poverty. The key priority for the education sector is reduction of the current inequities in the system, thereby providing better opportunities for the poor. Many of the recommendations set out in the *Report of the National Task Force on Education* (Republic of Trinidad and Tobago 1993) directly address these concerns and include increased access to early childhood care and education, reform of the common entrance examination system, rationalization of the secondary-level curriculum, and improved relations between parents, students, and communities. In the health sector, a major reform initiative is under way, with the assistance of the IADB, to address the existing inequities. The program is aimed at strengthening health-sector policies and planning, refocusing public and private health expenditures toward priority areas, promoting preventive health care, and achieving a high level of cost efficiency.

The third problem is the ramifications of the forces of globalization on employment creation. Alongside globalization, the continued diffusion of information and communications technology, with its bias toward skilled labor, will also shape the parameters of job creation. To exploit world and hemispheric trade liberalization, Trinidad and Tobago needs to upgrade the technological and skill base of its industries and services, including that of agriculture, which is diversifying into higher-value-added products. This will demand a more highly educated work force. Policies are therefore needed to increase secondary enrollment and to develop effective vocational and on-the-job training programs, thereby upgrading the skills of those who have left the formal education system. At the tertiary level, the education system needs to be made more responsive to the skill requirements of the labor market. More cooperation is needed between the public and private sectors to develop study programs that will meet the needs of the labor market.

The fourth problem relates to the paradigm of labor market flexibility. While the labor market has shown significant flexibility and can be expected to do so in the future, the political economy of labor market institutions suggests that achieving stability and growth in the future may be problematic. Singh (1995) argues that the post-1980s economic regime based on labor market flexibility and market supremacy cannot solely provide full employment with moderate inflation. Such an effort requires more cooperative institutional arrangements by economic actors, as well as more cooperative relationships between nation-states. Strategies for domestic job creation and increased productivity will almost certainly demand some kind of social contract involving both the unions and the state, and possibly business when extended to the level of trilateral collaboration. However, the difficulties of putting together such a social contract are formidable. The European experience suggests that an equitable process, a long-term commitment to the process by parties on all sides so that inequities in one deal can be compensated in the next, and a crisis serious enough to engage the attention of all parties are key to the success of such an effort.

The fifth problem arises from the replacement and enhancement of the stock of human resources. This is particularly relevant when one considers the observed substantial emigration, legally and illegally, of highly skilled professionals and technicians to the North during the economic crisis. Many of these migrants have been young men and women, thereby skewing the age distribution pyramid, raising dependency ratios, and increasing the fiscal burden of social services on those employed. The reversal of this "brain drain" process through the repatriation of skilled and educated workers is likely to be a costly and time-consuming exercise with some negative feedback for economic recovery and development.

The final problem concerns the disturbing situation of the socially and behaviorally destabilizing influences of unemployment. For an unemployed individual, a sense of frustration, hopelessness, and anger at and alienation from society can arise. For the unemployed in general, and the unemployed youth in particular, the vast waste of human resources is liable to be transformed into deviant social forms such as crime, juvenile delinquency, vandalism, lack of discipline, and substance abuse. Latent yet discomforting impulses can also be manifested in a withdrawal from society, indifference, low self-esteem, and suicidal tendencies. The fallout on the family from acute unemployment, especially where the sole breadwinner is unemployed, is likely to contribute to the vicious spiral of declining nutritional standards, greater demand for health services, lower educational performance, and possible disintegration of the family unit.

NOTES

1. Interpretation of unemployment rates published by the Central Statistical Office (CSO) requires some caution. Part of the sharp increase that occurred in the late 1980s is due to the adoption of a broader definition of unemployment.

Prior to 1987, those actively seeking a job during the reference period, the previous week, were counted as unemployed. Beginning in 1987, an additional category, of individuals who actually sought work at some time during the three months prior to the survey, has been classified as unemployed. This is also substantially higher than the job-seeking rate used to measure unemployment in many countries.

2. The Survey of Living Conditions (SLC) represents the first comprehensive attempt to measure income distribution and poverty in Trinidad and Tobago and was implemented on a national basis, incorporating information from 1,453 households.

3. In the strictest sense of the term, individuals are defined to be underemployed if their marginal productivity is below the wage rate. Given the measurement difficulty of this concept, the more common definition of underemployment is assumed, that is, if the individual works less than forty hours per week.

4. Though no universally accepted definition exists, the informal sector usually refers to small-scale labor-intensive production organized around an individual or small group that operates outside the ambit of governmental regulations. Additional characteristics include lack of fixed location, irregular time pattern of work, and exclusion from formal credit markets.

5. For each complete year of service up to four years, the separated employee is entitled to two weeks' basic pay for each year. For the fifth and subsequent years of service, the employee is entitled to three weeks' basic salary. Workers with less than a year's service receive a prorated payment.

6. The Gini coefficient is an index representing inequality in the distribution of welfare. The coefficient ranges from 0 to 1 and increases as income distribution becomes more skewed.

7. The poverty line was defined as TT$ 2,420 per person per year based on May/June 1992 prices for a minimum, low-cost food basket for a 2,400-calorie diet.

8. The population of Trinidad and Tobago is ethnically mixed, with approximately 40 percent each of African and East Indian descent, followed by those of mixed descent.

9. A growing recognition of the gender distributive effects of structural adjustment and the relationship between gender and macroeconomic outcomes is best exemplified in *World Development* 23(11), November 1995, which devotes the entire issue to gender, adjustment, and macroeconomics.

REFERENCES

Boltho, A., and A. Glyn. 1995. Can macroeconomic policies raise employment. *International Labour Review* 134(4–5):451–70.

Cagatay, N., and S. Ozler. 1995. Feminization of the labour force: The effects of long-term development and structural adjustment. *World Development* (Special Issue on Gender, Adjustment, and Macroeconomics) 23(11): 1883–94.

Central Bank of Trinidad and Tobago. *Annual Economic Survey*, various issues, (1982–95). St. Augustine, Trinidad and Tobago: Central Bank of Trinidad and Tobago.

Central Statistical Office (CSO). *Economic Indicators Report*, various issues, 1982–95. St. Augustine, Trinidad and Tobago: Central Statistical Office.

———. *Labour Force Report*, various issues, 1982–95. St. Augustine, Trinidad and Tobago: Central Statistical Office.

Cornia, G. A., R. Jolly, and F. Stewart. 1987. *Adjustment with a Human Face*. Oxford: Oxford University Press.

Haddad, L., et al. 1995. The gender dimensions of economic adjustment policies: Potential interactions and evidence to date. *World Development* 23(6):881–96.

Henry, R., and J. Melville. 1989. *Poverty Revisited: Trinidad and Tobago in the Late 1980s*. St. Augustine, Trinidad and Tobago: University of the West Indies.

Hilaire, A. 1989. Economic reaction to a sectoral boom in Trinidad and Tobago, 1973–1985. Ph.D. thesis, University of Colombia.

Jolly, R., and G. A. Cornia. 1984. *The Impact of World Recession on Children*. Oxford: Pergamon Press.

Rambarran, A. 1992. Economic policy and agricultural performance in an open petroleum economy: Trinidad and Tobago, 1966–1982. Central Bank of Trinidad and Tobago, St. Augustine. Mimeographed.

Republic of Trinidad and Tobago. 1992. *Survey of Living Conditions (SLC)*. St. Augustine, Trinidad and Tobago.

———. 1993. *Report of the National Task Force on Education*. St. Augustine, Trinidad and Tobago.

Singh, A. 1995. Institutional requirements for full employment in advanced economies. *International Labour Review* 134(4–5):471–95.

Standing, G. 1989. Global feminization through flexible labour. *World Development* 17(7):1277–95.

Stewart, F. 1991. The many faces of adjustment. *World Development* 19(12):1847–64.

Teekens, R. 1989. Poverty data from two family budgetary surveys in Trinidad and Tobago. Central Bank of Trinidad and Tobago, St. Augustine. Mimeographed.

10
Labor Adjustment in Structurally Adjusting Economies: The Case for Unemployment Insurance in the Caribbean

Dhanayshar Mahabir

The economies of the Caribbean are usually described as small and open. They are small because they are unable to influence by their singular actions (and perhaps even by their concerted actions) the international price for traded goods. They are also unable to influence the international capital market and, hence, cannot alter international interest rates in a significant way. These economies are also highly open, with export to gross domestic product (GDP) ratios frequently in excess of 40 percent.

The openness of these economies implies a high reliance on international trade for economic welfare and growth. This trade dependence is also inevitably associated with hazards which can, on occasions, cause severe dislocations within these economies. These hazards can arise from trade in goods as well as trade in capital.

THE HAZARDS OF TRADE AND ADJUSTMENT

The small open economy (SOE) can experience the following kinds of undesirable shocks:

1. A fall in the international price of its principal exports would reduce the country's foreign exchange receipts if export volume does not simultaneously increase. This has been the experience of the larger economies in the Caribbean, namely, Trinidad, which suffered revenue losses consequent upon the declines in oil prices, and Guyana and Jamaica, which experienced a similar fate when the prices of bauxite and sugar collapsed in the late 1970s. In this situation, the country can try to increase its

output over the medium term to compensate for the price falls. In the presence of supply inelasticity, however, the country may have no option but to adjust to the decline in price if such a decline is seen to be quasi-permanent in nature. A similar type of shock emerges if the prices of imports rise while the prices of exports fall or stagnate. Such a long-run decline in the terms of trade suggests that the import bill must be reduced or export volume increased in order to stave off a balance-of-payments crisis. However, such a reduction in imports need not necessarily reduce welfare if domestic industries can tailor their productive apparatus to service the domestic market in the short period.

2. Rises in international interest rates which may result from the desire of the industrial countries to combat inflation via tight monetary policy can result in a deflation of the domestic economy—for such interest rate shocks preempt a greater proportion of foreign exchange earnings for foreign debt servicing, leaving less for the financing of the SOE's developmental needs. Few Caribbean economies have been spared the agony of a rising debt service ratio within recent times.

3. Exchange rate fluctuations can also create difficulties in the form of import shocks. An appreciation of, say, the pound sterling vis-à-vis the U.S. dollar can increase the domestic cost of imports from the United Kingdom to those countries with an exchange rate that is pegged to the U.S. dollar. Additionally, an appreciating U.S. dollar can adversely affect the tourist trade if large numbers of visitors originate from the nondollar areas. Responding to these shocks is complicated. As argued by Krugman (1988), if these shocks are assumed to be temporary, the countries may opt to borrow on the international market or else draw down on reserves in order to finance their external payments deficits. Where the shocks are likely to be permanent, however, the country has little choice but to reduce its demand for foreign exchange in the short run and introduce measures aimed at increasing export receipts over the medium term.

RESPONDING TO ADVERSE SHOCKS: REDUCING THE DEMAND FOR FOREIGN EXCHANGE

A reduction in the demand for foreign exchange can be achieved in both a direct and an indirect manner. For example, imports can be reduced directly via the use of commercial policy, namely, the imposition of quotas on imported, goods, the creation of a list of the types of goods which cannot be imported and the imposition of higher tariffs aimed at reducing the demand for price-elastic goods.

These commercial policies have been increasingly frowned upon by lending agencies, as they are believed to reduce the efficiency of domestic firms, which are then prevented from developing an ability to compete internationally. Accordingly, their use in the region has been dwindling over time.

Measures aimed at reducing the demand for foreign exchange can also take an indirect form. In particular, a reduction in domestic economic activity will reduce the demand for all goods, including foreign goods. Such a policy of deflation can be accomplished by tax increases, public expenditure cuts, and a reduction in the domestic money supply so that credit is more difficult and expensive to obtain. Such measures, which basically amount to tight monetary and fiscal policy, will reduce the demand for imported goods and, hence, the import bill. Unfortunately, these measures will also result in an increase in unemployment and, with it, the risk of unemployment hysteresis, which has, to date, not received much attention in the adjustment literature. Unemployment hysteresis refers to the situation where, the longer the period of time spent in unemployment, the lower the chances of the unemployed person to find a job in the formal sector of the economy.

The reduction in foreign exchange outflows can also be achieved via a debt management strategy. Some debts can be rescheduled, some can be forgiven, and some which carry very high rates of interest can be liquidated. In practice, however, this policy of debt restructuring is possible only where a program of expenditure reduction has already been implemented.

RESPONDING TO ADVERSE SHOCKS—INCREASING EXPORTS: EXPENDITURE SWITCHING

Successfully adjusting to a balance-of-payments crisis normally involves increasing the country's foreign exchange earnings. Such an increase in export earnings in the short period is usually not possible due to the existence of important supply inelasticities. However, these earnings can be enhanced over the medium term if the economy can alter its productive structure so as to produce more tradable goods. This would entail the gradual shift away from goods which cannot be easily exported to those products which can be internationally marketed. Such a policy may be achieved via a depreciation of the real exchange rate, which makes domestic goods cheaper to the foreigner and foreign goods more expensive to the domestic residents. Changing relative prices will certainly create incentives to change the structure of the economy.

Nevertheless, price incentives alone cannot achieve the desired results in the open developing economy since firms may possess inflexible capital equipment which yields revenues that are sufficient to at least cover variable costs. Where firms are covering variable costs, they may not be as eager to invest in new facilities but, rather, may choose to continue their traditional operations in the hope that their fortunes will improve. In addition, displaced labor may not be able to adjust with ease to the technical demands of the tradable goods sector. Finally, firms which produced largely for a domestic market and which collected significant rents from the high effective protection rates, which arose out of a protectionist commercial policy, may find it extremely difficult to begin to successfully penetrate foreign markets in the medium term. Programs of adjustment, thus, need to seriously examine these structural difficulties which may seriously hinder the attainment of simultaneous internal and external balance.

Stimulating exports from countries which have not had a very diversified economy, and the difficulties posed by a capital stock that is inappropriate for greater tradables production, are critical areas of investigation which need to be pursued in detail. This chapter focuses on some labor market aspects of the design of policies which can enhance the ability of the labor force to successfully adjust in the medium term to the challenges of greater tradable goods production. Notwithstanding this focus, it must be emphasized that domestic policy must also be targeted to the capital stock in order for the country to resume growth with payments equilibrium.

THE LABOR MARKET

Expenditure reduction policies, which reduce the import bill indirectly, frequently result in a dislocation of the labor market. In particular, new entrants to the labor force will normally find that their period of waiting, or their search time, is longer than expected. Those workers who are laid off may, after a period of waiting, find that their old job is lost forever and join the pool of the unemployed. Workers who quit voluntarily, hoping to find another job or to become self-employed, may also find that their search time is longer than they had planned.

This increase in the duration of unemployment arises as a direct consequence of adjusting to the crisis in the balance of payments, and a significant percentage of the unemployed may have to be placed into an unorthodox category termed "adjustment unemployment." Adjustment unemployment thus arises when the country, facing an external payments difficulty, is forced to deflate the domestic economy to reduce payments on the current external account. During the period of time which must elapse before the external equilibrium is restored by expenditure-switching policies, the unemployment problem then becomes protracted. This phenomenon, known as the J curve effect in the literature, can last for many years. In Trinidad, for example, after the 1985 devaluation, a decade had to elapse before expenditure-switching policies began to show fruit.

Given the time taken to find work, it is expected that large numbers of workers will become discouraged. These workers will either cease to look for work in the formal sector and engage in legal informal-sector activities, where their marginal productivities are low, or turn to the illegal informal sector, where they may be engaged in the narcotics trade or in petty and major crime. This drift toward the informal sector is also due to the presence of hysteresis, where the longer the period of time spent unemployed, the lesser the chances of finding employment in the formal sector, as employers view the long-term unemployed as possessing obsolete skills and a lack of discipline after being absent from formal employment for an extended time period. The persistence of high levels of unemployment also suggests serious ramifications for the future labor force, as unemployed parents find it increasingly difficult to cater adequately to the educational, nutritional, and other needs of their children. These children may then turn out to be "despondent" workers who, upon reaching working age, do not seek work in the formal sector but rather choose to obtain employment in the underground economy, which is usually easier to obtain. The existence of this category of workers who do not even bother to look for work in the formal sector, due to the size of the unemployment pool, can compromise the accuracy of the official unemployment rate, since their numbers will not be represented in the unemployment figures.

ADJUSTMENT PROGRAMS AND THE LABOR MARKET

Our preceding discussion suggests that policymakers in the small open economy need to seriously address the critical question of the impact of economic adjustment on the labor market. Measures aimed at preventing the emergence of discouraged workers, minimizing search time, reducing the quantity of despondent young workers, and generally making the spell of unemployment more bearable seem necessary. This is all the more necessary if the labor force itself is to be preserved so that unemployed members can retool and retrain to participate in export-related activities. Failure to address these labor market concerns will leave the affected countries with less ability to resume export-led economic growth. A technique which can be employed to preserve the formal-sector labor force is the introduction of an unemployment insurance scheme as part of the overall package of adjustment.

UNEMPLOYMENT INSURANCE: A REVIEW OF CHARACTERISTICS

Unemployment insurance (UI) schemes form an important component of the welfare programs of countries in the North Atlantic. These schemes have come under close scrutiny within recent times. Accordingly, it is imperative to identify the problems which these industrial economies have experienced with their own schemes so that the implementation of a similar scheme in the small open economy can avoid some of the major difficulties which have been found to exist.

Unemployment insurance (UI) which requires the employee to make frequent contributions to a fund, providing income relief during a period of unemployment, is a scheme which will not normally be provided by the private sector for the following reasons:

1. Moral hazard can easily exist since workers can engage in actions which will cause them to be fired from their job. For example, workers can display insubordination, arrive late for work, or engage in a host of activities which will enable them to lose their job and collect benefits. Insofar as those workers who are prone to engage in moral hazard activities cannot be easily identified and removed from the insurance plan, private firms will not readily offer this type of coverage.

2. If the scheme is operated by the private sector, only low-risk individuals might obtain coverage since firms will not hesitate to offer insurance to those individuals in the labor force who possess some degree of security of tenure. However, these individuals may not be interested in participating in UI. At the same time, the large numbers of persons who work in the insecure sector of the economy may wish to purchase insurance, but the associated premium may be so high that they are, in effect, barred from participating. Consequently, the market would fail to supply this valuable product to those who are deemed to be in greatest need of it.

3. Private firms will only offer to cover a particular contingency if the likelihood of the undesirable event arising is purely random. Given the insured pool, randomness implies that not all in the group should suffer the event simultaneously. Hence, based on historical data and comparing its own insured pool with other pools of similar characteristics, the firm can then predict the average monthly payout. (Rothschild and Stiglitz 1976).

With respect to unemployment, the key question pertains to whether unemployment is a random event, in which case coverage can be offered by private firms, or whether it tends to be correlated, that is, large numbers of persons tend to become unemployed at the same time. Recent experience suggests that in the undiversified small open economy, large sections of the labor force tend to become unemployed simultaneously due to the vagaries of international trade. In Trinidad and Tobago from 1982 to 1994, for example, the annual unemployment rate was about 10 percent. Private firms would have found it difficult to honor the claims of all those persons who became unemployed as a result of the adjustment measures undertaken by the government.

As a result of these characteristics, state involvement in the scheme appears necessary, but, as expected, such involvement raises its own particular concerns (Corak 1994; Atkinson and Micklewright 1991).

IMPLEMENTING A UI SCHEME: UI AS INCOME DISTRIBUTION

A state-sponsored UI scheme can allow voluntary participation so that only those workers who believe themselves most at risk would join the plan. However, given this large pool of high-risk workers, the annual payout of the plan is then likely to exceed the plan's income, with the deficit being amended by subventions from the state. In a regime of adjustment, however, such demands on the state resources are to be avoided given the necessity of the central government to reduce its own spending in an attempt to reduce the country's import bill. Reliance on the public finances for additional funding is then certain to precipitate a collapse of the scheme.

In the situation of weak public finances, therefore, the state will insist upon compulsory participation so that all employed persons in the labor force, be they high- or low-risk, will be required to contribute to the plan. Indeed, the state may even require that high-income earners pay a greater fraction of their income as a premium than the low-income earners. The percentage of one's income that is paid will, of course, depend on the size of the fund which is calculated to be sufficient for the program to be self-financing.

Compulsory participation is associated with an element of income distribution where the low-risk workers contribute in excess of their benefits while the high-risk workers who experience more frequent bouts of unemployment benefit to an extent that is greater than their contributions. This income redistribution component must thus be borne in mind, and, accordingly, it is necessary for the state to clearly articulate its policy on the redistribution of income from those who are more or less permanently employed to those who will be in and out of jobs on a regular basis. In particular, this policy will also have to include some offsetting reliefs to the high-income earners so that the incentives to evade taxes are reduced.

THE LIKELY IMPACT OF UI ON THE LABOR MARKET OF THE SOE

Apart from the characteristics which were outlined, maximizing behavior suggests that the introduction of a UI scheme can cause individuals and firms to modify their behavior, thus introducing distortions in the labor market (Milbourne et al. 1991; Shavell and Weiss 1979). It is, therefore, important to design the scheme so that these distortions are minimized. A list of these distortions include the following:

- The system can be abused by outright fraud, dishonest practices, and cheating. Here persons may engage in covert employment while collecting UI benefits. Both workers and firms are culpable, but corrupt administrative officers may also facilitate the collection of these benefits.

- Workers may also engage in moral-hazard behavior; that is, they will precipitate their job loss in order to collect UI benefits.

- Some workers may be induced to remain idle while they collect benefits and to begin a job search only when benefits are nearly exhausted. This practice will tend to increase the duration of unemployment.

- The labor force itself will expand as despondent workers, homemakers, young persons in full-time training, and retirees begin to actively seek work in order to qualify for benefits. The unemployment rate can therefore rise in the presence of UI.

- Firms, as maximizing agents, will attempt to reduce their wage bill in the presence of the UI scheme. It is expected that firms will employ as many part-timers as possible, provide employment for the time necessary to qualify for UI and then lay off workers who will be rehired when UI benefits cease. This cycle of hiring, layoffs, and rehiring will benefit those firms which encounter fluctuations in demand for their output and consequent slack periods during the year, as exist, for example, in the tourism sector. This practice suggests, further, that the low-risk workers will subsidize the wage expenses of those firms, a feature of UI which clearly is contrary to the intention and philosophy of the scheme.

The above-mentioned distortions suggest that UI can create considerable problems of its own. Nevertheless, in the small open economy, which is subject to shocks, the benefits of a properly devised plan seem to outweigh the costs. These benefits include:

- A reduction in the incentive to participate in the informal sector, which does not, by its very nature, generate significant government revenues.

- The existence of a cushion which allows the unemployed to receive income while they look for another job or retrain for a new position. This will reduce the tendency for persons to drop out of the labor force and prevent the emergence of a large class of "lost" workers.

- Income support during the period of unemployment which will enable workers who are heads of households to furnish the basic nutritional and other requirements to their dependents. This will ensure that the next generation of workers that will be called upon to participate in the tradable goods sector are provided with the basic material requirements which constitute a necessary precondition for the acquisition of human capital.

DESIGNING THE UI SCHEME

It has to be recognized that, despite the attendant benefits, a UI scheme will add to the administrative burdens of the state in the typical Caribbean economy. This is a serious problem since administrative capability is relatively weak in these economies. It is recommended that the adjustment program should include, as a key component, the establishment of labor offices where those manning these offices are trained to manage the scheme.

A structural adjustment loan should include a component for establishing these offices, as well as a technical assistance component where experienced personnel from countries with long-established schemes can be hired to train staff in administering the labor office. The design of such a scheme will then include the following six features:

First, the establishment of labor offices manned by competent labor officers who can be redeployed from within the existing public services from areas where they may be less in demand. Such persons can also be paid out of general tax revenues, as the bulk of UI funds should be used to contribute to genuine unemployment relief and not to defray the administrative costs of government. This argument is premised on the notion that any attempt to make the program self-financing, inclusive of administrative costs, will tend to undermine the purpose of the scheme as these administrative costs may come to appropriate a larger and larger share of workers' contributions. A variant of this position is simply that at least 90 percent of all contributions to UI will be distributed to the unemployed, or if the unemployment rate is falling, any surplus will be invested for, and on the behalf of, those who will become unemployed in the future.

Second, the self-employed, who naturally are required to contribute to the scheme, pose a particular problem of moral-hazard activity, especially where they can declare bankruptcy and access funds from the program. Such actions can be reduced if benefits can be collected only where clear proof of bankruptcy or business closure exists. In any event, the self-employed below a certain income level should be able to collect no more than, say, 25 percent more than they have contributed to the plan; those at another income level will collect exactly how much they contributed, while the high-income earners can collect up to a maximum of 75 percent of their contributions. The exact percentages would naturally be determined only after detailed actuarial studies have been completed. However, this measure, while imperfect, should act as an incentive to prevent abuse of the plan while still honoring the income redistribution aspect of the program.

Third, workers who quit work solely to collect UI benefits can be discouraged from such actions if an eligibility period of some specified duration is imposed. Applicants, for example, must have worked for at least twenty-six weeks prior to applying for benefits. This time period can be either continuous or accumulated with other employers, but it is meant to ensure that workers contribute a fairly significant sum to the fund and have actually been engaged for a considerable period of paid employment prior to a claim so that taking short-term jobs, getting fired, collecting UI, and then finding another job will not be a financially rewarding practice.

Additionally, workers who have been found guilty of defrauding the plan should be required to return all monies collected. In addition, they can also be required to wait for a period of, say, four weeks after another claim is filed before collecting payments. This waiting period should act as some disincentive to those who abuse the system.

Fourth, benefits should decline with the passing of each month spent in unemployment. Hence, if the benefits amount to 75 percent of the last wage earned, then for each month unemployed benefits can decline by, say, 5 percent so that, at the end of the fifteenth month, all benefits should cease. This measure will hopefully prompt the unemployed person to look for work early in his or her spell of unemployment.

Fifth, where the economy is in a state of protracted decline and jobs are not easily found, UI benefits may easily disappear and workers will still be unemployed despite their efforts to find work. In this situation, the state may seek to create work for such individuals and use this avenue as a means of retraining such persons. For example, unemployment relief programs which are administered by the state can include a significant training component into their design so that workers receive income support while they are acquiring new skills.

Workers whose UI benefits have been exhausted can access these make-work projects if they show evidence that they are engaged in some type of retraining. In order to obtain additional short-term employment, the applicant must provide evidence that he or she is in some form of training program. In order to ensure equity, the maximum number of these short-term jobs (normally lasting for two weeks) which an individual may obtain in any one year may be limited to, say, six.

It has to be recognized, however, that retraining for the tradable goods sector is a task which has to be shared by both the state and the private sector, since it is the private sector which is charged with the responsibility for increasing the production of goods for export. Firms must therefore possess an incentive to offer apprenticeship programs and to hire persons on a part-time basis so that the skill base of the labor force is maintained. The wages of workers who are engaged in retraining can be partly defrayed by the state, or fiscal incentives can be offered to firms so that a tax credit can be earned for each trainee on the payroll.

Finally, contributions to the UI fund are not necessarily confined to employees. Firms may also be required to contribute a proportion of the workers' wages into the fund. The exact size of such contributions would depend, for example, on the effect of these contributions on the choice of technique to be employed by the firm. If the elasticity of substitution of capital for labor is high enough, these contributions may actually induce firms to employ more labor-saving techniques. Hence, the size of a firm's contributions must necessarily be sensitive to this issue.

The overall objective of unemployment insurance is to provide a cushion so that during the difficult expenditure-switching phase of adjustment, the unemployed are induced to remain in the labor market and continue to seek jobs or else engage in retraining opportunities for emerging jobs. At the same time, this scheme signals to the despondent workers that employment in the formal sector is beneficial since this sector provides a cushion which buffers some of the unpleasant consequences of unemployment. Thus, when complemented with training and coupled with a state-sponsored unemployment relief program, the labor market will stand a good chance of being better prepared for the challenges of adjustment.

ADDITIONAL POLICIES TO ASSIST THE UNEMPLOYED

In addition to the introduction of UI as a means of maintaining the skill base of the labor force, certain other reforms can be introduced to minimize the amount of frictional unemployment which exists. In particular, for new entrants into the labor force and for those who are looking for a better job, the basic problems may revolve around exactly where new work should be sought. Inexperience in a job search may hinder such individuals from finding available jobs. In this situation, the UI office can also act as a repository for vacancies which are continually arising in the economy.

Labor officers may also be required to help these unemployed persons to prepare resumes and complete other application material which will signal their availability to recruiters. With such a measure, an unemployed person may simply register at a center, obtain the current listing of available jobs requiring his or her skill, and focus the job search on this list of openings. This should enable the inexperienced job searcher to find work with a minimum of delay.

A concept which has been implemented with varying degrees of success in both the United States and Canada, but which has not been tried in any meaningful way in the Caribbean, is that of work sharing. Work sharing is attractive since it is possible to increase net employment without placing a burden on the public purse. One may implement the idea along the following lines. Employed persons in both the private and the public sectors should find it relatively easy to obtain no-pay leave to pursue their private objectives. Enterprises in both the public and the private sector should then possess a queue of prescreened candidates who can, on short notice, be called in to fill these temporary vacancies. The wages of these newly hired persons will then be sourced from the salaries which are released by those who are on leave. Such a measure will then generate job opportunities, income, and experience for persons who are qualified but who, because of the depressed state of the economy, cannot find full-time employment. While this proposition is attractive, its implementation can be problematic, especially where trade unions demand that all temporarily vacant positions be filled by in-house workers who will either benefit from higher overtime rates or, if they are junior workers, from experience gained while they are employed in this acting position. This largely explains why work sharing is not a popular option in the Caribbean.

Fiscal policy can also be amended to mitigate the unemployment problem. The fiscal structure in the small open Caribbean economy has traditionally favored tax incentives to firms to stimulate investments. However, such investment incentives, while they do tend to create employment, may display results only after a significant time lag. In addition, these fiscal incentives may display a bias toward capital-intensive technologies. To overcome this bias, the tax structure of these economies can be amended so that firms will possess an incentive to increase net employment. For example, firms can obtain a tax rebate equivalent to a percentage of the salary paid to new workers who were hired during a fiscal year. This incentive may make it worthwhile for the firm to continue to increase its labor force by either expanding its operations or by using technologies which are relatively more labor-intensive.

Finally, the state itself can play its part in keeping the labor force employed. A special unemployment relief tax can be levied on high-income earners or on firms which pollute the environment. The proceeds of this tax can then be dedicated to unemployment relief. Central and local government bodies could then prepare on, say, an annual basis a list of projects which can be completed with these funds. These projects, which may consist mainly of maintaining the country's capital stock, can then be completed with these funds. This public-sector maintenance program can lead to enhanced employment, provide funds for training, and also ensure that the capital stock of the country is maintained.

CONCLUSIONS

It is important to recognize that the labor market plays a critical role in the success of adjustment programs. Accordingly, it is necessary to study the idiosyncrasies of this market and to devise policies which will ensure that the labor force is prepared to handle the challenges posed by expenditure switching and the penetration of foreign markets. A neglect of these issues is certain to result in a decline in the stock of the country's intellectual assets, a rise in the informal sector, and the emergence of the highly undesirable class of discouraged and despondent workers. These developments have been observed in those Caribbean economies which have implemented adjustment programs in the recent past. Our analysis of the dynamics of the labor market and the policy recommendations which were suggested are specifically rooted in the experiences of these small open Caribbean economies. However, while the solutions offered in this paper are region specific, they may, nonetheless, still be applicable to other countries which are small, open and highly susceptible to external shocks.

For such an economy, an unemployment insurance scheme furnishes a valuable mechanism to maintain its skills base while it adjusts to its payments crises. If such a scheme is accompanied by programs such as work sharing, the establishment of a public-sector maintenance program to complement the country's public-sector investment program, and some alteration of the fiscal structure in favor of labor-using technologies, the labor market will stand a better chance of responding to the challenges ahead.

REFERENCES

Atkinson, A. B., and J. Micklewright. 1991. Unemployment compensation and labour market transitions: A critical review. *Journal of Economic Literature* 29(4):1679–1727.

Corak, M. 1994. Unemployment insurance, work disincentives and the Canadian labour market: An overview. In *Unemployment Insurance: How to Make It Work*, edited by J. Richards and W. Watson. Toronto, Canada: Howe Institute.

Krugman, P. 1988. External shocks and domestic policy responses. In *The Open economy*, edited by R. Dornbusch and L. Helmers, 54–79. New York: Oxford University Press.

Milbourne, R. D., D. D. Purvis, and D. Scoones. 1991. Unemployment insurances and unemployment dynamics. *Canadian Journal of Economics* 24(4):804–26.

Rothschild, M., and J. Stiglitz. 1976. Equilibrium in competitive insurance markets: An essay on the economics of imperfect information. *Quarterly Journal of Economics* 90(4):630–49.

Shavell, S., and L. Weiss. 1979. The optimal payment of unemployment insurance benefits over time. *Journal of Political Economy* 87(6):1347–62.

11
Economic Liberalization and the Turkish Labor Market

Tevfik F. Nas and Mehmet Odekon

Since 1980, the Turkish economy has been undergoing a phenomenal transformation. An ambitious stabilization and liberalization program to combat the economic problems of the late 1970s by opening up the domestic and external sectors of the economy to competitive forces has led to a free-market economic environment with an impressive performance in growth and exports. One research area that has captured little attention in this transformation is labor markets and the impact of structural adjustment on employment performance. One possible explanation for the lack of interest in this area is that data on labor markets and employment are not as refined as those reported on other macroeconomic variables and, because of differences in labor survey methods, provide little when it comes to international comparisons.

It is also difficult to identify the effects of liberalization measures on job creation and then to separate those from the adverse effects of stabilization measures. Interpreting the variation in the unemployment rates is especially problematic when, over a period of time, liberalization and stabilization policies combined determine the macroeconomic outcomes. In Turkey, for example, the structural reforms were preceded by stabilization measures in 1980, and throughout the following decade and beyond, several austerity programs were instituted, all with complex contractionary outcomes. Despite these limitations, however, labor markets and the problem of unemployment are worth looking at, especially when current data show no significant change in labor market conditions since the inception of the 1980 reforms.

This chapter begins by introducing the important aspects of the 1980 liberalization and stabilization program. Next, we draw on the rather limited data to discuss the effects of the program on the labor market and employment. Then, a firm-level labor demand function is estimated, followed by conclusions and policy recommendations.

THE LIBERALIZATION AND STABILIZATION PROGRAM

The 1980 program rests on the assumption that opening the economy to free-market forces would enable prices to reflect the opportunity costs in all markets in the economy. The resulting reallocation of resources would raise economic efficiency, eliminate supply-side rigidities, and enhance the productive capacity of the economy. In addition, the stabilization component of the program would keep aggregate demand stable by means of contractionary fiscal and monetary policies. Consequently, the combination of higher output with restrained domestic demand would provide the incentive for the production of exportables and, thus, expedite the process of disengagement from the import substitution industrialization (ISI) policy that the Turkish economy had been accustomed to since the 1960s.[1]

The abrupt replacement of the ISI policy by the outward-looking, export promotion policy initially proved to be a success, albeit a short-lived one. It was a success because the import substitution policy of the previous two decades had brought the economy to the brink of collapse. By the end of the 1970s, inflation had reached 110 percent, unemployment peaked at about 15 percent, and growth in real gross national product registered a negative 1.1 percent (Nas and Odekon 1996:215). Overvaluation of the Turkish lira, foreign exchange shortages, and the inability to service the increasing foreign debt also led to the deterioration of external accounts. These adverse macroeconomic developments culminated in the inception of the liberalization and stabilization program in 1980 and in the military coup later that year.

The turnaround in the economy during 1981–87 was remarkable. The inflation rate declined to about 30 percent in 1981 and then stabilized at around 40 percent during the following few years. The output growth rate jumped to an annual average of 6.4 percent. During the same period, the trade deficit as a percentage of exports decreased from 1.6 percent in 1980 to 0.4 percent in 1987. Monetary expansion slowed down considerably, from 66.9 percent in 1980 to 41.7 percent in 1987. The expansion of credit, largely granted to state economic enterprises, was lowered from an annual increase of 101.4 percent to 52.4 percent in the 1980–87 period (Odekon 1992:155). The initial stop-and-go approach to interest rate liberalization was replaced with a more firm and consistent approach in the late 1980s and early 1990s. The resulting positive real interest rates encouraged savings, which, nonetheless, remained below expectations (Rittenberg 1988:116). This is one reason why the anticipated rise in manufacturing investment did not take place (Kepenek and Yenturk 1994:283).

At the micro level, large firms, accustomed to their monopoly power under the import substitution regime, were initially wary of the liberalization program. This sentiment, however, changed rapidly as these firms became aware of the opportunities in export orientation of production.[2] Having already established contacts through networking as importers, import substitution firms capitalized on their knowledge of foreign trade and markets to become successful exporters.

Two lessons are to be learned from this transformation. First, the rapid and smooth shift from an ISI to an export-oriented policy shows that ISI had been deliberately prolonged, more than necessary. These firms apparently had reached certain economies of scale already, at least enough to be successful exporters to European and other competitive markets. Second, one can argue that the success of Turkish export performance was partially the result of the ISI strategy, which provided the industrial base for exports. It should also be mentioned that not only did the existing ISI firms take advantage of the new policy orientation, but also a number of new firms, especially from Anatolia, joined the export bandwagon. Traditionally, private Turkish manufacturing, which had been monopolized by a few large elite families, consisted of family-owned holding conglomerates which worked with foreign know-how under royalty agreements. The new entrants into manufacturing not only altered the structure of the manufacturing sector, but also affected the entire political structure (Waterbury 1992; Sayari 1992). This transformation led to the emergence of a new elite whose grip on economic and political power intensified as a succession of right-wing governments ruled the country after 1981.

The strong performance of the Turkish economy began to falter in the late 1980s. The slowdown in growth, rise in inflation, increase in short-term foreign debt, and instability in the financial markets marked the end of a relatively short-lived but successful economic liberalization era. The standard textbook explanation of these adverse developments revolves around the inability or unwillingness of authorities to control the fiscal and monetary expansion. Indeed, in 1986-90, the public-sector deficit increased three fold, raising the ratio of the public-sector deficit to gross domestic product (GDP) from 3.7 percent in 1986 to 7.8 percent in 1990, according to the Organization for Economic Co-operation and Development, or OECD (1995:104). As a result of the accompanying monetization, the inflation rate increased to 75 percent in 1988. Apparently, inflationary expectations were affected adversely as well. In the early 1990s, foreign currency holdings in the economy rose at an ever increasing rate. Ultimately, this currency substitution led to a rapid depreciation of the Turkish lira, by about 232 percent from April 1993 to April 1994, and also to financial market volatility (OECD 1995:23).

On April 5, 1994, a new stabilization program was announced. The main targets of this program were controlling the public-sector deficit and stabilizing the Turkish lira and the financial markets. To this end, the program contained a wide range of policies: price increases for state economic enterprises, a public-sector wage freeze, renewed privatization efforts, and tax and social security reforms. These measures revived the economic activity. The GDP growth rate bounced back to 7.3 percent in 1995 from –5.5 percent in the previous year. The rate of inflation fell from a post-1980 peak of 106.3 percent in 1994 to 93.6 percent in 1995 (OECD 1996:136). The credibility of the Turkish economy in world financial markets improved somewhat. Inflow of foreign capital, which had been below expectations throughout the post-1980 period, increased, albeit still marginally. Consequently, external, particularly short-term, debt continued to rise. By the end of 1994, the total foreign debt-GDP ratio reached 50.4 percent, and the short-term debt-GDP ratio increased to 41.7 percent (OECD 1996:142). However, a surge in both workers' remittances from abroad and exports helped the buildup of substantial reserves, delaying any immediate foreign exchange shortage. To sum up, the April 5th measures served the short-term targets of stabilizing inflation and improving the external sector in the economy.

One other main feature of the 1980 program was its deemphasis on agriculture. In the 1980–94 period, the share of agriculture in GDP decreased from 23 percent to 16 percent, forcing Turkey to import food products. Turkey's dependency on food imports rose from 3.4 percent in 1969–71 to 109.9 percent in 1988–90, as Turkey became an importer of cereal, live animals, and other foodstuffs (United Nations Development Programme 1994:154). In the meantime, the share of the labor force in agriculture remained at about 50 percent (World Bank 1996:195). Rapid population growth and the shrinking capacity of the agricultural sector led to massive urbanization. Urban population, as a ratio to total population, increased from 44 percent in 1980 to 67 percent in 1994, with 19 percent of the total urban population living in Istanbul (United Nations Development Programme 1994:172). In spite of these imbalances, per capita income rose to about $2,500 in 1994, making Turkey a permanent member of the middle-income developing economies.

THE LABOR MARKET

The Turkish labor market, in particular before the 1980s, was characterized by substantial differences in rural-urban, formal-informal, and private-public labor markets as a result of government policies and regulations and labor organizations. One of the first actions of the military regime in 1980 was to limit labor activity by replacing collective bargaining with the so-called Supreme Arbitration Board. Two years later, a Wage Negotiations Coordination Board was formed, only to be abolished in 1987.[3] This new institutional environment contributed to the decline in real wages. In 1981–88, the average annual decline in real wages reached about 7 percent. Real wages in the private manufacturing sector dipped in 1986 to almost two-thirds of their 1981 level (OECD 1993:61). The share of labor cost in the total net value-added of the 500 largest firms decreased from 50 percent in 1980 to 33 percent in 1988 (OECD 1991/92:26).

The decline in real wages coincided with gains in productivity. The average annual increase in productivity in manufacturing in 1981–88 was about 4.1 percent. In 1989–92, however, with the relaxation of labor market restrictions, unions pressed for higher wages, raising the real wage level in 1989 to its 1981 level. Employers responded by replacing labor with capital or part-time labor (OECD 1993:64). In any case, the freeze on public-sector wages in 1994 made the wage gains temporary.

Unemployment followed its textbook behavior. As reported by both the Household Labor Force Surveys (conducted by the State Institute of Statistics) and the OECD, Turkish unemployment rates remained far above the OECD averages prior to 1980. Throughout the 1980s and during the first half of the 1990s, the unemployment rate fluctuated around 7 to 8 percent, rising to a little over 8 percent in 1994.[4]

Note that the spell of unemployment has been uneven. Urban unemployment remained higher than rural unemployment, and the urban female unemployment rate has been considerably higher than that of urban males, 28.5 percent and 9.8 percent, respectively. In addition, economic policies have disproportionately affected the youth, ages fifteen to twenty-four, raising the unemployment rate for this group to 17.3 percent in 1994 (OECD 1996:67). The high educational attainment level of unemployed youth makes the problem very serious. About 33.3 percent of the unemployed youth have secondary and 38.7 percent above secondary educational attainment (Turnham 1993:82). The real issue here is that the growth of the economy has not been high enough to absorb the unemployed. Of course, the rapid population growth is not helping the situation either.

Also note that, in spite of the fact that real wages declined considerably, unemployment remained fairly high. This is puzzling, given the fact that real depreciation of the Turkish lira stimulated labor-intensive exports. For example, the share of labor-intensive manufactured exports in total nonfuel exports increased from 26.8 percent in 1975 to 57.6 percent in 1986. During the same period, the share of textile and clothing in labor-intensive manufactured exports increased from 4.1 percent to 43.7 percent (OECD 1989/90, 1996). Clearly, failure to focus on overall economic growth, and economic and political uncertainty that kept domestic and foreign investment below the warranted level, are perhaps the main reasons unemployment remained high.

LIBERALIZATION PROGRAMS AND LABOR MARKETS

Economic liberalization programs give rise to short-term adjustment costs in the labor market.[5] Resource reallocation in response to program incentives and disincentives causes certain sectors to contract and some others to expand. Contracting sectors release labor, while expanding ones absorb it. The rate at which contracting sectors release labor, however, may exceed that of absorption. Hence, the result is unemployment, which is hypothesized to be temporary. Since export promotion plays a central role in liberalization programs, expanding sectors are those with export orientation.

In order for this policy to be successful, depreciation of the currency in real terms is a prerequisite. In a deflationary environment, real currency depreciation requires a decrease in real wages, and that, in turn, leads to increased competitiveness. Assuming that the expanding export sectors are labor-intensive, the increase in competitiveness raises production and therefore employment. Over time, unemployment would be absorbed, and the speed of absorption depends on the degree of real wage flexibility, as well as on the output and real wage elasticities of employment (International Monetary Fund 1996). This automatic adjustment worsens the distribution of income, at least in the short run, potentially contributing to social and political instability.

Other aspects of the liberalization program have contributed to potentially adverse developments in the labor market, making the adjustment period fairly long. Privatization usually adds to the already high structural unemployment, rendering the absorption more difficult. Furthermore, faced with external competition, the export sector substitutes capital for labor to become more competitive, also worsening unemployment. Finally, liberalization of financial markets and the influx of foreign bank and nonbank financial institutions lead to increased orientation of the domestic financial markets to the international markets, causing potential investment funds to be channeled to financial speculation. Consequently, domestic investment projections remain below the warranted rate, thereby prolonging the labor market adjustment.

Note that the stabilization policies that accompany the liberalization program could also adversely affect the labor markets. Contractionary monetary and/or fiscal policies could significantly add to unemployment. The downside of this possibility, coupled with declining real wages, is the negative impact of high unemployment on aggregate demand, pushing the economy into an undesirable low output–high unemployment–low real wage spiral.

Given these fairly complex linkages, it is difficult to quantify the main variables that impact unemployment levels. Also, as has been the case over the last several decades in Turkey, where there has been a high growth of the labor force due to rapid population growth, high rural-urban migration, and a high proportion of low-skilled labor, any connection between unemployment rates and the liberalization process should be treated cautiously. Some aspects of liberalization and its impact on the demand for labor, however, could provide some insight on the extent to which the labor markets were affected.

THE MODEL AND RESULTS

To analyze the effects of certain key aspects of the liberalization program on demand for labor, we used pooled cross-section and time series data on the 500 largest manufacturing firms in Turkey. Following Bruno and Sachs (1985) and Nas and Odekon (1990), we estimated the following labor demand function:

$$L = l(w, er, y, i, K, \Pi)$$

where w is the real wage, er the real exchange rate, y the real gross domestic product, i the real interest rate, K firms' capital-sales ratio, and Π firms' profit ratio.[6]

The two policy variables in the model are the real exchange rate and the real interest rate. The depreciation of the real exchange rate renders the exportables competitive and results in output expansion. On the other hand, the real depreciation raises the domestic cost of importables and further contributes to higher demand for labor because of the substitution effect associated with the rise in cost of capital. Thus, the expected sign on the real exchange rate is positive.

The real interest rate, assuming it reflects the cost of capital, would affect labor demand positively, again because of the substitution effect, at least in the short run. In the long run, the rise in savings in response to higher return may indeed increase the availability of loanable funds and lower the cost of capital. Given the stop-and-go nature of financial liberalization during a good part of the 1980s and the expansion of speculative financial markets thereafter, it will not be wrong to assume that there have been limited cost-of-capital-reducing effects of financial liberalization in Turkey. Hence, we expect to have a positive sign on the real interest rate pointing at the short-run substitution effect.

We also include real wage and real output variables in the equation. The real wage variable is hypothesized to have a negative sign, whereas real output is expected to have a direct effect on firms' labor demand.

The first of the two firm-specific variables, the capital-sales ratio, is expected to have a positive effect on labor demand, for a rise in the use of capital would raise the demand for labor as well. The profit variable is also expected to have a positive sign. As profits rise, investment from retained earnings would raise labor demand. On the other hand, one might argue that higher profits may lead to substitution of capital for labor to achieve economies of scale and, hence, could adversely affect the demand for labor.

The ordinary least square (OLS) results are presented in Table 11.1.[7] The first row gives the results for all of the 500 large firms in 1981-94. The second and third rows summarize the results for export and nonexport firms.[8] The real exchange rate, real GDP, and capital-sales ratio are consistently significant with the hypothesized sign. The profit variable in the first and last rows is significant and has a negative sign, confirming the substitution argument. The interest rate and wage rate variables, however, are insignificant throughout. The ambiguity here could be the result of the model not capturing the separate influences of stabilization and liberalization measures and, as in the case of the interest rate variable, failing to identify and separate the cost-push effects from the expansionary effects.

CONCLUSIONS

From the preceding preliminary findings, it is clear that the real growth in the economy and the real exchange rate are significant sources of variation in firms' demand for labor. By altering relative prices, the real currency depreciation is reinforcing Turkey's comparative advantage in labor-intensive exportables and raising the demand for labor in the export sector. However, it should be emphasized that real depreciation and output expansion alone are not enough to solve the labor market problems. Additional measures should include an effective family-planning program that would curb the high rate of population growth and would also be in harmony with the culture of local people, especially in rural areas. Furthermore, the pro-industry bias inherent in economic liberalization programs needs to be addressed, particularly if it takes the form of being anti-agriculture, as has been the case in Turkey. As a result of the rapid shift from agriculture to manufacturing, not only did unemployment increase, but also the extended-family system, which traditionally served economically disadvantaged masses as a safety net, began to dissolve. In addition, the state, another safety net, started to shrink in its role as the "provider" of last resort. Hence, it is important that the necessary institutions, such as unemployment insurance, be put in place if the pains of the transition to the market system are to be minimized.

Another major problem in the Turkish economy, at least in the past, has been the concentration of economic activity, especially industrial activity, in a few large cities, such as Istanbul, Adana, and Izmir. Recently, however, this has been changing. In addition to the emergence of new industrial cities in Anatolia, the currently underway Southeast-

Table 11.1
Labor Demand in Turkish Manufacturing Industries: OLS Regression Results, 1981-94

	Constant	er	y	i	w	K	Π	N	R^2
Aggregate	-4.41*	1.02*	1.21	-.13	.19	.55*	-.003*	4311	.47
	(-6.3)	(7.4)	(10.4)	(-1.0)	(1.4)	(60.7)	(-3.0)		
Export	-2.73	1.01*	1.14*	-.50	.12	.40*	.002	366	.36
	(-1.2)	(2.3)	(2.9)	(-1.2)	(.7)	(12.2)	(.83)		
Nonexport	-4.55*	1.02*	1.20*	-.89	.19	.57*	-.003*	3945	.47
	(-6.3)	(7.2)	(9.8)	(-.6)	(1.3)	(59.2)	(-3.2)		

Figures in parentheses are t-statistics.
* Denotes significance at 5 percent level.

ern Anatolia Project, the biggest project of its kind in the world, has already become the driving force of geographical diversification with its massive irrigation and hydropower complexes, including all necessary social and economic infrastructure. Geographical diversification of economic activity, which is the product of such a full-fledged strategy with massive infrastructure building, student work programs, and the provision of various public services facilitating people's access to basic needs, is definitely an important step in the right direction.

NOTES

1. The main features of the program include, along with the lowering of price and nonprice barriers in both the domestic and external sectors: direct and indirect subsidies to exporters; provisions enabling exporters to keep a portion of their foreign exchange earnings to import the necessary raw materials and/or capital goods; daily adjustments in the exchange rate; introduction of a value-added tax as part of a broader tax reform package; privatization of state-owned economic enterprises; and administrative reforms to minimize the role of the government in the economy. For a detailed analysis of the 1980 Turkish liberalization and stabilization effort, see Nas and Odekon (1988, 1992) and Aricanli and Rodrik (1990).

2. See Odekon (1992) for a discussion of firms' perceptions of several aspects of the liberalization program.

3. The new rules and regulations governing labor activities proved to be so limiting and undemocratic that the International Labor Organization censored Turkey (Kepenek and Yenturk 1994:397).

4. Turkish labor market data are not uniform and vary with the source used. For example, according to Edwards (1991), unemployment in 1979, the year preceding the inception of the liberalization program, was 9.4 percent and rose to an annual average of 11.7 percent in 1980–87 and reached 12.7 percent in 1989. Note that the OECD and Turkish figures are lower than Edwards's. They show a marginal drop in the 1980s relative to the 1970s and then a rise in the early 1990s. Nevertheless, these sources also confirm the high and persistent unemployment.

5. See International Monetary Fund 1996, Buffie 1995, Flanagan 1994, Robbins 1994, Burda 1992, and Commander et al. 1991 for a discussion of labor market effects of the liberalization policies.

6. The Bruno and Sachs (1985) model calls for the inclusion of the real price of imported materials. Due to the lack of data, we use the real exchange rate as a proxy. In the estimation, we used pooled firm-level data, combining it with annual macro data. Data sources are as follows:

L: employment, from various Journal of Istanbul Chamber of Commerce (ISO) issues

y: real GDP, from OECD

er: real exchange rate calculated as eP^*/P, where e is the nominal exchange rate, P^* is foreign producer price index and P, domestic producer price index (PPI), all from the International Monetary Fund i: lending rate, from Eczacibasi Holding Research Unit, Istanbul, Turkey

w: nominal wage rate deflated by PPI, from various OECD issues

K, Π : capital-sales and profit-sales ratios, from ISO

7. All variables are in natural logarithm. Two stage least square results are not significantly different from OLS results and are not reported here.

8. Firms with an export-sales ratio greater than 0.6 are classified as export firms. Data from ISO.

REFERENCES

Aricanli, T., and D. Rodrik, eds. 1990. *The Political Economy of Turkey*. New York: St. Martin's Press.

Bruno, M., and J. Sachs. 1985. *Economics of Worldwide Stagflation*. Cambridge: Harvard University Press.

Buffie, E. 1995. The long-run consequences of short-run stabilization policy. In *Labor Markets in an Era of Adjustment*, edited by S. Horton, R. Kanbur, and D. Mazumdar, 237–76. Washington, DC: World Bank.

Burda, M. 1992. *Unemployment, Labor Market Institutions and Structural Change in Eastern Europe*. London: Center for Economic Policy Research.

Commander, S., F. Coricelli, and K. Staehr. 1991. *Wages and employment in the transition to a market economy*. World Bank Economic Development Institute WPS 736. Washington, DC: World Bank.

Edwards, S. 1991. Liberalization and unemployment. In *Liberalizing Foreign Trade: Lessons of Experience in the Developing World*, edited by D. Papageorgiou et al., 71–84. Oxford: Basil Blackwell.

Flanagan, R. 1994. Labor market responses to a change in economic system. In *Proceedings of the World Bank Annual Conference on Development Economics*, 405–25. Washington, DC: World Bank.

International Monetary Fund. 1996. *Reinvigorating Growth in Developing Countries: Lessons from Adjustment Policies in Eight Economies*. Washington, DC: International Monetary Fund.

———. *International Financial Statistics*. Various issues, 1985–97. Washington, DC: International Monetary Fund.

Journal of Istanbul Chamber of Commerce. Various issues, 1981–95. Istanbul: ISO.

Kepenek, Y., and N. Yenturk. 1994. *Turkiye Ekonomisi*. Istanbul: Remzi Kitabevi.

Nas, T. and M. Odekon. 1990. Supply side response in liberalization. *Bogazici University Journal of Economics and Administrative Studies* 4(2):281–88.

———. 1996. Effects of post-1980 macroeconomic policies on Turkish manufacturing. *Journal of Developing Areas* 30:211–22.

———, eds. 1988. *Liberalization and the Turkish Economy*. Westport, CT: Greenwood Press.

———, eds. 1992. *Economics and Politics of Turkish Liberalization*. Bethlehem, PA: Lehigh University Press.

Odekon, M.. 1992. Turkish liberalization: From the perspectives of manufacturing firms. In *Economics and Politics of Turkish Liberalization*, edited by T. Nas and M. Odekon, 155–75. Bethlehem, PA: Lehigh University Press.

Organization for Economic Co-operation and Development. *Economic Surveys: Turkey*. Various issues, 1980–96. Paris: OECD.

Rittenberg, L. 1988. Financial liberalization and savings in Turkey. In *Liberalization and the Turkish Economy*, edited by T. Nas and M. Odekon, 115–27. Westport, CT: Greenwood Press.

Robbins, D. J. 1994. *Worsening relative wage dispersion in Chile during trade liberalization and its causes: Is supply at fault?* Harvard Institute for International Development Discussion Paper 484. Cambridge: Harvard University.

Sayari, S. 1992. Politics and economic policy-making in Turkey. In *Economics and Politics of Turkish Liberalization,* edited by T. Nas and M. Odekon, 26–43. Bethlehem, PA: Lehigh University Press.

Turnham, D. 1993. *Employment and Development*. Paris: Organization for Economic Co-operation and Development.

United Nations Development Programme (UNDP). 1994. *Human Development Report, 1994*. New York: Oxford University Press.

Waterbury, J. 1992. Export-led growth and the center-right coalition in Turkey. In *Economics and Politics of Turkish Liberalization*, edited by T. Nas and M. Odekon, 44–72. Bethlehem, PA: Lehigh University Press.

World Bank. 1996. *World Development Report, 1996: From Plan to Market*. New York: Oxford University Press.

References

Acuña, C. 1994. Politics and economics in the Argentina of the nineties (Or, why the future no longer is what it used to be). In *Democracy, Markets, and Structural Reform in Latin America: Argentina, Bolivia, Brazil, Chile, and Mexico*, edited by W. C. Smith, C. H. Acuña, and E. Gamarra, 31–73. New Brunswick, NJ: North-South Center/Transaction Books.

Adedeji, A. 1989. *African Alternative Framework to Structural Adjustment Programmes for Socio-Economic Recovery and Transformation*. New York: U.N. Economic Commission for Africa.

Adelman, I., and D. Sundings. 1987. Economic policy and income distribution in China. *Journal of Comparative Economics* 11(3):444–61.

Adjibolosoo, S. 1994. The human factor and the failure of economic development and policies in Africa. In *Perspectives on Economic Development in Africa*, edited by F. Ezeala-Harrison and S. Adjibolosoo. Westport, CT: Praeger.

Aghion, P., and O. J. Blanchard. 1993. *On the speed of transition in central Europe*. Working Paper 6. London: European Bank for Reconstruction and Development.

Alcorte, L. 1995. The impact of new technologies on industrial structure: Case studies from Brazil, Mexico and Venezuela. (Paper presented at the Latin American Studies Association Meetings) September 28–30, Washington, DC.

Alexakis, P., and M. Xanthakis. 1992. Export performance of Greek manufacturing companies: Export subsidies and other factors. *Economia Internationale* 45(2):143–52.

Allen, S. G., A. Cassoni, and G. J. Labadie. 1994. Labor market flexibility and unemployment in Chile and Uruguay. *Estudios de Economia* 21:129–45.

Anderson, S., J. Cavanaugh, and D. Ranney, eds. 1996. NAFTA's first two years: Myths and realities. Washington, DC: Institute for Policy Studies. Mimeographed.

Aricanli, T., and D. Rodrik, eds. 1990. *The Political Economy of Turkey*. New York: St. Martin's Press.

Aronskind, R. 1990. El salario dolarizado: Un mínimo que se hunde. *El Bimestre Político y Económico* 49(April):9–11.

Aspiazu, D., E. Basualdo, and M. Khavisse. 1986. *El Nuevo Poder Económico en la Argentina de los Años Ochenta*. Buenos Aires: Legasa.

Atkinson, A. B., and J. Micklewright. 1991. Unemployment compensation and labour market transitions: A critical review. *Journal of Economic Literature* 29(4):1679–1727.

———. 1992. *Economic Transformation in Eastern Europe and the Distribution of Income*. New York: Cambridge University Press.

Bagchi, A. K. 1989. Development planning. In *The New Palgrave: Economic Development*, edited by J. Eatwell, M. Milgate, and P. Newman, 98–108. London: Macmillan.

Baker, D., G. Epstein, and R. Pollin, eds. 1997. *Globalization and Progressive Economic Policy*. Ann Arbor: University of Michigan Press.

Barbeito, A., and C. Rodríguez. 1995. Empleo, remuneración del trabajo, y distribución del ingreso. In *Argentina Hoy: Crisis del Modelo*, edited by N. Minsburg and H. W. Valle, 283–310. Buenos Aires: Ediciones Letra Buena.

Batra, R. 1993. *The Myths of Free Trade*. New York: Charles Scribner's Sons.

Blanchard, O. J., and S. Fischer. 1988. *Lectures on Macroeconomics*. Cambridge, MA: MIT Press.

Blanchard, O. J., S. Commander, and F. Coricelli. 1994. Unemployment in Eastern Europe. *Finance and Development* 31(4):6–9.

Blanchard, O. J., K. A. Froot, and J. D. Sachs, eds. 1995. *The Transition in Eastern Europe 2* (National Bureau of Economic Research Project Report) Chicago: University of Chicago Press.

Blecker, R. A. 1996a. The political economy of the North American Free Trade Agreement. In *U.S. Trade Policy and Global Growth*, edited by R. Blecker, 136–76. Armonk, NY: M. E. Sharpe.

———, ed. 1996b. *U.S. Trade Policy and Global Growth*. Armonk, NY: M. E. Sharpe.

Bloom, D. E., and A. Brender. 1993. *Labor and the emerging world economy*. NBER Working Paper 4266. Washington, DC: National Bureau for Economic Research.

Bluestone, B. 1990. The great u-turn revisited: Economic restructuring, jobs, and the redistribution of earnings. In *Jobs, Earnings, and Employment Growth Policies in the United States*, edited by J. D. Kasarda. Boston: Kluwer Academic Publishers.

Bluestone, B., and B. Harrison. 1982. *De-industrialization of America*. New York: Basic Books.

Boeri, T. 1995. *Regional Dimensions of Unemployment in Central and Eastern Europe and Social Barriers in Restructuring*. EUI Working Paper 95/17.

Bolle, M. J. 1996. *NAFTA: Estimates of Job Effects and Industry Trade Trends after Two Years*. Washington, DC: Congressional Research Service, Economics Division.

Boltho, A., and A. Glyn. 1995. Can macroeconomic policies raise employment. *International Labour Review* 134(4–5):451–70.

Bour, J. L. 1995. Los costos laborales en la Argentina. In *Libro Blanco Sobre el Empleo en la Argentina*, edited by Ministerio de Trabajo y Seguridad Social, 179–98. Buenos Aires: Ministerio de Trabajo y Seguridad Social.

Bouzas, R. 1996. *The Mexican Peso Crisis and Argentina's Convertibility Plan: Monetary Virtue or Monetary Impotence?* Buenos Aires: FLACSO/ CONICET.

Bowles, S., and H. Gintis. 1995. Productivity-enhancing egalitarian policies. *International Labour Review* 134(4–5).

Brown, D. K. 1992. The impact of a North American free trade area: Applied general equilibrium models. In *North American Free Trade: Assessing the Impact*, edited by N. Lustig, B. Bosworth, and R. Lawrence, 26–68. Washington, DC: Brookings Institution.

Brown, D. K., A. Deardorf, and R. M. Stern. 1992. A North American free trade agreement: Analytical issues and a computational assessment. *World Economy* 15(1):11–30.

Brulhart, M. 1994. Marginal intra-industry trade: Measurement and relevance for the pattern of industrial adjustment. *Weltwirtschaftliches Archiv* 130(3):600–613.

Bruno, M., and J. Sachs. 1985. *Economics of Worldwide Stagflation*. Cambridge: Harvard University Press.

Bruton, H. J. 1970. The import substitution strategy of economic development. *Pakistan Development Review* 10:123–46.

Budhoo, D. L. 1990. *Enough Is Enough: Open Resignation Letter to IMF*. New York: The Apex Press.

Buffie, E. 1995. The long-run consequences of short-run stabilization policy. In *Labor Markets in an Era of Adjustment*, edited by S. Horton, R. Kanbur, and D. Mazumdar, 237–76. Washington, DC: World Bank.

Burda, M. 1992. *Unemployment, Labor Market Institutions and Structural Change in Eastern Europe*. London: Center for Economic Policy Research.

———. 1993. Unemployment, labor market institutions, and structural change in Eastern Europe. *Economic Policy* 16:101–38.

———. 1995. *The Impact of Active Labor Market Policies: A Close Look at the Czech and Slovak Republics*. London: Center for Economic Policy Research.

Cagatay, N., and S. Ozler. 1995. Feminization of the labour force: The effects of long-term development and structural adjustment. *World Development* (special issue on gender, adjustment, and macroeconomics) 23(11): 1883–94.

Calvo, G. A. 1978. Urban unemployment and wage determination in LDCs: Trade unions in the Harris-Todaro model. *International Economic Review* 19(1): 65–81.

Campbell, B., and J. Clapp. 1995. Guinea's economic performance under structural adjustment: Importance of mining and agriculture. *Journal of Modern African Studies* 33(3):425–49.

Canitrot, A. 1979. La disciplina como objetivo de la política económica: Un ensayo sobre el programa económico del gobierno Argentino desde 1976. *Estudios Cedes* 2(6).

———. 1995. Presentación general. In *Libro Blanco Sobre el Empleo en la Argentina*, 11–51. Buenos Aires: Ministerio de Trabajo y Seguridad Social.

Cavallo, D. 1982. *Volver a Crecer.* Buenos Aires: Sudamericana-Planeta.

Cavallo, D., R. Domenech, and Y. Mundlak. 1989. *La Argentina Que Pudo Ser: Los Costos de la Represión Económica.* Buenos Aires: Fundacion Mediterránea/Manantial.

Central Bank of Trinidad and Tobago. *Annual Economic Survey,* various issues, 1982–95. St. Augustine, Trinidad and Tobago: Central Bank of Trinidad and Tobago.

Central Statistical Office (CSO). *Economic Indicators Report,* various issues, 1982–95. St. Augustine, Trinidad and Tobago: Central Statistical Office.

———. *Labour Force Report,* various issues, 1982–95. St. Augustine, Trinidad and Tobago: Central Statistical Office.

Central Statistical Office (CSO) and F. Coricelli. 1995. *Unemployment, Investment and Sectoral Reallocation.* CEPR Discussion Paper Series 1110.

Chadha, B. 1994. *Fiscal Constraints and the Speed of Transition.* CEPR Discussion Paper Series 993.

Chadha, B., and F. Coricelli. 1995. *Unemployment, Investment and Sectoral Reallocation.* CEPR Discussion Paper Series 1110.

Clarín. Various issues, 1989–96.

Commander, S., F. Coricelli, and K. Staehr. 1991. *Wages and Employment in the Transition to a Market Economy.* (World Bank Economic Development Institute WPS) 736. Washington, DC: World Bank.

Corak, M. 1994. Unemployment insurance, work disincentives and the Canadian labour market: An overview. In *Unemployment Insurance: How to Make It Work,* edited by J. Richards and W. Watson. Toronto, Canada: Howe Institute.

Corbo, V. 1985a. Reforms and macroeconomic adjustment in Chile during 1974–1984. *World Development* 13(8). Washington, DC.

———. 1985b. *The Role of the Real Exchange Rate in Macroeconomic Adjustment: The Case of Chile 1973–82.* Discussion Paper DRD145. Washington, DC: World Bank.

Corbo, V., and F. Sturzenegger. 1988. Stylized facts of the macroeconomic adjustment in the indebted countries. Washington, DC: World Bank. Mimeographed.

Cornia, G. A., R. Jolly, and F. Stewart. 1987. *Adjustment with a Human Face.* Oxford: Oxford University Press.

Dabir-Alai, P. 1996. Planning in India: An overview of key objectives and a few achievements—the first 20 years. In *Study of Indian History and Culture,* edited by H. D. Vinod, 466–86. Bombay: Bhishma.

DeLancey, V. 1992. The economies of Africa. In *Understanding Contemporary Africa,* edited by A. A. Gordon and D. L. Gordon. Boulder and London: Lynne Rienner Publishers.

Dewatripont, M. 1992. The virtues of gradualism and legitimacy in the transition to a market economy. *Economic Journal* 102:291–300.

Dewatripont, M., and G. Roland. 1992. Economic reform and dynamic political constraints. *Review of Economic Studies* 59:703–30.

Di Tella, G., and R. Dornbusch, eds. 1989. *The Political Economy of Argentina 1946–1983.* Pittsburgh, PA: University of Pittsburgh Press.

Dornbusch, R. 1993. *Stabilization, Debt, and Reform: Policy Analysis for Developing Countries.* Englewood, NJ: Prentice-Hall.

Drèze, J. 1993. Dealing with famines. *Briefing Notes in Economics* 3 (March).
Drèze, J., and A. K. Sen. 1990. *The Political Economy of Hunger*. Oxford: Clarendon Press.
Droucopoulos, V., and S. Thomadakis. 1994. Globalisation of economic activities and small- and medium-sized enterprises development. Department of Economics, University of Athens. Mimeographed.
Easterly, W. 1989. *Policy Distortions, Size of Government and Growth*. NBER Working Paper 3214. Cambridge, MA: National Bureau of Economic Research.
Economic Commission for Latin America and the Caribbean (ECLAC). 1994. *Social Panorama of Latin America, 1994*. Santiago, Chile: ECLAC.
——. 1996. *Preliminary Overview of the Economy of LA and the Caribbean*. Santiago, Chile: ECLAC.
Edwards, S. 1985. Economic policy and the record of economic growth in Chile 1973–1982. In *The National Economic Policies in Chile: Contemporary Studies in Economic and Financial Analysis* 51, edited by G. M. Walton. Greenwich, CT: JAI Press.
——. 1991. Liberalization and unemployment. In *Liberalizing Foreign Trade: Lessons of Experience in the Developing World*, edited by D. Papageorgiou et al., 71–84. Oxford: Basil Blackwell.
Edwards, S., and A. Edwards. 1987. *Monetarism and Liberalization; The Chilean Experience*. Cambridge, MA: Ballinger Publishing Company.
Epstein, G. A. 1995. International profit rate equalization and foreign direct investment: A study of integration, instability and enforcement. In *Macroeconomics after the Conservative Era*, edited by G. A. Epstein and H. Gintis, 308–33. Cambridge, MA: Cambridge University Press.
Ezeala-Harrison, F. 1993. Structural re-adjustment in Nigeria: Diagnosis of a severe Dutch disease syndrome. *American Journal of Economics and Sociology* 52(2):193–208.
——. 1994. African subsistence labour allocation: A model with implications for rural development and urban unemployment. In *Perspectives on Economic Development in Africa*, edited by F. Ezeala-Harrison and S. Adjibolosoo. Westport, CT: Praeger.
——. 1995a. Africa's diploma disease: Diagnosis of the non-sequential agenda of education. Paper presented at the conference of the Canadian Association for the Study of International Development, Montreal, June.
——. 1995b. Canada's global competitiveness challenge: Trade performance versus total factor productivity measures. *American Journal of Economics and Sociology* 54(1):57–78.
——. 1995c. Human factor issues in the history of economic underdevelopment. *The Review of Human Factor Studies* 1(1):1–25.
——. 1995d. Over-stretched economic underdevelopment in sub-Saharan Africa. *Briefing Notes in Economics* 14 (January).
——. 1996. *Economic Development: Theory and Policy Applications*. Westport, CT: Praeger.
Ezeala-Harrison, F., and S. Adjibolosoo, eds. 1994. *Perspectives on Economic Development in Africa*. Westport, CT: Praeger.

Faux, J., and T. M. Lee. 1992. *The Effect of George Bush's NAFTA on American Workers: Ladder Up or Ladder Down?* Washington, DC: Economic Policy Institute.

Ferraro, R., and L. Riveros. 1994. *Historia de Chile: Una Vision Economica.* Santiago: Departmento de Economia, Universidad de Chile.

Filgueira, C. 1984. El estado y las clases: Tendencias en Argentina, Brasil y Uruguay. *Pensamiento Iberoamericano* 6(July–December):35–61.

Fischer, S. 1993. The role of macroeconomic factors in growth. *Journal of Monetary Economics* 32(1):485–512.

Flanagan, R. 1994. Labor market responses to a change in economic system. In *Proceedings of the World Bank Annual Conference on Development Economics,* 405–25. Washington, DC: World Bank.

Folbre, N. 1995. *The New Field Guide to the US Economy.* New York: The New Press.

Foreign Broadcast Information Service (FBIS)—*Latin America.* 1992a. 29, 15 July.

———. 1992b. 20, 3 December.

———. 1993. 25–26, 5 March.

———. 1994. *Constitution of the Argentine Nation—1944.* 14 October.

Gambrill, M. 1995. La politica salarial de las maquiladoras: Mejoras posibles bajo el TLC. *Comercio Exterior* 45(7):543–49.

García, N. 1993. *Ajuste, Reforms y Mercado Laboral. Costa Rica (1980–1990); Chile (1973–1993); México (1981–1991).* Santiago: PREALC-OIT.

García-Vázquez, E. 1995. *La Política Económica Argentina en los Últimos Cincuenta Años.* Buenos Aires: Ediciones Macchi.

Garfunkel, J. 1990. *59 Semanas y Media Que Conmovieron a la Argentina.* Buenos Aires: EMECE.

Gaudio, R., and A. Thompson. 1990. *Sindicalismo Peronista / Gobierno Radical: Los Años de Alfonsín.* Buenos Aires: Fundación Friedrich Ebert—Folios.

Gavin, M. 1993. Unemployment and the economics of gradualist policy reform. Columbia University. Mimeographed.

Gerchunoff, P., and J. C. Torre. 1996. *Argentina: La Política de Liberalización Económica Bajo un Gobierno de Base Popular.* Buenos Aires: Instituto Torcuato Di Tella.

Ghanem, H., and M. Walton. 1995. Workers need open markets and active governments. *Finance and Development* 32(3):3–6.

Giannitsis, T. 1988. *Accession to EEC and Effects on Industry and Trade: Foundation of Mediterranean Studies (Idryma Mesogeiakon Meleton)* (in Greek). Athens, Greece.

Gillis, M., D. H. Perkins, M. Roemer, and D. R. Snodgrass. 1996. *Economics of Development.* New York: Norton.

Glytsos, N. P. 1994. Greek labour market adaptability in the EC integration. In *Participation, Organizational Effectiveness and Quality of Work Life in the Year 2000,* edited by L. Nikolaou-Smokoviti and G. Szell. Frankfurt, Germany: Peter Lang.

Goldin, I., O. Knudsen, and D. van der Mensbrugghe. 1993. *Trade Liberalization: Global Economic Implications.* Washington, DC: OECD/World Bank.

Goodno, J. B., and J. Miller. 1996. Which way to grow? Notes on poverty and prosperity in Southeast Asia. In *Real World International*, edited by M. Breslow et al. Somerville, MA: Dollars and Sense.

Graham, C. 1994. *Safety Nets, Politics, and the Poor: Transitions to Market Economies*. Washington, DC: The Brookings Institution.

Greenaway, D., and R. C. Hine. 1991. Intra-industry specialization, trade expansion and adjustment in the European economic space. *Journal of Common Market Studies* 29(6):603–22.

Greenaway, D., and C. Milner. 1983. On the measurement of intra-industry trade. *The Economic Journal* 93:900–908.

——. 1986. *The Economics of Intra-Industry Trade*. Oxford: Basil Blackwell.

Grubel, H. G., and P. Lloyd. 1975. *Intra Industry Trade*. London: Macmillan.

Hachette, D., and R. Luders. 1987. Aspects of the privatization process: The case of Chile, 1974–85. World Bank. Mimeographed.

Haddad, L., et al. 1995. The gender dimensions of economic adjustment policies: Potential interactions and evidence to date. *World Development* 23(6):881–96.

Hanson, A. H. 1968. Power shifts and regional balances. In *The Crisis of Indian Planning*, edited by P. Streeton and M. Lipton, 19–60. London: Oxford University Press.

Henry, R., and J. Melville. 1989. *Poverty Revisited: Trinidad and Tobago in the Late 1980s*. St. Augustine, Trinidad and Tobago: University of the West Indies.

Hilaire, A. 1989. Economic reaction to a sectoral boom—Trinidad and Tobago, 1973–1985. Ph.D. thesis, University of Colombia.

Hine, R. C., D. Greenaway, and C. Milner. 1994. Changes in trade and changes in employment: An examination of the evidence from UK manufacturing industry, 1979–87. University of Nottingham. Mimeographed.

Hinojosa, R. et al. 1996. North American integration three years after NAFTA. University of California, Los Angeles. Mimeographed.

Hodd, M. 1992. *The Economies of Africa*. London: G. K. Hall and Co.

Horton, S., R. Kanbur, and D. Mazumdar, eds. 1995. *Labor Markets in an Era of Adjustment*. Washington, DC: World Bank.

Hufbauer, G. C., and J. Schott. 1993. *NAFTA: An Assessment*. Washington, DC: Institute for International Economics.

Husain, I. 1994. Results of adjustment in Africa: Selected cases. *Finance and Development* 31(2):7–12.

Hutton, W. 1986. *The Revolution That Never Was: An Assessment of Keynesian Economics*. London: Longman.

Instituto Nacional de Estadísticas y Censos (INDEC). 1989. *La Pobreza en el Conurbano Bonaerense*. Buenos Aires: Estudios INDEC 13.

International Bank of Reconstruction and Development (IBRD). 1991. *World Development Report*. Washington, DC: World Bank.

International Labor Organization. 1991. *The Challenge of Employment Promotion: Trinidad and Tobago in the 1990s*. Geneva: International Labor Organization.

——. 1996. *World Employment 1996/97: National Policies in a Global Context*. Geneva: International Labor Organization.

———. 1995. *World Employment 1995 Report*. Geneva: International Labor Organization.

International Monetary Fund (IMF). 1994a. *International Financial Statistics*. Washington, DC: International Monetary Fund.

———. 1994b. *World Economic Outlook*. Washington, DC: International Monetary Fund.

———. 1996. *Reinvigorating Growth in Developing Countries: Lessons from Adjustment Policies in Eight Economies*. Washington, DC: International Monetary Fund.

———. *International Financial Statistics*. Various issues. Washington, DC: International Monetary Fund.

Jabbaz, M. 1995. El debate sobre la flexibilidad y la precarización del trabajo en la Argentina. In *Argentina Hoy: Crisis del Modelo*, edited by N. Minsburg and H. W. Valle, 311–34. Buenos Aires: Edicions Letra Buena.

Jadresic, E. 1990. Salarios en el largo plazo: Chile, 1960–1989. *Coleccion Estudios CIEPLAN* 29:9–34.

Johnson, H. G. 1967. The possibilities of income losses from increased efficiency or factor accumulation in the presence of tariffs. *Economic Journal* 77(305):151–54.

Jolly, R., and G. A. Cornia. 1984. *The Impact of World Recession on Children*. Oxford: Pergamon Press.

Jones, C., and M. A. Kiguel. 1994. Africa's quest for prosperity: Has adjustment helped? *Finance and Development* 31(2):2–5.

Journal of Istanbul Chamber of Commerce. Various issues, 1989–95. Istanbul: ISO.

Katseli, L. T. 1990. Economic integration in the enlarged European community: Structural adjustment of the Greek economy. In *Unity with Diversity in the European Economy: The Community's Southern Frontier*, edited by C. Bliss and J. B. de Macedo. Cambridge: Cambridge University Press for the Centre for Economic Policy Research.

Katsos, G., and N. I. Spanakis. 1983. *Industrial Protection and Integration*. Athens: Center for Planning and Economic Research.

Kehoe, T. J. 1992. *Modeling the Dynamic Impact of North American Free Trade*. Working Paper 491. Minneapolis, MN: Federal Reserve Bank of Minneapolis.

Kepenek, Y., and N. Yenturk. 1994. *Turkiye Ekonomisi*. Istanbul: Remzi Kitabevi.

Khan, M. H., and M. S. Khan. 1995. *Agricultural Growth in Sub-Saharan African Countries and China*. (IMF Papers of Policy Analysis and Assessment) 95/7. Washington, DC: International Monetary Fund.

Kim, K. S. 1993. An alternative strategy for equity with growth—case of Mexico. *Hitotsubashi Journal of Economics* 34(1):45–66.

Kim, K. S., and P. Voraspontaviporn. 1989. International trade, employment, and income: The case of Thailand. *Developing Economies* 27(1):60–74.

Koechlin, T. 1992. The responsiveness of domestic investment to foreign economic conditions. *Journal of Post Keynesian Economics* 15(1):63–83.

———. 1993. NAFTA and the location of North American investment: A critique of mainstream analysis. *Review of Radical Political Economics* 25(4):59–71.

———. 1997. The limits of globalization. In *Political Economy of Globalization*, edited by D. Gupta, 59–79. Boston, MA: Kluwer Academic Publishers.

Koechlin, T., and M. Larudee. 1992. The high cost of NAFTA. *Challenge* 35(5): 19–26.

Kornai, J. 1992. The post-socialist transition and the State: Reflections in the light of Hungarian fiscal problems. *American Economic Review, Papers and Proceedings*, 82(2):2–21.

Koster, M. H., and M. N. Ross. 1988. *The Quality of Jobs: Evidence from Distributions of Annual Earnings and Hourly Wages*. Washington, DC: American Enterprise Institute.

Köves, A., and P. Marer. 1991. *Foreign Economic Liberalization: Transformations in Socialist and Market Economies*. Boulder, CO: Westview Press.

Krueger, A. O. 1974. The political economy of rent-seeking. *American Economic Review* 64(3):291–323.

Krugman, P. 1987. Is free trade passe? *Journal of Economic Perspectives* 1(2):131–43.

———. 1988. External shocks and domestic policy responses. In *The Open Economy*, edited by R. Dornbusch and L. Helmers, 54–79. New York: Oxford University Press.

Lall, S. 1995. Structural adjustment and African industry. *World Development* 23(12):2019–31.

Larrain, F. 1988. Public sector behavior in a highly indebted country: The contrasting Chilean experience, 1970–1985. Washington, DC: World Bank. Mimeographed.

Larrain, F., and P. Meller. 1990. The socialist-populist Chilean experience: 1970–73. Santiago. Mimeographed.

Larudee, M. 1996. Integration and income distribution under the North American Free Trade Agreement (NAFTA). Paper Presented at Conference on Globalization and Progressive Economic Policy, sponsored by the Economic Policy Institute, June 21–23, Washington, DC.

Lauro, A. 1990a. Extinción de la clase media Argentina. *Clarín—Edición Internacional* 10, 27 August–2 September.

———. 1990b. Los rostros de las dos Argentinas. *Clarín—Edición Internacional* 9, 26 November–2 December.

Leamer, E. 1993. Wage effects of a US-Mexico free trade agreement. In *The Mexico-US Trade Agreement*, edited by P. Garber, 57–125. Cambridge, MA: MIT Press.

Levy, S., and S. van Wijnbergen. 1994. Agriculture in the Mexico-US free trade agreement: A general equilibrium analysis. In *Modeling Trade Policy*, edited by J. Francois and C. Sheills, 151–94. New York: Cambridge University Press.

Lewis, W. A. 1955. Economic development with unlimited supplies of labor. *The Manchester School* 22:139–91.

Lianos, T., A. Sarris, and L. Katseli. 1996. Illegal immigration and local labour markets: The case of northern Greece. *International Migration* 34(3):449–84.

Lo Vuolo, R. 1994. *Análisis de la Actual Situación del Mercado de Trabajo y Su Probable Proyección Futura*. Buenos Aires: PRONATASS—Ministerio de Trabajo y Seguridad Social/Secretaría de Seguridad Social.

Lozano, C. and R. Feletti. 1995. Convertibilidad y desempleo: Crisis ocupacional en la Argentina. *Cuadernos del Sur* 11(20):25–45.

Lucas, R. E. 1988. On the mechanics of economic development. *Journal of Monetary Economics* 22(1):3–42.

MacDougall, D. 1960. The benefits and costs of private investment from abroad: A theoretical approach. *Economic Record* 36(1):13–35.

Machinea, J. L. 1990. *Stabilization under Alfonsín's Government: A Frustrated Attempt.* Buenos Aires: Documentos CEDES 42.

Majul, L. 1990. *Por Que Cayó Alfonsín: El Nuevo Terrorismo Económico.* Buenos Aires: Sudamericana.

Manzetti, L. 1992. *The Political Economy of Privatization through Divestiture in Lesser Developed Economies: The Case of Argentina.* Miami, FL: North-South Center.

Marc, A., C. Graham, and M. Schacter. 1994. *Economic Reforms and the Poor: Social Action Programs and Social Funds in Sub-Saharan Africa: Findings* 12. Washington, DC: World Bank.

Mardas, D. 1992. *The Consequences of the Unified Market on Greek Export Trade: An Intra-Industry Analysis* (in Greek). Athens: Greek Center for European Studies (EKEM).

Mardas, D., and N. Varsakelis. 1988. Greece in commission of European communities: "The cost of non-Europe" basic findings. *European Economy.*

Marquez Padilla, C. 1995. El sector manufacturero, politicas comercial y cambriaria y la cuestion ocupacional, 1980–1992. *Economia Mexicana, Nueva Epoca* 4(1):151–70.

Menem, C., and R. Dromi. 1990. *Reforma del Estado y Transformación Nacional.* Buenos Aires: Ciencias de la Administración.

Milanovic, B. 1996. *Income, Inequality, and Poverty During the Transition.* Washington, DC: World Bank.

Milbourne, R. D., D. D. Purvis, and D. Scoones. 1991. Unemployment insurances and unemployment dynamics. *Canadian Journal of Economics* 24(4):804–26.

Minsburg, N., and H. W. Valle, eds. 1995. *Argentina Hoy: Crisis del Modelo.* Buenos Aires: Ediciones Letra Buena.

Minujín, A., ed. 1992. *Cuesta Abajo: Los Nuevos Pobres.* Buenos Aires: UNICEF/Losada.

Minujín, A., and G. Kessler. 1995. *La Nueva Pobreza en la Argentina.* Buenos Aires: Planeta Argentina.

Monza, A. 1995. Situación actual y perspectivas del mercado de trabajo en la Argentina. In *Libro Blanco Sobre el Empleo en la Argentina*, by Ministerio de Trabajo y Seguridad Social, 137–62. Buenos Aires: Ministerio de Trabajo y Seguridad Social.

Mwase, N. 1993. The liberalization and deregulation of the transport sector in sub-Saharan Africa. *African Development Review* 5(2):74–86.

Nas, T., and M. Odekon, eds. 1988. *Liberalization and the Turkish Economy.* Westport, CT: Greenwood Press.

———. 1990. Supply side response in liberalization. *Bogazici University Journal of Economics and Administrative Studies.* 4(2):281–88.

———, eds. 1992. *Economics and Politics of Turkish Liberalization.* Bethlehem, PA: Lehigh University Press.

———. 1996. Effects of post-1980 macroeconomic policies on Turkish manufacturing. *Journal of Developing Areas* 30:211–22.

Nun, J. 1987. Cambios en la estructura social de la Argentina. In *Ensayos Sobre la Transición Democrática en la Argentina*, edited by J. C. Portantiero and J. Nun, 117–37. Buenos Aires: Puntosur.

Odekon, M. 1992. Turkish liberalization: From the perspectives of manufacturing firms. In *Economics and Politics of Turkish Liberalization*, edited by T. Nas and M. Odekon, 155–75. Bethlehem, PA: Lehigh University Press.

Organization for Economic Co-operation and Development (OECD). *Economic Surveys: Turkey*. Various issues, 1980–96. Paris: OECD.

———. 1996. *Economic Surveys, 1995–96*. OECD.

———. 1997. *OECD Economic Surveys: Mexico, 1997*. Paris: OECD.

Paredes, R., and L. Riveros. 1993. El rol de las regulaciones en el mercado laboral: El caso de Chile. *Estudios de Economía* 20(1):41–68.

Peralta-Ramos, M. 1992. *The Political Economy of Argentina: Power and Class since 1930*. Boulder, CO: Westview Press.

Phelps, E. S. 1991. Distributive justice. In *The New Palgrave: The World of Economics*, edited by J. Eatwell, M. Milgate, and P. Newman, 164–67. London: Macmillan.

Pickett, J. 1990. *The Low-Income Economies of Sub-Saharan Africa: Problems and Prospects*. Research Paper 12. Abidjan, Ivory Coast: African Development Bank.

Pissarides, C. A. 1990. *Macroeconomic Adjustment and Poverty in Selected Developed Countries*. Discussion Paper 13. London: London School of Economics and Political Science, Center for Economic Performance.

———. 1997. Learning by trading and the returns to human capital in developing countries. *The World Bank Economic Review* 11(1):17–32.

Portantiero, J. C. 1987. La crisis de un régimen: Una mirada retrospectiva. In *Ensayos Sobre la Transición Democrática en la Argentina*, edited by J. C. Portantiero and J. Nun, 57–80. Buenos Aires: Puntosur.

Portantiero, J. C., and J. Nun, eds. 1987. *Ensayos Sobre la Transición Democrática en la Argentina*. Buenos Aires: Puntosur.

Porter, M. 1990. *Competitive Advantage of Nations*. London: Macmillan.

Prebish, P., ed. 1950. *The Economic Development of Latin America and its Principal Problems*. Lake Success: United Nations.

Przeworski, A. 1991. *Democracy and the Market: Political and Economic Reforms in Eastern Europe and Latin America*. Cambridge University Press.

Rahman, A., K. Griffin, C. Riskin, and R. W. Zhao. 1992. Household income and its distribution in China. *China Quarterly* 1(132):1029–61.

Rambarran, A. 1992. Economic policy and agricultural performance in an open petroleum economy: Trinidad and Tobago, 1966–1982. Central Bank of Trinidad and Tobago, St. Augustine. Mimeographed.

Ranney, D. 1993. NAFTA and the transnational corporate agenda. *Review of Radical Political Economics* 25(4):1–9.

Republic of Trinidad and Tobago. 1992. *Survey of Living Conditions (SLC)*.

———. 1993. *Report of the National Task Force on Education*.

República Argentina, Ministerio de Economía. 1989. Discurso del Ministro de Economía, 07/9/89 and Principales medidas económicas del 07/9/89. Press Release 2/89. Buenos Aires: Ministerio de Economía, July 9.

Resource Center of the Americas. 1997. *Labor Report on the Americas*. Minneapolis, MN. Mimeographed.

Rich, P. NAFTA and Chiapas. 1997. *Annals of the American Academy of Political and Social Science* 551:72–84.

Rittenberg, L. 1988. Financial liberalization and savings in Turkey. In *Liberalization and the Turkish Economy*, edited by T. Nas and M. Odekon, 115–27. Westport, CT: Greenwood Press.

Riveros, L. 1986. Labor market mal-adjustment in Chile: Economic reforms and friction among sub-markets. *Analisis Economico* 1(1).

———. 1994. Labor markets in an era of adjustment: Chile. In *Labor Markets in an Era of Adjustment*, edited by S. Horton, R. Kanbur, and D. Mazumdar. Washington, DC: World Bank EDI Development Studies.

———. 1997. Chiles structural adjustment: Relevant policy lessons for Latin America. In *Adjustment and Equity Impact in Latin America*, edited by A. Berry (Forthcoming).

Riveros, L., and C. E. Sánchez. 1990. *Argentina's Labor Markets in an Era of Adjustment*. Policy, Research and External Affairs Working Paper 386. Washington, DC: World Bank, Country Economics Department.

Robbins, D. J. 1994. *Worsening Relative Wage Dispersion in Chile during Trade Liberalization and Its Causes: Is supply at Fault?* Harvard Institute for International Development Discussion Paper 484. Cambridge, MA: Harvard University.

———. 1995. *Trade, Trade Liberalization, and Inequality in Latin America and East Asia: Synthesis of Seven Country Studies*. Discussion Paper. Cambridge, MA: Harvard Institute for International Development.

———. 1996. *Evidence on Trade and Wages in the Developing World*. OECD Development Centre Technical Paper 119. Paris: Organization for Economic Development and Co-operation.

Robinson, S., M. E. Burfisher, R. Hinojosa-Ojeda, and K. E. Thierfelder. 1992. Agricultural policies and migration in a U.S.-Mexico free trade area: A computable general equilibrium analysis. In *Economy-Wide Modeling of the Implications of a FTA with Mexico and NAFTA with Canada and Mexico*, edited by US ITC, 455–507. Washington, DC: US ITC.

Rodrik, D. 1995. *The Dynamics of Political Support for Reform in Economies in Transition*. CEPR Discussion Paper Series 1115.

Romer, P. 1989. Capital accumulation in the theory of long run growth. In *Modern Business Cycle Theory*, edited by R. Barro. Cambridge, MA: Harvard University Press.

Rothschild, M., and J. Stiglitz. 1976. Equilibrium in competitive insurance markets: An essay on the economics of imperfect information. *Quarterly Journal of Economics* 90(4):630–49.

Sachs, J. D., and H. J. Schatz. 1996. U.S. trade with developing countries and wage inequality. *American Economic Review* 86(2):234–39.

Sachs, J. D., and A. Warner. 1995. *Economic Convergence and Economic Policies*. Development Discussion Paper 502. Cambridge, MA: Harvard Institute for International Development.

Sapelli, C. 1990. Ajuste estructural y mercado del trabajo. Una explicacion de la persistencias del desempleo en Chile: 1975–1980. *Estudios de Economía* 17(2):257–77.

Sarris, A. H. 1988. Greek accession and EC commercial policy toward the south. In *European Trade Policies and the Developing World*, edited by L. B. M. Mennes and J. Kol. London: Croom Helm.

Sarris, A. H., Z. Anastassakou, and S. Zografakis. 1995. *Social Accounting Matrix of the Greek Economy for the Year 1980* (in Greek). Research report to the Greek General Secretariat for Research and Technology. Athens: University of Athens.

Sarris, A. H., G. Kordas, and P. Papadimitriou. 1994. Intra-industry trade of Greece in the course of European integration. Department of Economics, University of Athens. Mimeographed.

Sarris, A. H., P. Papadimitriou, and A. Mavrogiannis. 1994. Manufacturing trade, specialization and adjustment of Greece in the course of European integration. Department of Economics, University of Athens. Mimeographed.

———. Forthcoming. Intra-industry trade and industrial adjustment of Greece under European union membership. *OIKONOMIKA*.

Sayari, S. 1992. Politics and economic policy-making in Turkey. In *Economics and Politics of Turkish Liberalization*, edited by T. Nas and M. Odekon, 26–43. Bethlehem, PA: Lehigh University Press.

Schadler, S. 1996. How successful are IMF-supported adjustment programs? *Finance and Development* 33(2):14–17.

Schvarzer, J. 1981. *Expansión Económica del Estado Subsidiario, 1976–1981.* Buenos Aires: CISEA.

———. 1983. *Martínez de Hoz: La Lógica Política de la Política Económica.* Buenos Aires: CISEA.

Serpell, R. 1993. *The Significance of Schooling: Life Journeys in an African Society.* New York: Cambridge University Press.

Shaiken, H. 1990. *Mexico in the Global Economy.* Monograph Series 33. University of California, San Diego Center for U.S.-Mexico Studies.

Shavell, S., and L. Weiss. 1979. The optimal payment of unemployment insurance benefits over time. *Journal of Political Economy* 87(6):1347–62.

Singer, H. W. 1950. The distribution of trade between investing and borrowing countries. *American Economic Review* 40(1):470–85.

———. 1993. Alternative approaches to adjustment and stabilization. *Third World Economics* 72:12–14.

Singh, A. 1995. Institutional requirements for full employment in advanced economies. *International Labour Review* 134(4–5):471–95.

Skott, P., and M. Larudee. 1997. Uneven development and the liberalization of trade and capital flows: The case of Mexico. *Cambridge Journal of Economics.*

Smith, W. C. 1989. *Authoritarianism and the Crisis of the Argentine Political Economy.* Stanford, CA: Stanford University Press.

———. 1990. Democracy, distributional conflict, and macroeconomic policymaking in Argentina (1983–1989). *Journal of Interamerican Studies and World Affairs* 32(Summer):1–42.

Sourrouille, J. V., and J. Lucangell. 1983. *Política Económica y Procesos de Desarrollo: La Experiencia Argentina Entre 1976 y 1981*. Santiago, Chile: CEPAL.

Standing, G. 1989. Global feminization through flexible labour. *World Development* 17(7):1277–95.

Stanford, J. 1993. Continental integration: The impact on labor. *Annals of the American Academy of Political and Social Science*.

Stewart, F. 1991. The many faces of adjustment. *World Development* 19(12):1847–64.

Tanzi, V. 1993. *Fiscal Policy and the Economic Restructuring of Economies in Transition*. Working Paper 93/22. Washington, DC: International Monetary Fund.

Teekens, R. 1989. Poverty data from two family budgetary surveys in Trinidad and Tobago. St. Augustine, Central Bank of Trinidad and Tobago. Mimeographed.

Tinakorn, P. 1995. Industrialization welfare: How poverty and income distribution are affected. In *Thailand's Industrialization and Its Consequences*, edited by M. Krongkaew. London: Macmillan.

Torres, C. 1982. *Evolución de la Política Arancelaria: Período 1973–1981*. Central Bank Report 16. Santiago: Central Bank of Chile.

Toye, J. 1995. *Structural Adjustment & Employment Policy: Issues and Experience*. Geneva: International Labor Office.

Tsounis, N. K. 1992. The effects of European economic integration on the Greek economy and the pattern of Greek international trade. Ph.D. Diss., University of Manchester.

Turnham, D. 1993. *Employment and Development*. Paris: Organization for Economic Co-operation and Development.

United Nations. 1993/1994. *Africa Recovery*. Geneva: UN Department of Public Information.

United Nations Development Programme. 1994. *Human Development Report, 1994*. New York: Oxford University Press.

United States International Trade Commission (US ITC). 1991. *The Likely Impact on the United States of a Free Trade Agreement with Mexico*. Washington, DC: US ITC.

———. 1992. *Economy-Wide Modeling of the Implications of a FTA with Mexico and NAFTA with Canada and Mexico*. Washington, DC: US ITC.

Vacs, A. C. 1986. The politics of foreign debt: Argentina, Brazil and the international debt crisis. Ph.D. Diss., University of Pittsburgh.

———. 1990. Argentina. In *Latin American and Caribbean Contemporary Record 7:1987–1988*, edited by J. Malloy and E. Gamarra, B3–B9. New York: Holmes and Meier.

———. 1996. Argentina: The melancholy of liberal democracy. In *Establishing Democracies*, edited by M. E. Fischer, 149–77. Boulder, CO: Westview Press.

Valle, H., and M. Marcó del Pont. 1995. Dolarización, convertibilidad, y soberanía económica. In *Argentina Hoy: Crisis del Modelo*, edited by N. Minsburg and H. W. Valle, 59–84. Buenos Aires: Ediciones Letra Buena.

Verbitsky, H. 1991. *Robo Para la Corona*. Buenos Aires: Planeta.

Villareal, J. M. 1987. Changes in Argentine society: The heritage of the dictatorship. In *From Military Rule to Democracy in Argentina*, edited by M. Peralta-Ramos and C. H. Waisman, 69–89. Boulder, CO: Westview Press.

Vona, S. 1991. On the measurement of intra-industry trade: Some further thoughts. *Weltwirtschaftliches Archive* 127:678–700.

Walton, G. M., ed. 1985. *The National Economic Policies in Chile: Contemporary Studies in Economic and Financial Analysis* 51. Greenwhich, CT: JAI Press.

Waterbury, J. 1992. Export-led growth and the center-right coalition in Turkey. In *Economics and Politics of Turkish Liberalization*, edited by T. Nas and M. Odekon, 44–72. Bethlehem, PA: Lehigh University Press.

Weintraub, S. 1992. Modeling the industrial effects of NAFTA. In *North American Free Trade: Assessing the Impact*, edited by N. Lustig, B. Bosworth, and R. Lawrence, 109–43. Washington, DC: Brookings Institution.

Wolff, E. N. 1995. *Top Heavy: A Study of the Increasing Inequality of Wealth in America*. New York: Twentieth Century Fund Press.

Wood, A. 1994. *North-South Trade, Employment, and Inequality: Changing Fortunes in a Skill-Driven World*. Cambridge, U.K.: Oxford University Press.

———. 1995. How trade hurt unskilled workers. *Journal of Economic Perspectives* 9(3):57–80.

———. 1997. Openness and wage inequality in developing countries: The Latin American challenge to East Asian conventional wisdom. *The World Bank Economic Review* 11(1):33–58.

World Bank. 1993. *Argentina: From Insolvency to Growth*. Washington, DC: World Bank.

———. 1994a. *Adjustment in Africa: Lessons from Country Case Studies*. Washington, DC: World Bank.

———. 1994b. *Adjustment in Africa: Reforms, Results, and the Road Ahead*. Washington, DC: World Bank.

———. 1995a. *Labor and Economic Reforms in Latin America and the Caribbean*. Washington, DC: World Bank.

———. 1995b. *The World Bank Atlas—1996*. Washington, DC: World Bank.

———. 1995c. *World Development Report 1995: Workers in an Integrating World*. Washington, DC: World Bank.

———. 1996a. *Social Dimensions of Adjustment*. Washington, DC: World Bank.

———. 1996b. *World Development Report 1996: From Plan to Market*. New York: World Bank.

World Bank and United Nations Development Programme. 1989. *Africa's Adjustment and Growth in the 1980s*. Washington, DC: World Bank.

Zografakis, S. 1997. Economic policy and impacts on the distribution of income in Greece: Analytical approach with the use of a computable general equilibrium model. Ph.D. Diss., University of Athens.

Index

About the Contributors

FABRIZIO CORICELLI holds a Ph.D. in economics from the University of Pennsylvania. He is currently associate professor of monetary economics at the University of Siena and professor of economics at the Central European University in Budapest. From 1987 to 1993 he worked at the International Monetary Fund and at the World Bank. He has published extensively on issues concerning the transition from central planning to a market economy. He is a research fellow at the Centre for Economic Policy Research, London, and at the Davidson Institute, University of Michigan, and a member of the editorial board of the *Journal of Comparative Economics*.

PARVIZ DABIR-ALAI is a senior lecturer in economics at Richmond—The American International University in London. He has fifteen years of teaching, research, and writing experience. Substantial portions of this experience have been acquired in the United Kingdom, United States, and most recently in the West Indies. He is the founding editor of *Briefing Notes in Economics* and has been a consultant to the Inter-American Development Bank.

FIDEL EZEALA-HARRISON is associate professor of economics at the University of New Brunswick, Saint John, Canada. His research interests include all areas of international economics development, regional development, and labor market problems, especially in microeconomic applications to the study of issues in these areas. Dr. Ezeala-Harrison is the author of many journal articles in the areas mentioned. In addition, he is the author of *Economic Development: Theory and Policy*

Applications (Praeger, 1996) and the co-editor of *Perspectives on Economic Development in Africa* (Praeger, 1994).

KWAN S. KIM is professor of economics and a fellow of the Kellogg Institute for International Studies at the University of Notre Dame. He has published several books and over fifty articles in the areas of development studies, international economics, and econometrics.

TIM KOECHLIN teaches economics at Skidmore College. He has written and spoken on the determinants of direct foreign investment, the mobility of productive capital, the North American Free Trade Agreement and the effects of economic integration on wages, employment, and state policy.

DHANAYSHAR MAHABIR lectures in economics at the University of the West Indies in Trinidad and Tobago. He is also chairman of the Public Utilities Commission of Trinidad and Tobago. Dr. Mahabir's rich public-sector experiences include a three-year term at the Caribbean Development Bank in Barbados. His academic work covers contestable markets and the theory of potential competition, unemployment and social-sector reform, and economic philosophy. His articles have been published in *Briefing Notes in Economics*, *Economica* and *McGill Journal of Political Economy*.

TEVFIK F. NAS is Professor in the Economics Department at the University of Michigan, Flint. His recent contributions include *Cost Benefit Analysis: Theory and Application*; two co-edited books, *Liberalization and the Turkish Economy* and *Economics and Politics of Turkish Liberalization*; and a number of articles on macroeconomic and public policy issues published in various journals, including the *American Political Science Review*.

MEHMET ODEKON is an associate professor of economics at Skidmore College. He has co-edited two books, *Liberalization and the Turkish Economy* and *Economics and Politics of Turkish Liberalization*. He authored several articles and book chapters on the Turkish economy.

ANSTON RAMBARRAN is an economist attached to the Research Department of the Central Bank of Trinidad and Tobago. Early on in his career he served as a research assistant at the University of the West Indies at St. Augustine. Rambarran holds a master of science in financial economics from the University of London, and his recent research has focused on the financial aspects of adjustment, especially debt and exchange rate management strategies. His research has resulted in the production of a number of high-quality monographs published by the Central Bank.

TRUDI J. RENWICK has been employed by the Public Utility Law Project of New York as an economic policy analyst since 1993. Dr. Renwick provides expert testimony on low-income energy assistance and utility rate design issues in numerous proceedings before the New York State Public Service Commission. She earned her Ph.D. in economics from the American University in 1991. She is currently completing an analysis of poverty and single-parent families which will be published by Garland Press. Dr. Renwick holds an M.A. in Ibero-American studies from the University of Wisconsin and has lived in Argentina, Ecuador, and Brazil.

LUIS A. RIVEROS is the dean of the School of Economics and Business Administration at the University of Chile. He is the author of more than thirty articles in professional journals and of several books on labor economics. He worked for seven years at the Research Department of the World Bank and is now an international consultant on labor issues for the World Bank, International Development Bank, and other organizations. He is the president of the Latin American Council of Business Schools, Director of the International Federation of Scholarly Associations of Management (IFSAM), director of the Chile-Pacific Foundation, and president of the Program Committee, Latin American branch of the Econometric Society.

ALEXANDER SARRIS received his Ph.D. in economics and electrical engineering from the Massachusetts Institute of Technology. He taught at the University of California, Berkeley, and since 1982 has been professor of economics at the University of Athens, Greece. His interests are in the areas of applied international and development economics, agricultural economics, and structural macro-micro modeling. He has published ten books and monographs and over fifty articles in professional journals and books. He has advised many international institutions and governments and has done extensive work in developing, West European and East European economies.

ALDO C. VACS is associate professor and chair at the Department of Government, Skidmore College. He teaches courses on international political economy, Latin American politics, and relations with the United States. Vacs completed his Ph.D. in political science at the University of Pittsburgh. He also holds degrees in sociology, planning and economic policies, and political science from institutions in Argentina, Chile, and Brazil. He is a research associate at the Center for Latin American Studies of the University of Pittsburgh, a contributing editor of the

Handbook of Latin American Studies, and a contributor to *Argentina: A Country Study* for the Country Studies series/Area Handbook Program sponsored by the Library of Congress. His publications include studies of Latin America's relations with Russia and the United States, the process of Latin American democratization, economic liberalization, and structural reform. He is currently doing research on the global processes of political and economic liberalization, on the evolution of Latin America's foreign policies since the end of the Cold War, and on the process of political economic transformation under way in the Southern Cone countries.

ISBN 0-313-30358-4

EAN

9 780313 303586

90000>

HARDCOVER BAR CODE